COMING TO TERMS

Throwing Light on Words
Used in the Church's Debate
Over Same-Sex Behaviors

Coming to Terms

Throwing Light on Words
Used in the Church's Debate
Over Same-Sex Behaviors

David J. Landegent

Table of Contents

Introduction

You're in a robust discussion about a controversial issue when something is said that you would like to comment on. But before you get a chance to speak, three other points have been raised by others that you'd also like to comment on, only to see the whole conversation move in another direction. Perhaps you've had that experience before. I have—many times—through decades of being involved in the LGBT debate that has raged in my denomination (the Reformed Church in America). This book contains some of the things I would have said if it were possible to hit a pause button during a discussion and give some input.

I have never hidden my "conservative" viewpoints on this issue,[1] but I have immensely appreciated the give-and-take of discussion with the other "side."[2] Often during discussions, I can't help but notice how often we are speaking past each other because we are using key words differently.

Although I would love to be so persuasive that those who disagree with me would change "sides," my more realistic hope for these essays is that they would at least understand my perspective better. I'm also hoping that those who are already on my "side" would be able to better articulate their perspective when they get into discussions about LGBT issues.

But why a volume of essays instead of a straight-forward book that develops a thesis and builds a case for it? Partly because of the multi-faceted dimensions of this discussion. The issue is not an immoveable object out there that we can slowly dissect one layer at a time, but a rapidly moving entity that can be viewed from many angles.

That's what prompted me to look at LGBT matters from many angles through various essays, some of which are more tangential to the LGBT issue, but all of them relevant. And I should warn you that since we are looking at the same thing from many angles, it is inevitable that there will be repetition here and there, but always with different nuances.

I thought about ordering them in a way to make a more persuasive case, but in the end, I decided to just present them in alphabetical order by

---

[1] For more this, see the essay "Conservative" on page 61.
[2] For more this, see the essay "Sides" on page 233.

title (which is why I'm starting with such a negative essay about "abomination"—sorry). Occasionally I will include notes that point the reader to other essays in this volume that have common elements. I should also note that while some of the essays will argue for the case that same-sex behavior is sinful, other essays simply assume that to be true and look at other implications of that belief.

So I invite you to join me in thinking through these matters using the words of Isaiah 1:18, "Come now, let us reason together, says the LORD: though your sins are like scarlet, they shall be as white as snow; though they are red like crimson, they shall become like wool" (ESV). We are not reasoning together simply so we can have a jolly good time debating. Nor are we reasoning with each so that we can establish who's right and who's wrong. Rather, we are reasoning together with the Lord so that we can find grace and truth in the midst of a contentious issue.

Abomination

S ticks and stones may break bones, but words have the power to break hearts. The English language has a number of words to describe when something is bad, some of which are more potent than others. Bad, evil, naughty, wicked—these words work well in describing negative behaviors and people. That is, until somebody starts using words in their opposite sense. In some contexts, it might be a compliment to describe someone as "one bad guitar player" or a movie as "wicked sick."

But other "bad" words have even more negative power. I'm thinking of words like atrocious, vile, abhorrent, disgusting, loathsome, and repugnant. Two very negative words have found their way into the discussions about same-sex behaviors because of a few Bible verses. In the Holiness Code of Leviticus 17-26 we find a number of sins labeled as *to'ebah*, which is a noun often translated as either "abomination" (KJV, NRSV, ESV) or something that is "detestable" (NIV).

Same-sex behaviors receive this designation in Leviticus 18:22 and 20:13. It is harsh language intended to convey the truth that these sins are morally repugnant to God, and that we should be repulsed by them as well. Compared to such severe wording, it seems mild (and even polite) to call them "sinful" instead.

In discussions with members of the LGBT community, I avoid using terms like "detestable" and "abomination." In today's climate such words can be regarded as an insult, even if they have a good biblical pedigree.

It might soften things if we came to see that the Bible only tags objects and actions as abominations, but *not* the people who do those actions. But that's not actually the case. Although about 90% of the abominations in the Bible *are* objects and actions, there are a few cases of the people themselves being called abominations (see Deuteronomy 22:5; 25:6; Proverbs 3:32; 6:16-19; 11:20; 16:5; 17:15; 24:9; 29:27; Isaiah 41:24). This point may not make much difference to the LGBT community anyway, since they regard their identity and their actions as all rolled together. They do not merely think of themselves as those who *do* same-sex behaviors; rather, they see those actions as defining who they *are*. In their minds, they don't just engage in gay or lesbian sexual actions; they *are* gays and lesbians. So to call their behavior an abomination means, to them, that they themselves are being called abominations. And that doesn't feel like love or grace to them. It wouldn't to me either.

Nevertheless, I also have to admit that it's not a positive step when our culture attempts to eliminate words that express moral abhorrence. If sin is only described as a little indiscretion, a mistake, or a lapse of good judgment, we have become blind and deaf to how deeply offensive sin is to our high and holy God. The Lord's "eyes are too pure to look on evil" (Habakkuk 1:13, NIV11).

Perhaps it would help if we noticed that it's not just same-sex behaviors that are called an abomination in the Bible. The following sins are also called abominations to God (mostly found in Leviticus, Deuteronomy, Proverbs, Ezekiel, and texts about King Manasseh):

- incest and bestiality (Leviticus 18:26-27, 29-30; Ezekiel 22:11)
- adultery (Ezekiel 33:26)
- idols and idolatry (Deuteronomy 7:25-26; 13:14; 17:4; 20:18; 27:15; 32:16; 2 Kings 21:2, 11; 23:13; 2 Chronicles 33:2; 34:33; 36:8, 14; Ezra 9:1, 11; Isaiah 41:24; Jeremiah 16:18; 44:3-4, 22; Ezekiel 5:9, 11; 6:9, 11; 7:20; 8:6, 9, 13, 15, 17; 9:4; 11:18, 21; 14:6; 16:2, 22, 36; 44:13)
- male cult prostitution (1 Kings 14:24)
- child sacrifice (Deuteronomy 12:31; 2 Kings 16:3; 2 Chronicles 28:3; Jeremiah 32:35)
- occult practices (Deuteronomy 18:9, 12)
- eating unclean animals (Deuteronomy 14:3)
- sacrificing damaged animals (Deuteronomy 17:1)
- offering earnings made from prostitution (Deuteronomy 23:18)
- offerings made by a wicked person (Proverbs 15:8; 21:27; Isaiah 1:13)
- cross-dressing (Deuteronomy 22:5)
- remarrying an ex-wife (Deuteronomy 24:4)
- economic sins (Ezekiel 18:12-13, 24)
- using dishonest weights (Deuteronomy 25:16; Proverbs 11:1; 20:10, 23)
- intermarrying with idolaters (Ezra 9:14; Malachi 2:11)
- general evil (Proverbs 3:32; 8:7; 11:20; 15:9; 16:12; Jeremiah 6:15; 8:12; Ezekiel 7:3-4, 8-9; 12:16; 16:43, 47, 50-51, 58; 20:4; 22:2; 33:29; 36:31), including lists of various sins like pride, lying, murder, scheming and stirring up dissension (Proverbs 6:16-19); idolatry, adultery, lying, and violence (Jeremiah 7:1-11); adultery, idolatry, child sacrifice, and sabbath-breaking (Ezekiel 23:36-39)

- lying (Proverbs 12:22)
- pride (Proverbs 16:5)
- injustice (Proverbs 17:15)
- Temple-desecration (Ezekiel 43:8; 44:6-7)

A few of these abominations (like cross-dressing or eating unclean animals) may strike us as not deserving such a terrible label, but we would agree that many of them are based on the Ten Commandments and are morally repulsive. So it's not just same-sex behaviors that are called abominations in the Bible—all kinds of sins receive that label. All of us—same-sex attracted or not—need to remember that *all* our sins are an abomination to God.

We don't need to remember this so that we can feel like abominations ourselves, detested by God. Rather, we remember how horrible sin is so that we can turn from it and be amazed at the great steadfast love of God for sinners like ourselves. "But God demonstrates his own love for us in this: While we were still sinners, Christ died for us" (Romans 5:8, NIV11).

The fact that human sin is an abomination to God is not a myth, like the abominable snowman of the Himalayas. The abomination of sin is very real; but the cross of Jesus shows us the even greater reality of God's love.

Against [1]

A Christian musician once said something in an interview that I've heard expressed many times and perhaps even said myself: "We [Christians] shouldn't be known for the things we're against, but for the things we love."

I know what he means. The world already has a negative picture of Christians as people who live by the principles of "NO" and "DON'T." In their eyes, we are self-righteous prudes who don't watch movies, don't dance, don't smoke and don't drink...and a whole bunch of other things we don't do. And it doesn't help when the media shines the spotlight on the angriest Christians they can find. They're scowling about liberals, shouting about abortion, and getting mad about the LGBT community. So I can understand why that Christian artist said we should be known for what we love, not for what we're against.

But in my more clear-minded moments I realize that such a goal is an illusion. In order to be in favor of something, you have to be against its alternatives...unless, of course, you're willing to be in favor of everything, which can only result in total moral chaos. In order to be in favor of something, you have to be against its alternatives.

Just a quick glance at the Sermon on the Mount will show you that Jesus stood in favor of some actions and attitudes, but also against others. Here's a quick list from part of that sermon (Matthew 5) of what Jesus stood *for*: humility, meekness, hungering for righteousness, mercy, purity, peace, shining the light, obeying commands, surpassing righteousness, reconciliation, speaking the truth of "Yes" and "No," giving to those who are needy, loving enemies, and being perfect. These are wonderful things the Lord wants to see happen in our lives and our world.

But there's also a list in that same chapter of activities and attitudes that the Lord is *against*: losing our saltiness, hiding the light, ignoring the commands, murdering, hating, calling people fools, adultery, lust, divorce, oath-taking, revenge, and loving only your friends.

---

[1] Based on an editorial entitled "What We're Against" which I wrote for *The Sunday School Guide,* Vol. 87, January 31, 2010, 65, 78-79. Used by permission.

It's great to accent the positives, the good things we should do. But this can turn into a sentimental blob of warm fuzziness if we don't also put some teeth into it by talking about what the kingdom of God opposes. What we're against helps us define what we're for, and it's an illusion to overlook this fact.

The Christian artist I alluded to earlier was responding to a controversy about one of his songs. The purpose of his song was to stir lackadaisical Christians to be more concerned about social justice, and he decided to use a vulgar term as a way to jolt them out of their apathy. But his recording company refused to release the song because of the vulgar term, and people quickly took sides on the issue. He couldn't help but wonder why Christians should be so *against* a vulgar term, but not really care about being in favor of social justice. Perhaps he was thinking of Jesus' words in Matthew 23:24, spoken to the Pharisees who tithed little spices, but forgot about justice: "You blind guides! You strain out a gnat but swallow a camel" (NIV11). Partly in response to the outcry against his vulgar language, the artist said that we should be known more for what we love instead of what we're against.

But even in this situation, it's not correct to say that the artist is one who admirably shows what he's in favor of (social justice), while his detractors are the ones who spitefully show what they're against (vulgarity). It would be more accurate to say that both the artist and his detractors are both for and against things. The artist is *for* social justice and *against* injustice (and maybe his detractors wondered if he was also against civil language). Likewise, those who disagreed with the artist are also for and against things: they are *for* civil language and *against* vulgarity (and perhaps the artist also wondered if they were against justice).

Since there's a general tendency to dislike negative people and negative terms, we often play games with labels so that our side receives positive press and our opponents get stuck with a negative label. This has happened in the controversy over abortion. My side of the controversy prefers to be known as a "pro-life" movement, instead of an "anti-abortion" or "anti-choice" movement, because the latter sounds so negative. And it's tempting for us to refer to the positions of the other side of the controversy as "anti-life," "pro-abortion," or even "pro-death." They, of course, don't want to be known for such negative things, so they would rather be called "pro-choice," and say that we are against choice. And so the debate over terms continues.

But if cooler heads prevailed, both sides in this moral controversy (and others) would calmly declare what they favor and what they oppose. Then we at least know what we're talking about. A positive label alone does not bring a lot of clarity. I might call myself pro-life, for instance, but that term won't be very clear unless I also tell you what I'm against. It might mean only that I'm against abortions, but pro-life might also mean I'm against nuclear weapons, all forms of war, capital punishment, child abuse, and hunger. As I said earlier, what we're against helps us define what we're for.

I remember a regional church meeting in which someone attempted to change our by-laws so that it listed the kinds of behaviors that would be unfitting for pastors and elder delegates. This didn't go through because someone objected to the legalistic tone of having lists of forbidden vices. I can understand why we'd want to avoid a legalistic tone, but to reject something only because it contains a list of what you're against is not a sufficient reason to reject it. The Ten Commandments contain a list of mostly negative immoral actions that the Lord is against. Paul often spelled out lists of behaviors that Christians should not do (see Romans 1:29-32, 1 Corinthians 6:9-11, or Galatians 5:19-21). Even Jesus could make lists of what he opposed: "For from within, out of the heart of man, come evil thoughts, sexual immorality, theft, murder, adultery, coveting, wickedness, deceit, sensuality, envy, slander, pride, foolishness. All these evil things come from within, and they defile a person" (Mark 7: 21-23, ESV). Obviously, to stand for Jesus, you have to stand against those things that are opposed to Jesus.

The real problem is not that we're against things, but the *way* we are against them and the *manner* we often choose to express our opposition. Opposing sin must be done in a way that is marked by the fruit of the Spirit growing in our hearts—love, joy, peace, patience, and more (Galatians 5:22-23).

Consider love. Our opposition to any sinful action needs to be built upon a foundation of loving our neighbor and wanting the best for them. But if we oppose a sin because we hate those who practice it, we will quickly find ourselves warring against Jesus himself. Or how about joy? Christians should oppose sin, not in a spirit of despair and hopelessness, but with a spirit of joy—knowing that victory is sure in Jesus Christ. If we oppose sin in a peaceful way, we will remain calm, speaking softly and without anxious fear. As for patience, opposing sin calls for the same patience God has toward a rebellious world.

What I'm saying here also applies to LGBT discussions.

My hunch is that the Christian artist who said, "We shouldn't be known for the things we're against, but for the things we love," said this because he had seen too many Christians lash out in anger, despair, fear and impatience. If we truly follow Jesus, however, we will not operate in this way. We must express our deep opposition to sinful actions in our world, in our churches (and even in our own hearts), but we must do so in way that shows we are ambassadors of Christ, God making his appeal through us with a message of reconciliation (see 2 Corinthians 5:19-20).

In a world hostile to the gospel, it's unavoidable that we Christians will be known for what we are against. But hopefully we will *also* be known for the loving way that we are against the unrighteousness all around us and within us.

Allies

Because you happen to have the same opinion as another person on a particular controversial issue, you could perhaps be thought of as allies. But I have to admit that I don't appreciate some of my allies in the debate over same-sex behavior. Some of them are an embarrassment. Some of them are outright appalling. I want to distance myself from them completely.

A few years back a pastor named Fred Phelps made lots of headlines for orchestrating an effort in his church to picket funerals of servicemen (who were not even gay) with signs that read, "God hates fags" and "God hates America." It was horrendous. He and I may have had the same belief that same-sex behavior was not God's will for human life, but we had nothing else in common. His hatred and his style of expressing it was evil and abhorrent, and if the only choice was between his stance and the progressive one, I know where I would go.

Other "allies" who believe same-sex behavior is sinful seem to think it is their calling to administer God's judgment by mocking, beating up, and generally mistreating the LGBT community. Again, their response is evil and must be repudiated.

Then there are other "allies" who are an embarrassment, the kind who make you roll your eyes, look the other way, and try to think of what you can say at that moment to get them to be quiet. I can remember a large denominational meeting in which some delegates believed they had been anointed by God to function like a Jeremiah or John the Baptist. When they came to the microphone it was with a torrent of judgmental words spoken with a harsh tone of voice.

Later at that same meeting I was walking with a friend, who is moderate on the issue of same-sex relationships, and we were accosted by one of my "allies." The accoster wanted—almost demanded—to know where my friend stood, and when my friend failed to readily pledge his allegiance to the cause, this man proceeded to read him chapter and verse (literally) from the Bible—informing him about the Greek words that backed his interpretation. The content of his message may have been correct, but his tone certainly undermined any chance of being persuasive.

I imagine that conservatives are not alone in having allies that they wish would keep quiet. I'm guessing that some progressives are also embarrassed by what some of their allies say. A few years ago, a progressive friend of mine said that it bothered him when one of his allies said on the floor of our national denominational meeting that Jesus doesn't care what anyone does in the privacy of their bedroom.

I know during our national meetings, both conservatives and progressives who feel strongly about these issues will gather together after hours to "caucus." Some regard this as wrongful politicking, and some of that probably happens. But speaking as a conservative here, I see two good reasons to "caucus." One is that many of the delegates are relatively new to the process, and some of them are stunned, bewildered, and/or discouraged by the progressive ideas spoken on the floor. "How can people possibly think like that?" they wonder. So caucusing gives an opportunity for those of us who are more acquainted with the debate to help them understand it better and to encourage them.

A second good thing that can happen in caucusing is that if there is an ally there who conveys a nasty, sarcastic tone toward the "other side," it gives the rest of us an opportunity to help him or her see that there are more helpful ways to speak.

Caucusing is also a time to provide information, but not so the group can strong-arm people into voting lock-step with the rest of the caucus. We need to let each delegate sense how God—not the caucus—would have them speak and vote on any given issue. Hopefully, we are providing information so that they know what it is they are voting on, rather than just blindly casting a vote about something they don't understand.

Sometimes we are afraid to criticize or rebuke an ally because we think that might hurt our cause, but it may actually hurt our cause to remain silent. That bully of an ally may be giving the other side the wrong impression that we all agree with their overbearing approach. Allies like that are not true allies at all.

Analogies

When trying to explain something to another person, it's common to look for some analogy that would help them understand what we mean. Some of the analogies work for us, and others don't.

For instance, when a business person tells me that my work as a pastor is similar to theirs in that we're both trying to sell something, I try to keep my body language from giving away my revulsion at such a thought. Paul's words in 2 Corinthians 2:17 loom large in my mind: "Unlike so many, we do not peddle the word of God for profit" (NIV11).

But I have to admit, there are some points of contact in the analogy. We both have something valuable that we want to persuade another person to desire, and we know how to help them fulfill that desire. But for me, there are a number of things that don't work in the analogy. The salesman offers a valuable item, while I am offering a valuable relationship with the living God. The salesman hopes to make a monetary profit from the transaction, while I—even though I receive a paycheck for my pastoral work—do not regard an individual who needs Jesus as a potential donor. So even though I like many people involved in sales, I don't like the analogy that ministry is like merchandising.

Similarly, in discussions about LGBT concerns, both sides try to explain their position by comparing same-sex behaviors to some other action. The hope is that the analogy will illuminate some facet of the discussion, so we can understand what the behavior is and how those who do it should be treated by others.

Let's look at just a few of those analogies.

Bestiality

Although I do not hear this analogy very much anymore, it used to be fairly common to hear a conservative say something like, "If we give the green light to same-sex behaviors, the next thing you know people will want to start having sex with animals."

They probably resort to this analogy for three reasons. First, both bestiality and same-sex behaviors receive the same label of "abomination" in Leviticus 18:22-23.[1] Secondly, they both are about actions that involve the sexual organs. And thirdly, the analogy is intended to convey the idea that both actions should be seen as deeply repulsive. If society is becoming more accepting of same-sex behaviors, then the hope is that the comparison will wake people up to how terrible it is: it's as bad as bestiality.

This analogy is deeply offensive to the LGBT community, however, because it seems to cast them as the lowest of the low. Maybe both actions involve the sexual organs and can be found together in Leviticus 18, but they are different in a very important respect, namely, the matter of personal relationships. While it's true that some people treat their animals as if they were people, it's an illusion. There may be a form of communication between people and animals, but not true conversation and interpersonal sharing. The conversation with an animal is one-sided, and the relationship is one of dependence and even coercion. There may be some same-sex (and opposite-sex) encounters that are also impersonal and coercive (which makes them quite a bit like bestiality), but gays and lesbians would contend that there are also many same-sex relationships that are deeply personal.

So if one's goal is to build bridges of understanding between conservatives and progressives—even if there is no hope of agreement—this analogy is not very helpful. Nonetheless, even if it is not voiced, conservatives cannot help but wonder if society is sliding toward accepting nearly every form of sexual behavior there is, including bestiality.

Divorce

Sometimes progressives suggest that same-sex behaviors should be accepted in the same way that we have learned to accept divorce. It used to be that we treated divorced people as second-class citizens, and a divorced pastor was almost unheard of. We did this because we saw a clear biblical condemnation of divorce—from the mouth of Jesus even. But now that divorce has become so common that divorced people are found in nearly every extended family, we have learned to be more merciful. We allow divorced people to belong to our churches and to be ordained as leaders.

So if we have learned how to do that, ask progressives, why can't we offer the same mercy and grace to the LGBT community, accepting them into our churches and welcoming them into ordained leadership? While biblical commands appear to forbid it, there are biblical commands forbidding divorce too—and yet we have opened our arms.

Conservatives have no one to blame but themselves for the strength of this analogy. Our moral track record on divorce and our easy acceptance of it have done nothing but open the door for other sexual sins to be accepted as well. Not that we want to return to the day when divorced people were

---

[1] For more on this, see the essay "Abomination" on page 3.

rejected and treated like outcasts; that was wrong. But we have not been very good at figuring out how to be gracious and firm at the same time. It's a difficult balancing act.

Yet there are some respects in which this analogy fails to hold.

First, although the church has become more tolerant of divorce in its actions, the standard has nonetheless remained unchanged. No one is arguing that divorce is no longer a sin. We may still quibble about whether in some situations, one of the two partners bears the full weight of that sin and the other is a victim of it (as may be the case when a man runs off with a co-worker and leaves his wife and two kids). Nonetheless, divorce is still regarded as a sin.

If progressives were arguing, then, that same-sex behavior is a sin, but we need to be more merciful toward those involved in it (as we have been toward divorced people), then we would at least be operating with the same moral standard, even though we might differ on how that works out in pastoral care and church discipline. But that's not at all what most progressives are advocating. Many of them would rather that we celebrate same-sex relationships as a good variation within God's created world.

So when progressives use this analogy, it may wake up conservatives to their own possible hypocrisies, but it doesn't actually represent how the progressives want the church to respond to the LGBT community.

Race and ethnicity

Various ethnic and racial minorities have suffered injustices during the course of American history. Simply because of one's genetic heritage, people have been cruelly mistreated. Efforts continue to be made to put the nation on a better path of treating all people equally, but there's a long way to go until we look past the color of someone's skin to see the content of their character (to paraphrase Martin Luther King, Jr.).

Progressives have sometimes used this issue as a way of supporting the LGBT community. Their analogy contains three parts. First, both ethnic minorities and members of the LGBT community have experienced injustices and harsh treatment. Second, the progressives contend that both ethnic minorities and the LGBT community have been mistreated simply because of their genetic heritage. African Americans, Hispanics, Asians, gays and lesbians were simply born that way, and yet have been mistreated through no fault of their own. And then, thirdly, just as the church is called to work toward racial justice and equality, so it must work toward justice and equality for the LGBT community.

How should conservatives view this analogy? As for the first part of the analogy, we must confess to our own shame that we have indeed been a part of that history of mistreating the LGBT community, just as we have done to various racial and ethnic minorities. And as for the third part of the analogy, churches should generally be on the side of according equal civil rights to the LGBT community. They should not be slandered, denied housing, or have their rights to free speech, voting, or assembling taken away. Conservatives, however, will have a few reservations here. For instance, because they think marriage is by definition between a man and a woman, they will generally reject the notion that it's a civil right for men to marry men or for women to marry women. They would also reject any idea that the rights given in civil society must extend to the church, so that churches would be required to marry same-sex couples or ordain same-sex people. But with these exceptions, most conservatives would support civil rights for the LGBT community.

It's with the second part of the analogy that conservatives would have the greatest reservations. In general, they do not think that being gay, lesbian, bisexual, or transgendered is a genetic given in the same way that being "red and yellow, black and white" is a genetic given (as the old Sunday School song put it). I know that some studies have been made suggesting a genetic element, but nothing definitive has come forth. I can't help but wonder if the ones doing the study had a vested interest in reaching a foregone conclusion.

This doesn't mean conservatives necessarily think that engaging in same-sex behavior is simply a moral choice that someone has made (although some do).[2] There are likely many factors that contribute toward bringing a person to that point, with genetic predisposition being one of them. But a genetic predisposition does not require anyone to actually engage in same-sex behavior—not any more than a genetic predisposition to alcoholism requires one to drink. It seems like an easy way out to claim, "I was born this way," and then cave in to whatever desires you feel you were born to have. Most men are genetically predisposed toward sexual promiscuity, but they have learned for a variety of reasons why they should not give free rein to this genetic predisposition.

It would seem wiser to say that some genetic markers create a given, unalterable body trait (such as a very visible skin color or an invisible time bomb that will trigger a genetic disease). Other genetic markers create a bodily trait that can be somewhat altered (one's height, for instance, can be affected to a degree by diet). Other genetic markers seem to create a predisposition toward a certain set of behaviors, but do not of necessity make those behaviors happen (like alcoholism, musical ability, or same-sex attraction). [3]

---

[2] For more on this, see the essay "Choices" on page 42. .
[3] For more on this, see the essay "Genetics" on page 104.

So ultimately, the analogy between race and same-sex behavior doesn't work for conservatives because it presupposes the very thing that they see differently. And on a side note, a number of people who belong to minority ethnic groups are insulted by the comparison. It's true that there are some people who belong to ethnic minorities who have accepted the analogy because they have understandably developed a built-in sympathy toward any group that is treated unjustly. But in my experience, a majority of Christians from ethnic and racial minority groups do not appreciate the comparison.

Addiction

Conservatives sometimes like to compare same-sex attraction to an addiction. They realize that if you think about something long enough and often enough, it will actually alter the pathways in the brain, so that an addiction develops. Life begins to revolve around this very thing, like cocaine or video games. Conservatives can easily imagine this happening to someone who had a same-sex attraction thought flit through their brain. Maybe they tried not to think about it, but it often happens that the very thing you try not to think about is what you think about. And if they derived any pleasure (or horror) from the thought, then the brain returns to it again and again.

This analogy is an attempt by conservatives to try to understand how a person could become same-sex attracted. Heterosexual conservatives might be very aware of how this kind of addictive thinking could happen to them with pornography, so it's not too big of a step for them to see how this could happen with same-sex attraction as well.

I'm guessing, however, that the LGBT community doesn't like this analogy for at least a couple of reasons. For one, we usually associate addictions with something that's bad for us in the long term, and most of them do not think of their same-sex attraction as bad. Secondly, they probably think this explanation is too simplistic, if not completely erroneous. They have no awareness of this being the process by which they became aware they were same-sex attracted.

Still, I can't help but wonder if there is something to this analogy.

Anger

This analogy may surprise you, but it can be helpful because it's not about a sexual activity (like bestiality), and thus eases tensions often found in these discussions. And anger is also something everyone has experienced. We haven't all been addicted or divorced, or committed bestiality, or experienced life as part of an ethnic minority, but we've all been angry. Perhaps both sides in the LGBT discussions could find the analogy of anger helpful in trying to understand same-sex behavior—though we will likely find it helpful in different ways.

The part I find helpful is in trying to comprehend the possible genetic component. It's based a little on my interaction with my son when he was a child. At that age, he had a fiery temper that he certainly didn't learn from watching my wife and I interact. (I sometimes wonder if I even have a temper.) But whenever something happened that displeased him, I could almost see the chemicals pouring into his brain causing him to explode in fury. I figured it was how he was genetically wired. But of course, I was not going to encourage him to be himself and let his rage come to full expression whenever he wanted. So I figured it was my job (and the Lord's job) to help him learn how to control his temper. I could not make it disappear, but he could certainly learn to control it—and he did learn.

I look on same-sex attraction in a similar light. There may be some genetic predisposition for some people to be attracted to the same sex, but that doesn't mean it should be given free rein. Rather, a person must learn to control it, with the Lord giving the power to do so.

But of course, analogies can take us in many directions. Progressives may look at the same analogy and say, "Anger is something all people experience. In itself, it's neither right nor wrong. What matters is what you do with it. If you let anger go unchecked in a destructive direction, it's bad. But if you channel your anger in constructive directions, it can be good. Likewise, same-sex attraction is something all people experience to a greatly varying degree. Most people easily learn to snuff it out completely. Others let it loose so that it pulls them into very destructive patterns in life. But still others can learn to channel their same-sex attractions in constructive ways so that they become faithful to one partner."

As you might guess, I'm not too keen on pulling the analogy in that direction because of my conviction that God forbids any same-sex activity. It would seem better to me to channel same-sex attractions in a constructive way that does not involve acting upon those attractions.

But regardless, these are just a few analogies that some have found helpful in trying to explain their position to those who think differently. If you have a better one, share it.

Answers [1]

When I was an adolescent, humanity was in search of "answers" to all kinds of problems. Scientists found answers in the laboratory; politicians found answers in sociological analysis; students found answers in the library. Figure the right equations and you could land on the moon. Add the right chemicals together and you could cure a disease. There were answers for all the problems of the world, and humanity just needed enough perseverance to find those answers.

Gradually, however, people sensed that something was amiss. While science, education, capitalism, democracy, and technology had brought many good things—they alone would not be able to find the answers needed for the world's problems. For in spite of all the progress, the early 1970's still had to contend with war, pollution, racism, and homegrown terrorism (sounds a lot like today, doesn't it?). So where could answers be found?

In my early days of faith, I would often listen to a live album by André Crouch, in which he sang repeatedly, "Jesus is the answer for the world today." That line made a lot of sense to me at that time, and it still does. The answer to perplexing issues would be found in Jesus, not in better laws, more education, new political leaders, or improved technology.

Today, however, the whole notion of finding "answers" is dismissed as a left-over notion from the past. Modernism taught us that the answers are out there, but post-modernism teaches us to believe that no one really knows the truth. So if anyone claims to have the answers, they're just using words to get their way. Even among Christians, influenced by post-modernism, there is a reluctance to describe Jesus as the answer.

I hear this in discussions about same-sex issues. Conservatives like myself offer what we perceive as biblical answers, while progressives would rather stay with the questions. Or maybe more accurately, conservatives want to reach some conclusive answers about same-sex behaviors, while progressives are more comfortable living with the tensions posed by the

---

[1] Based on an editorial entitled "Answers" which I wrote for *The Sunday School Guide,* Vol. 87, October 12, 2008, 17, 30-31. Used by permission.

questions—probably because they either expect the answers to be too harsh and final, or they don't think there are any answers. I once heard a young post-modern Christian say, "We need to quit offering answers to the world and just live with the questions."

Aside from the ironic fact that his statement is actually his "answer" to what the world needs, I would like to put in a good word for giving "answers," and in particular, I want to explore what kind of "answer" Jesus is.

But to begin, we need to go back to the "Answer Book," the Bible, and observe how the English word "answer" is used in God's Word (in at least 570 references in the NIV). And the main thing I noticed is that the word "answer" is mostly used as a relationship word in the Bible. It describes what happens when two or more persons converse; they answer each other. It's usually in the form of a verb. The Lord answers Abraham (Genesis 18:32). Moses answered the Lord (Exodus 4:1). The tribes of Israel answer Joshua (Joshua 24:16). In the New Testament, we find the same relational kind of answering. Jesus answers Peter's question about how often to forgive an offender (Matthew 18:22). The disciples answer Jesus' question about feeding 5,000 (Mark 8:4). Jesus answers his critics (Luke 22:67), and they answer him (John 7:20). "Answer" is not so much a noun to describe a solution; rather, it is a verb to describe what happens when people talk.

This relational aspect of knowing and sharing "answers" is an important one to hold on to. Perhaps one of the reasons today's post-modern Christians are wary of answers is that answers in the past have been shared in a non-relational way. I can remember an old *Peanuts* cartoon in which Linus triumphantly announces to Charlie Brown, "The answer to life is 5." But, like Charlie Brown, people don't find that kind of answer very satisfying. The answer to a math problem doesn't care less about who you are. And sometimes our Christian answers seem as cold and comfortless as a mathematical answer.

We can't just throw a Christian slogan at someone who is searching for God, and congratulate ourselves on giving them the right answer. To truly "answer" them, we must involve ourselves in conversation—getting to know them, and listening for what their real concerns are. 1 Peter 3:15 says, "Always be prepared to give an answer to everyone who asks you to give the reason for the hope that you have. But do this with gentleness and respect" (NIV11). That means more than throwing true statements about Jesus at people. It means answering them as persons loved by God.

The second thing I observed, especially in the Gospels, is how Jesus answers in unexpected ways. We might expect Jesus' answers to provide a systematic set of statements that satisfy our curiosity about theological issues, or to lay out the blueprints for righteous living. But instead Jesus answers in unusual ways. Sometimes, he answers with a command: "Jesus answered, 'If you want to be perfect, go, sell your possessions and give to the poor, and you will have treasure in heaven. Then come, follow me.'" (Matthew 19:21, NIV11). Sometimes his answer is a question: "Jesus answered, 'Do you think that these Galileans were worse sinners than all the other Galileans because they suffered this way?'" (Luke 13:2, NIV11), or, "'Why do you call me good?' Jesus answered." (Luke 18:19, NIV11). Occasionally Jesus answers with a stinging rebuke (see Luke 13:5). Sometimes Jesus even answers with initial silence, as he did in Matthew 15:23.[2]

So even though Jesus is the answer, he's not like any "answer man" you've heard before. His answers are not tidy little solutions containing three easy steps to achieve a desired result. Although his answers are simple in the sense of being concise and understandable, they are not simple in terms of what it takes to respond. Jesus' answers are often blunt, personal challenges designed to put our sinful self to death and transform our heart into a new creation—none of which goes down easily.

At this point, the post-modern Christians who thinks, "We need to quit offering answers to the world and just live with the questions," might be okay with what I'm saying. They might resonant with the idea that Jesus is not an impersonal solution kind of answer, but instead he's an answer that is interpersonal and challenging. Nevertheless, the biblical witness also points out one more thing, namely, to say Jesus is the answer also means there is a place for statements of fact and truth. Just because the answers Jesus gives are relational does not mean they are less-than-objectively true. Just because Jesus sometimes answers our questions with more questions does not mean we are only left with questions and no answers.

Jesus also answers questions with statements of truth that do not permit an infinite multitude of interpretations. "Verily, verily," he says to us concerning the truth. So we dare not hide behind some "pop philosophy" that says "What's true for me may not be true for you." What Jesus says is true, whether you accept it or not.

Here are some examples of Jesus giving answers that are statements of truth. "Very truly I tell you,' Jesus answered, 'before Abraham was born, I am!'" (John 8:58, NIV11). "Jesus answered, 'Everyone who drinks this water will be thirsty again, but whoever drinks the water I give them will never thirst. Indeed, the water I give them will become in them a spring of water welling up to eternal life'" (John 4:13-14, NIV11). "Jesus answered, 'I am the way and the truth and the life. No one comes to the Father except through me'" (John 14:6, NIV11). "Jesus answered, 'Very truly I tell you, no one can enter the kingdom of God unless they are born of water and the Spirit'" (John 3:5, NIV11). And these are just a few examples.

---

[2] For more on this, see the essay "Why do you ask?" on page 283.

Are there still questions and ambiguities beyond some of these answers? Undoubtedly so. But the answers given do form a path in the right direction; they also rule out false answers.

I'm willing to admit that the line from that old praise song, "Jesus is the answer," might be misinterpreted as a slogan in today's world. It might make people think Jesus is nothing but a quick-fix religious solution, not too much different than swallowing the right kind of pill. In order to keep the focus on relationships, it might be wise for us to say not only that "Jesus is the answer" (which means that the answer is personal, even a person), but we could also say that "Jesus answers" (Jesus is a person who responds to us). Jesus answers all who seek truth, forgiveness, comfort, strength, and direction. Jesus answers.

If we would look to Jesus for answers, or rather, if we would look to Jesus to answer us, we will find ourselves just as amazed as the religious leaders were long ago, listening to him as a boy in the temple: "Everyone who heard him was amazed at his understanding and his answers" (Luke 2:47, NIV11).

Bible [1]

D ialogues and debates over the issue of same-sex behaviors can be frustrating for everyone involved. Those who regard such behavior as sinful are quick to quote Bible verses. Those who approve of at least some forms of same-sex behavior get frustrated with this move and say something like, "But I believe the Bible too." And then we reach an impasse. My belief in the Bible leads me to say same-sex behavior is sinful, but their professed belief in the Bible leads them to the opposite conclusion. Is there any way forward in understanding each other?

Perhaps we could just chalk this up to differences of interpretation: "I believe the Bible, you believe the Bible—we just interpret it differently." This seems reasonable on the face of it. We're well acquainted with how two Bible-believing people can draw very contradictory interpretations. Bible-believers can be found on all sides of debates about baptism, ordaining women to ministry, warfare, capital punishment, and the Second Coming. But in spite of these different interpretations, we usually are willing to admit that our theological opponents still believe the Bible.

But when it comes to same-sex issues, many of us have a hard time understanding how those who affirm same-sex behavior can possibly say they believe the Bible. Any and all references to same-sex behavior in the Bible are unrelentingly negative. There is no commendation of such behavior anywhere, but only condemnation. Even the coming of Jesus, which transformed much of what we read in the Old Testament, did not change this negative assessment of same-sex behavior. From Genesis to Revelation we find no crack in the monolithic witness of Scripture against it.

And this is very much unlike other issues. Take baptism, for instance. We might interpret the Bible as supportive of infant baptism, but we would have to admit that some texts seem more supportive of "believer baptism." Or consider warfare. We might believe the Bible makes allowance for "just wars," but we know other Scriptures lend themselves to an ethic of non-violence. There are many controversial issues for which both sides of the

---

[1] Based on an editorial entitled "What Do We Mean By 'I Believe the Bible'?" which I wrote for *The Sunday School Guide,* Vol. 84, June 11, 2006, 15, 26-27. Used by permission.

debate can find supportive verses, and then it becomes a matter of weighing the interpretive force of those verses. But when it comes to the issue of same-sex behaviors, we can find no countervailing witness of Scripture.

So what do people who affirm same-sex relations mean when they say they believe the Bible? What is it that they believe the Bible is? Or more specific to this issue, what would a progressive have to believe the Bible is in order for them to still affirm same-sex behavior? I'm in danger here of putting words in their mouths, but here are some guesses.

Maybe, for instance, a person believes the Bible is a mixture of fallible human words and the divinely-inspired infallible Word of God. If that's the case, then it's the job of believers to pray for the Holy Spirit to help them discern which parts of the Bible can be safely ignored and which need attentive obedience. Those who believe this about the Bible might conclude that the verses about homosexuality were merely human words from that time which did not accurately convey God's real intentions. God's Word is not found in the verses that oppress others, but instead is to be found in the verses about social justice, grace, and not judging others. The problem with this perspective is that Paul said, "*All* Scripture is God-breathed" (2 Timothy 3:16, NIV11, italics mine), not just some Scripture (which of course, raises the issue of the canon, but that's too big of an issue for this essay).

Or perhaps a person believes the Bible is a true and inspired record of God's dealings with the world two thousand years ago—and therefore very helpful to us—but the Spirit of God is still at work in the world, and so we must be open to the fullness of truth that God continues to teach us.[2] With this approach, it would be simple to conclude that because humanity was not yet ready in biblical times for good expressions of same-sex behaviors, God spoke against it in the Bible. But now, through the Spirit's work, times have changed, and we are ready for the truth that love can find expression in same-sex relations. While it's true, however, that Jesus did talk about sending the Spirit to lead us into all truth (John 16:13), we should be wary of any message from the Spirit that undermines what the Spirit has already inspired in the Bible—with the notable exception of what the Spirit has already changed in Scripture (like the requirement of circumcision). For Jesus himself said that "Scripture cannot be broken" (John 10:35, ESV).

Then again, it could be that a person believes the Bible is inspired by the Holy Spirit to give both general principles (which are always relevant) and concrete examples (which may or may not be as directly relevant). We learn from Scripture the big truths of grace, holiness, forgiveness, life, love, and justice. We also see many specific examples (in narratives as well as laws) of those big truths, but in some cases the examples no longer apply. Here again, someone who approves of same-sex behavior would emphasize

---

[2] For more on this, see the essay "Teachings of the Spirit" on page 248.

the big truths about love and justice, while downplaying specific examples of laws and stories that rejected same-sex behavior. Those who take this position would also likely be aggravated by conservative Christians who, in their opinion, are neglecting the weightier matters of Scripture.

Admittedly, there's a sense in which all of us use larger themes of Scripture to interpret specific details of Scripture, but we'll fall into error if we focus only on those larger themes. That's because the concrete details of Scripture are what keep the larger themes from being distorted by our own ideas. For instance, today people hear the big word "grace" and think of unconditional tolerance that pays no attention to whether something is sinful or not. The concrete details of Scripture, however, show that biblical grace not only extends acceptance to sinners, but also empowers them to change.[3] While conservatives might run the risk of becoming Pharisees who major on minor things and neglect what's most on God's heart, I would hesitate to describe a person's sexual actions as being of minor importance to God. God knows our sexual behavior shapes nearly everything about us, with great potential for joy or disaster.

Or how about the person who believes the Bible is a true revelation from God, but it must take its proper place in the larger scheme of revelation. For example, the Bible is *special* revelation that must work in tandem with the *general* revelation of creation. And on the other end of the spectrum, the Bible is only the written Word that points to the fuller revelation found in Jesus, who is even more properly called the Word of God. Supporters of same-sex behavior who believe this about the Bible would argue that we must pay attention to what creation and culture—not just the Bible—are revealing to us about same-sex behavior. Also, since Jesus carries more revelatory weight than Scripture, it should give us pause to realize that Jesus never talked about homosexuality.[4] But the underlying problem with this approach is the belief that revelation in Christ and creation might possibly contradict Scripture. Conservatives, however, believe that cannot happen. Instead Christ, creation, and Scripture all re-affirm one another. Those who hope creation and Christ will veto the biblical ban on same-sex behavior are waiting in vain.

Those who favor and those who oppose same-sex behavior might both claim to believe the Bible, but they probably do not believe the same things about the Bible. All Scripture is God-breathed, alive and active, sharper than any two-edged sword, true and unbreakable, a lamp to our feet and a light to our path, bread for the journey, able to accomplish that for which it has been sent, and useful for equipping the people of God for righteousness.

---

[3] For more grace, see the essay "Fifty shades of grace" on page 86.

[4] For more on these themes, see the essays "Creation" and "Red letters" on pages 65 and 194, respectively.

Binary

Sometimes a new label comes along, and it takes a few hearings before you start to understand what it's about. One that's fairly new to me (but maybe not to others) is the adjective "binary." Until recently, it was mostly heard in conversations about computers that use binary code.

Binary code is founded on the base-2 numeral system in which the only two numbers are 1 and 0. Most of us are far more accustomed to the base-10 numeral system, which has ten different digits (0-9). In base-10, the right-most number is in the one's column, the next column over is the ten's column, the next column is the 100's column, etc. In base-2, with only two digits, the right-most column is the one's column, the next column is the two's, then the four's, the eights, the sixteen's, the thirty-two's, etc. So whereas base-10 would write the number 39, base-2 would translate that same number as 100111 (which is equivalent to 32 + 0 + 0 + 4 + 2 +1). Whether you understand that or not is not that critical. But where this is helpful for computers is that 0's and 1's translate into off's and on's, so that by turning a signal off and on in different sequences, the computer can send rapid messages.

But now the word "binary" is getting used in other contexts to signify situations in which there are only two options. A binary person, for instance, does not see things in zeros and ones, but they might see the world through the lens of various polar opposites: black and white, right and wrong, conservative and liberal, Republican and Democrat, capitalist and socialist, red states and blue states, and—with regards to gender—men and women.

This term is not normally used by conservatives (who tend to be binary people), but by progressives as a subtle (or not-so-subtle) form of criticism. "Why do you have to be so binary?" they might ask. Or they might criticize a conservative as a binary person. The implication is that the binary approach to life is too simplistic (with the additional implication that binary people are simple-minded). Progressives might say, "The world is far more complicated than many think. There's a whole rainbow of colors, not just black and white; and even a whole rainbow of skin colors. And there's a whole range of political options. Since Europeans function with multiple political parties, why are Americans so in love with the two-party system, with all third-party attempts crumbling to the ground?"

And for that matter, some progressives wonder why we take such a binary approach to gender. They prefer to see a whole rainbow (or should we say alphabet) of gender options available to people. Yes, there are straight men and women, but there are also LGBTQA+. Some prefer to delineate all the different types of genders out there so you can find your true self, but others prefer to say there's a whole spectrum of genders. For instance, although we commonly distinguish seven colors in rainbows (ROYGBIV), they actually contain a multitude of shade variations between each color. In the same way, a progressive might say, there's no need to set up a certain number of genders, but instead each person can find their place within an entire spectrum of gender variations.

In response I would have to say that if we truly want to avoid being simplistic, we need a bigger picture yet. One simplistic solution has been to see everything from a binary perspective, so that everything is black and white (and thus we miss out on all the wild colors of God's world). But the other simplistic solution has been to see everything from a spectrum perspective, as if everything is a rainbow. This too is simplistic because the rainbow is missing two important colors: black and white.

The truth is that some things are binary: they are black and white, right and wrong. While other things are more like a spectrum or kaleidoscope. Wisdom knows how to discern which is the appropriate way to view the different parts of creation.

On the level of creation you can see this. For example, it's a binary part of creation that some things are alive and others are not. There's a binary distinction also between the Creator and the creation. But the spectrum aspect is also seen in creation, as we see a myriad of animals, amphibians, reptiles, insects, birds, etc. Paleontologists are still trying to figure out if dinosaurs are more like reptiles or birds, or something else altogether. Physicists attempt to see if light is more like a wave or a particle. Some things are binary, some are not.

And this is true on a moral level as well. Some things are black and white. Ritualistic sexual abuse of children is purely evil. Rescuing a child from that danger is completely right. Other things are more on a spectrum, such as the manner in which God calls people to observe the sabbath. This principle also applies to doctrine and biblical interpretation. Some doctrines and interpretations are binary, clearly right or wrong. But a number of things can be doctrinally and biblically correct along a spectrum of acceptable options.

So, on the one hand, if we make everything a spectrum, then we lose the right to oppose any action or say that any interpretation is incorrect. And on the other hand, if we make everything black and white, we would descend into endless prideful arguments over small matters, with no allowance for circumstances or different perspectives. Because of temperament and background, it will vary from person to person how much they see the world in terms of a spectrum or in a binary matter. That will happen. But no one should try to eliminate the spectrum or the blacks and whites.

I'm not going to make a case for it in this essay (that's covered by plenty of other essays), but I regard the morality of same-sex behavior from a binary perspective (to use other people's terms). It's sin. I also use the term "gender" in a similar binary fashion. With regards to humanity, God only made two genders: men and women—even the exception of hermaphroditism testifies tragically to the duality of the genders. What is not as clear to me, however, and here I would shift to a spectrum perspective, is the question of the best pastoral care and evangelistic practices for ministering to the LGBT community. I can see a wide spectrum here ranging from tough talk (but be careful to do it in love) to subtle nudges toward the truth.

All in all, the term "binary" might be useful in this debate, but I would avoid using it as a near-synonym for "simplistic." A lot of very complex and worthwhile things can be accomplished with binary code on a computer, and a lot of complex and worthwhile ministries can be accomplished even when done from a binary perspective.

Celibacy

A young woman I know is now approaching her late 30's. She has never married; she has never had sex; she has never really even dated. She would dearly love to do all those things, but it has not happened. Yet, she has not been in turmoil about that. She has managed to press on in life, following Jesus, making a positive difference in her church and in her world. There has been no moaning or groaning about not meeting Mr. Right.

Some might think she has the so-called gift of celibacy, but it's not a gift she asked for, cultivated, was born with, adopted as her lifestyle, or heard as a calling from God. If the right man and opportunity came along, I believe she would be glad to marry him. She's only celibate because so far there has been no other choice—at least within the framework of obedience to Jesus.

Some might look at her situation and think, "Well, you know, everyone deserves to find some sexual satisfaction, if not fulfillment, in life. If there's no marriage on the horizon, there are other ways to find sexual fulfillment. You could make yourself available and hopefully find a stable situation for living together. Or maybe you could find a lesbian partner. Or pornography might be of some solace. If there's no option for marriage, we'd all understand if you found sexual fulfillment in some other way."

As far as I know, no one has ever voiced that to her. But if they did, I'm confident she would immediately reject such ideas. She's a follower of Jesus, and he only allows for sex within marriage between a man and a woman. She'd rather find fulfillment in Christ than in sexual disobedience.

I bring this up because of an argument I've heard a few times in favor of same-sex behavior. The argument goes something like this (and I hope I'm being fair in how I present it). "Here are these people who have no recollection of being anything other than attracted to their same sex. They have a human need to experience sexual intimacy with another human being. But you're telling them that if they are not attracted to marrying someone of the opposite sex, then their only option is to live without sexual fulfillment. You can say all you want that they should follow a celibate lifestyle, but in 1 Corinthians 7:7 Paul said that celibacy is a spiritual gift, and if they don't have that gift, then it's hardly fair or humane to expect them to live without sexual intimacy—especially since our society is clearly more comfortable with same-sex marriage being an option."

An example of this argument can be found in Jim Brownson's book *Bible, Gender, Sexuality*. He critiques the traditionalist position because it "requires us to assume that *all* gay and lesbian Christians who cannot change their sexual orientation are called and gifted for a life of celibacy." But that's neither true nor helpful, says Brownson. He contends, in fact, that it's counterproductive, for "asking Christians not called to celibacy to remain unmarried is opening the door to sexual immorality."[1]

I completely disagree with this contention. The young woman I mentioned earlier is part of a segment of single heterosexual Christians out there who may or may not have the gift of celibacy, but they still refrain from sexual relations simply out of obedience to the Lord. For Jesus to ask them to do this, even if it may become a permanent situation, is not asking the impossible. They may be tempted to lose their virginity, but Christ would ask them to resist this temptation, even if they have no special calling to celibacy. He would say the same to those tempted by same-sex relationships, whether they have a special gift of celibacy or not.

Obedience is not a special calling; it is the Lord's call on every believer. And so to all people—whether same-sex attracted or opposite-sex attracted—the Lord issues a call to obedience, and obedience means sex only happens within the marriage of one man and one woman.

---

[1] James V. Brownson, *Bible, Gender, Sexuality* (Grand Rapids: Eerdmans, 2013), 144.

Certainty [1]

Elsewhere in this book, I contend that the primary reason that conservatives do not want to compromise on LGBT issues is our certainty about what God has revealed about it. [2] We may not be as certain about the best way to approach the matter pastorally, but we are certain about what the Bible teaches on this.

Many progressives might be shocked that anyone could claim certainty in this matter. But my sneaking suspicion is that even if they never would say such a thing about themselves, many of them are just as certain about their position as I am about mine. If they were uncertain, why would they affirm someone in engaging in same-sex behavior or perform a same-sex marriage? If they were uncertain, why would they ordain those involved in same-sex relationships or risk splitting a denomination over the issue? If they were uncertain, why would they be willing to depart from a moral teaching that the church has held since the first century?

So I don't believe that conservatives are the only ones who are certain about their position on this issue; it's just that we may be more willing to say so.

Unfortunately, certainty has become a dirty word, an obscenity not to be uttered in polite theological conversation. When a believer says, "I know" or "I'm sure," some theologians recoil as if they had just heard a four-letter word. Christians are urged to break away from the vulgar masses who have a "lust for certitude," a seductive idol living in sin with synonyms like fanatical, uncompromising, intolerant, and dogmatic. In today's environment of pluralistic tolerance, doubt may have an honored place in the household of faith, but theological certainty is in danger of being disinherited.

Before it's too late, I would like to put in a good word for theological certainty. Even though the word "certainty" has been burdened with ugly connotations, Christians should not give up on it or its positive synonyms, like assurance, assuredness, confidence, conviction, and sureness.

---

[1] Most of this essay, starting at the fourth paragraph, comes from an article I wrote entitled "The Lust for Certitude," which appeared in *Perspectives: A Journal of Reformed Thought,* Vol. 14 (June/July 1999), 11-13. Used by permission.

[2] For more on this, see the essay "What's the big deal?" on page 275.

According to the Scriptures, theological certainty is a good thing. Luke writes his gospel so that his friend Theophilus "may know the certainty of the things you have been taught" (Luke 1:4, NIV11). Paul's colleague Epaphras prays for the Colossians that they may stand "mature and fully assured" (Colossians 4:12, ESV). Hebrews 10:22 invites us to "draw near to God with a sincere heart and with the full assurance that faith brings" (NIV11). The next chapter even includes certainty in its definition of faith, "Now faith is being sure of what we hope for and certain of what we do not see" (Hebrews 11:1, NIV).

The Bible celebrates many certainties of faith. It is certain that God is alive, that God's love is forever, that God's Word is true, and that God's promises are reliable. "You know with all your heart and soul that not one of all the good promises the LORD your God gave you has failed. Every promise has been fulfilled; not one has failed" (Joshua 23:14, NIV11).

The gospel of Jesus Christ is also filled with certainties. "Here is a trustworthy saying that deserves full acceptance: Christ Jesus came into the world to save sinners" (1 Timothy 1:15, NIV11). "For to be sure, he was crucified in weakness, yet he lives by God's power" (2 Corinthians 13:4, NIV11). "Let all the house of Israel therefore know for certain that God has made him both Lord and Christ, this Jesus whom you crucified" (Acts 2:36, ESV). Jesus is the cornerstone laid in Zion "for a sure foundation; the one who trusts will never be dismayed" (Isaiah 28:16, NIV).

The certainty of judgment on the wicked is also emphasized in Scripture. Proverbs 11:21 says, "Be sure of this: The wicked will not go unpunished, but those who are righteous will go free" (NIV11). "For of this you can be sure: No immoral, impure or greedy person—such a person is an idolater—has any inheritance in the kingdom of Christ and of God" (Ephesians 5:5, NIV11).

We could multiply other scriptural references to certainty and sureness, but these should be sufficient to show that there is no gospel if there is no certainty. Certainty itself is not the problem. Uncertainty is not the solution. What's needed is for God's people to be certain in a particular way. All certainty is not created equal. Some kinds of certainty are more desirable than others. It might be helpful to contrast three kinds of undesirable certainty with the theological certainty which is appropriate for Christians.

Ideological certainty versus the certainty of faith
Ideological certainty is that which has lost (or is in the process of losing) its connection with living faith in God. It finds certainty in slogans, statements, positions, and propositions. A person who is ideologically certain may vigorously defend the virgin birth, but not know new birth in Christ. A man may be certain of "once saved, always saved," but not really know the Sav-

ior. A woman may be certain that same-sex behavior is a sin, but not pray to the Friend of Sinners.

God, however, calls us to a certainty that grows out of a vital relationship of faith in him. We don't just trust propositions that God will save, we trust God himself to save. As we place our trust in God and experience his reliability and faithfulness, we then learn the certainty of faith. P. T. Forsyth said our certainty is based on God's certainty which we come to know through faith. We do not arrive at certainty; it arrives at us. Certainty comes to us in the person of Jesus Christ, who not only speaks truth but is the Truth. [3]

This does not mean we are pitting propositional truth against personal truth. They need to work in tandem. Because Christians have certainty in God by faith, we can also have certainty in propositions that arise out of the relationship of faith. Perhaps we could call them relational propositions. Our certain trust in God cannot help but lead us to see the certainty of relational propositions like God is alive ("Jesus lives in my heart"), God hears ("the Lord answered my prayers"), God forgives ("my guilt was lifted"), and God speaks the Scriptures ("that Bible verse spoke to my need").

We are not certain of some minimalist theism, but certain of the fullness of the gospel. All the truths of the Scripture are relational propositions. We are certain that biblical statements are true because we have placed our confidence in the God who speaks them. In spite of the various interpretations we have of the Bible, and the uncertainty that that seems to create, Christians can be united in being certain that God speaks the Scriptures to us. We cannot, then, dispense with propositional truth, but we do need to ground our certainty of it in the faithfulness of the God we trust. If we don't, we end up with ideological certainty, instead of the certainty of faith.

Ideological certainty is always a temptation for Christians. Those who are ideologically certain often begin with the certainty of faith, but then slowly move away from it. While in college, Max was introduced to Jesus Christ. He trusted Jesus, and so he trusted what Jesus said in the Bible. Because of unbelieving professors and friends who questioned him, however, he wondered whether the Bible was a subjective truth that he only believed because it met his needs or an objective truth that stood whether he believed it or not. Thinking those were the only two choices, Max opted to regard the Bible as objective truth. He took this Bible object in hand and studied it even more, learning to defend its propositions against all doubters. Max was becoming very sure of biblical truth (and also very sure of himself), but in the meantime, he began neglecting his personal relationship

---

[3] Peter Taylor Forsyth, *The Principle of Authority in Relation to Certainty, Sanctity and Society: An Essay in the Philosophy of Experimental Religion* (New York & London: Hodder and Stoughton, 1913), 43, 81.

of faith with the Lord. Max was moving from the certainty of faith to ideological certainty.

Max's problem arose because of the false choice between objective and subjective truth. Of course, God's Word is not subjective truth, subject to our emotions and tastes. But to say that the Word is objective truth is to say too little. The term "objective truth" rightly highlights that the Word is true whether we believe it or not, but it easily happens that objective truths become objects over which we have control—a piece of mental furniture to move where we wish. Instead of looking at God's Word as subjective truth or objective truth, we should consider God's Word as the Subject, in the grammatical sense of being the active agent. God's Word is alive and active, a sharp sword proceeding directly from the mouth of God. It is not an object that can be separated from God like a verbal orphan. It is not a spear that shoots from God's mouth and leaves him. It is a sword that is always in God's grasp. You can't have the Word without the God who speaks it.

As Eugene Peterson said, "Words, separate from the person who speaks them, can be beautiful just as seashells can be beautiful; they can be interesting just as skeletons can be interesting; they can be studied with profit just as fossils can be studied with profit."[4] But God did not speak his words to be beautiful, interesting or profitable. He spoke them so we would get in touch with him by faith. There is no certainty in the Word without faith in the certain God who speaks it. According to P. T. Forsyth, the goal of the Christian is not to be certain of being certain, but of being certain of Someone beyond our certainty. Certainty is not found within ourselves, but in the God we trust.

Fortress certainty versus the certainty of hope

Some object to certainty because it appears to immobilize people. Because of their certainty, they see no need to change, grow, or learn anything new. Why should they set out on a quest of knowledge when they have already arrived? Why should they consider a new idea when they are already safely in the shelter of truth? This is a fortress kind of certainty in which everything is explained and in order. Since the truth is immutable, fortress certainty assumes that our thoughts should be just as immutable.

It's understandable why we might treat certainty like a fortress. Whenever disorder breaks into our lives, we seek security, and we find it in the certainty of God's truth—not the uneasiness fostered by human opinions.[5] But certainty does not have to cut us off from growth and change. Theological certainty is not only something we have by faith, but also something we

---

[4] Eugene Peterson, *Reversed Thunder: The Revelation of John and the Praying Imagination* (San Francisco: Harper & Row, 1988), 13.

[5] Herman Bavink, *The Certainty of Faith* (St. Catherines, Ontario: Padeia Press, 1980), 20.

move toward in hope. Although we are absolutely certain of truth in Jesus Christ, we do not attach the same absolute certainty to our present understanding of him. Paul already knew Jesus Christ, but he did not consider himself to have arrived in complete knowledge and certainty. He pressed on "to know Christ and the power of his resurrection and the fellowship of sharing in his sufferings" (Philippians 3:10, NIV).

Paul's certainty of hope is in marked contrast to a song from the early days of the Jesus movement, which said, "My ideas about Jesus will always be the same, because it says in my Bible that He doesn't change." This is a classic misunderstanding. It's what some have called an "immunity of current understanding," thinking that whatever we're certain of right now is the final truth.

Although the truth of Jesus does not change, how we understand that truth will. Although there is absolute truth in Jesus, no Christian can yet claim to know it absolutely. The certainty we have in the Lord is always there, but it undergoes change and growth. Hope energizes us as we move from present certainty to the fuller certainty of the future.

But if our knowledge is in a state of change, how can we be certain of anything? This question is especially baffling to those who are ideologically certain (as discussed in the previous section). Ideological certainty has no room for growth and change—propositions and slogans are either true or false. But the certainty of faith, with its focus on the reliability of the person of God, does have room for growth and change. Just as a husband can have certain knowledge of his wife, but continue to grow in his understanding of her, so we can have certain knowledge of God, but continue to grow in our understanding of him.

That certainty and change can co-exist is suggested by 2 Peter 1:19. Before Jesus came, the disciples were certain that the prophets spoke the truth about the Messiah. But when they heard the Father testify about Jesus on the Mount of Transfiguration, they changed in their understanding of the Messiah. This new truth, however, did not undermine their former certainty, but expanded it. According to 2 Peter 1:19, "We have the word of the prophets made more certain" and our certainty will increase even more "until the day dawns and the morning star rises in our hearts" (NIV).

The certainty of hope freely admits that it doesn't know all the answers at present. We do not know on what day the Lord will return. We do not know what we ought to pray for. Like Abraham, we do not know where God is leading us. Like Job, we do not understand all the mysteries of the universe. Like Jacob we don't always recognize that "the Lord is in this place" (Genesis 28:16, NIV). The certainty of hope doesn't have all the answers, but it does have *some* answers from God. The certainty of hope may see through a glass darkly, but it still sees.

The certainty of hope also has room for questioning and wrestling with God. We question God, as Job did, because we are certain God has the answers. We wrestle with God, as Jacob did, because we are certain that God gives the blessing. It is not doubt, but theological certainty that makes us press on through our trials to a fuller knowledge of God. Doubt is not the great fertilizer of faith that some people claim. According to the Bible, doubt is not so much a matter of the intellect (being partly-convinced), but of the will (being partly-committed). The half-hearted commitment of doubt does not help people grow. It only immobilizes people. Instead, that which brings growth and transformation is sure and certain commitment, pressing on in hope through the questions and wrestlings.

In one sense, being certain is like standing on the rock of truth instead of the shifting sands of opinion. Some people, however, use this metaphor to justify a fortress mentality, in which we are fixed to one spot, incapable of change and growth. Perhaps we could follow P. T. Forsyth's suggestion that while rock is better than sand, soil is even better yet.[6] When we are certain, we not only stand on a rock, but also grow in the vital soil of truth. Like a rock, the soil of truth will not give way, but unlike a rock, the soil of God's truth will nourish and transform our lives.

If we think all truth is relative, we will be stuck in a bog of uncertainty. If we think we have already arrived at all truth, we will be stuck in a fortress. But if we live by the certainty of hope, we will grow and flourish in the garden of God.

Arrogant certainty versus the certainty of love

Many people today object to certainty because it sounds so arrogant. How can anyone but the proud think they know what's true? How can anyone but the conceited claim to have the answers?

Many of those brimming with certitude are guilty as charged. They pompously talk down to their opponents. Like Elihu, they claim, "Be assured that my words are not false; one who has perfect knowledge is with you" (Job 36:4, NIV11). They are unable to admit they could be wrong, or that their knowledge is incomplete.

Even worse, if they are in positions of power, they might use their power to pressure, silence, censor, imprison, banish, or even kill their foes. The arrogant quickly become intolerant. Because of arrogant certainty, Saul of Tarsus tried to destroy the church. Because of arrogant certainty, Christians have conducted inquisitions, waged holy wars, and killed heretics. No wonder John Locke believed that the only way to create a tolerant society was by demonstrating that no one can have complete certainty about matters of faith.

---

[6] Forsyth, 37.

But certainty does not always have to lead to arrogance and intoler-ance. Love has the power to bring certainty to its knees in humility and ser-vice. We are not called to be certain so that our side wins denominational debates and culture wars. We are not called to be certain so that we can as-sert our rights to be right. God calls us to be certain for the sake of others, especially for the sake of a lost world. "For Christ's love compels us, because we are *convinced* that one died for all...that those who live should no longer live for themselves but for him who died for them and was raised again" (2 Corinthians 5: 14-15, NIV11, italics mine).

The world needs us to be certain—not with the certainty of arrogance and intolerance, but with the certainty of love. The world does not need moralistic lecturers pointing their fingers; rather, the world needs confident witnesses who will speak the truth clearly and fearlessly. The world does not need high-handed control freaks trying to dominate discussions; rather, the world needs poised servants who know what needs to be said and done. The world does not need self-appointed authorities; rather, the world needs God-assured ambassadors for Christ.

Love is what equips Christians to be the witnesses, servants, and ambassadors so needed by the world. Notice, however, that love does not eliminate certainty from these roles. Love only brings certainty to its knees. Who would believe an uncertain witness? Who wants to be helped by a servant who doesn't know what she is doing? Who would trust a vacillating diplomat? The world needs and wants Christians who live in the certainty of love.

Perhaps a paraphrase of 1 Corinthians 13 would help us understand this certainty of love:

If I speak assuredly in the tongues of men and of angels, but have not love, I am only a resounding gong or a clanging cymbal. If I am certain of all mysteries and all knowledge, but have not love, I am nothing. If I am so certain that I am willing to make great sacrifices, but have not love, I gain nothing.

The certainty of love is patient and kind with those who believe differently. The certainty of love will not envy when falsehood gets better press. The certainty of love will not boast or be proud of having a corner on the truth. The certainty of love will not be rude, hot-headed, or engage in power plays to promote the truth. The certainty of love will rejoice in the truth and weep over falsehood.

Instead of crushing opponents, the certainty of love always protects. Instead of suspecting conspiracies, the certainty of love always trusts. Instead of taking desperate measures, the certainty of love always hopes that God's truth will prevail. Instead of writing off an opponent, the certainty of love always perseveres.

Theologies, doctrines, catechisms, and debates will one day cease. All our certainties are only partial, but when Jesus returns, we will leave behind our childish certainties and embrace certainty in its fullness. Yes, we do see now, but only dimly. We do know now, but not fully—at least not until we see Jesus face-to-face. Until that day, we have the certainty of faith, hope, and love—and the greatest of these is love.

Certainty does not take on this loving quality through human determination. This kind of certainty is the result of experiencing the gracious love of God in Christ Jesus. Every Christian knows what it means to be turned from the false certainty of being right in our own eyes to the true certainty of being right in the gracious eyes of the Father. We know the heart's power of self-deception. We know that Jesus was crucified by people like us, who were sure they were helping God's cause. We know that when Jesus prayed, "Father, forgive them, they know not what they do," he was forgiving cocksure people like us. Because we are so sure of these gospel truths, we dare not be certain in an arrogant, intolerant way. We need the certainty of love.

The certainty of love not only humbles us, but it also makes us tolerant of others. But it's not the tolerance of contempt or aloofness. It's not the tolerance that closes its eyes and ignores others. It's not the tolerance that gives people an unconditional right to be wrong. It's not the tolerance that hides the truth so as not to offend others. Since God loved us so much that he could not let us deceive ourselves, we must have the same love for others.

Rather, we show a tolerance shaped by that word's etymological roots, meaning "to bear or carry." Love bears all things. Jesus bore the cross. Jesus bore our sins. Jesus continues to bear with sinners. Out of the certainty of love, the Lord carries (tolerates) the erring world into the future. Rather than dropping the curtain on a depraved world, the Lord carries it along, providing ample opportunity for repentance. "The Lord is patient with you, not wanting anyone to perish, but everyone to come to repentance" (2 Peter 3: 9, NIV11).

Tolerance does not mean approving others. Tolerance does not mean ignoring others. Tolerance does not mean leaving people be. Tolerance means investing yourself in others, taking their burden upon yourself and carrying them from one place to another. Tolerance means we carry the world to God in our prayers. Tolerance means carrying the lost sheep close to our hearts. Tolerance means we carry the paralyzed world to the Great Physician, even if we have to break through the roof to get them to Jesus (see Mark 2:1-12). Tolerance means we hold up and support a world which would otherwise collapse under the weight of lies. Without the presence of tolerant, burden-bearing Christians, the world would quickly descend into post-modern tribal warfare, with every brand of so-called truth at war against all others.

The certainty that God desires to instill in us must be filled with love, even for those who err. Without love for others, we become like the false teachers described in Titus 1:16, "They claim to know God, but by their actions they deny him" (NIV11). John added, "Whoever says, 'I know [God],' but does not do what he commands is a liar, and the truth is not in that person" (1 John 2:4, NIV11). Where there is no love, there is no true certainty. Where there is no love, certainty is nothing but self-assertion.

We have seen, then, three seductive forms of certainty. Ideological certainty lures us away from our relationship with God. Fortress certainty hinders us from growing and being transformed by the Lord. Arrogant certainty causes us to disobey God's call to love. The pursuit of these seductive certainties could indeed be condemned as a "lust for certitude." But not all certainty prostitutes itself like this. God wants us to know him and his will in the certainty of faith, hope, and love.

Change [1]

In the daily comic strip "Grand Avenue," the brother shares his philosophy about change with his sister in three panels: "There is nothing permanent except change. The only constant is change. Change is all around us. Change is everywhere." His cynical sister answers in the last panel, "Great...so how about if you *change* the subject."

I'm feeling the same way. Can't we change the subject? Yes, I know everything is changing. The world, media, technology, music, youth culture, the economy, education, the job market, political parties, the family, people's expectations, denominational loyalty—it's all changing, and churches need to make changes to address the new situations.

This issue enters into the same-sex debate because some say that conservatives are just afraid of change. If they would just learn to go with the flow and the changes happening in society concerning same-sex relationships, we would all be better off. But I can't help but wonder if by riding the waves of change, we might be missing the boat.

When we focus on change as the hallmark of being a missional church, it quickly becomes apparent that we'll always be hopelessly behind. We might restructure our church or denomination to better relate to our culture, only to find that our culture has already moved in a new direction, and all our radical changes are dismissed as "old school." We are told by experts that what worked in youth ministry three years ago doesn't work anymore, and that what helped churches grow five years ago no longer appeals to the target audience. As a matter of fact, talking about a target audience is already passé.

Trying to keep up with an ever-changing culture sounds to me like a recipe for ongoing frustration on the part of churches and their leaders. The only ones who will like this mad scramble to stay current will be the marketers and consultants who sell books, DVD's, and curricula to help churches that are afraid of getting left behind.

---

[1] Based on an editorial entitled "Change: The Subject," which I wrote for *The Sunday School Guide,* Vol. 87, September 14, 2008, 17, 30-31. Used by permission.

Someone might write me off as a victim of *Future Shock,* a condition Alvin Toffler wrote about long ago in which changes happen so rapidly that we are unable to keep up. But I can't help but wonder if all this talk of change is all that helpful.

When I looked up the English word "change" and related terms in my Bible, I was surprised by what I found. None of the biblical references to change were about cultural changes or the corresponding need for the church to change its missional strategy to that culture. Many of the biblical references to change are negative. The evil ruler of Daniel 7:25 is accused of trying to change set times and laws. Pharaoh is shown to be evil because he changes his mind about letting the Hebrews go. Jeremiah rebukes the Judean king for changing his mind and allying with Egypt against Babylon. In the New Testament, we are warned about "godless men, who change the grace of our God into a license for immorality" (Jude 4, NIV). And worst of all are the people who try to change gods, exchanging the true God for worthless idols (Jeremiah 2:11; Psalm 106:20; Hosea 4:7; Romans 1:23).

Then we find verses in which it is a good thing *not* to change. We are often told that God is not a human being who changes his mind and fails to keep his promises (see Numbers 23:19; 1 Samuel 15:29). Unlike a shifting shadow that continually changes (James 1:17), Jesus Christ is the same yesterday, today, and forever (Hebrews 13:8). The reason we have been saved instead of destroyed is because God does not change in his love for us (Malachi 3:6).

There are, of course, good kinds of changes in the Bible. Saul was changed into a different kind of person, at least while God's Spirit fell upon him (see 1 Samuel 10:6-9). The prophets called the people to change their ways through repentance (see Jeremiah 7:5) and rebuked them for their unwillingness to change (see Psalm 55:19; Jeremiah 13:23; 15:7). Jesus told us to change and become like little children in order to enter God's kingdom (Matthew 18:3). And even though he did not use the word "change," Paul talked about being transformed by the renewing of our minds into the Lord's likeness by reflecting his glory (see Romans 12:2 and 2 Corinthians 3:18). Finally, we hear of the great change that will happen on the last day when our bodies will be changed through resurrection (see 1 Corinthians 15:51 and Philippians 3:21).

The biblical use of the English word "change" does not seem to give any backing to those who say the church must change in order to meet a changing culture, for the Bible does not talk about sociological change or changes in missional strategy. When the Bible talks about change, it's mostly talking about moral and spiritual changes: condemning bad changes and advocating good ones.

Of course, there is a place for talking about changes needed to better reach the world with the gospel. Without using the word "change," the book of Acts does describe how the church changed in order to bring the gospel to the Gentiles. Also, without using the word "change," Paul describes in 1 Corinthians 9 how he changes evangelistic methods, depending on whether he's talking to those under the law or those without the law. So changes of methods and strategies are needed for evangelism, but I'm not convinced that this means we must focus on constantly changing in order to reach a constantly-changing world. Perhaps the best way to reach a world in flux is by focusing on what does not change.

The characters on the stages of history may change, but the character and grace of God do not change. The ways of technology may change, but the way of salvation does not change. Medical procedures may change, but the heart of God to reach the lost does not change. The economy may fluctuate, but the price paid for redemption does not change. Celebrities may change by the minute, but Jesus Christ is the same yesterday, today, and forever. Cultural mindsets may be on the move, but the human heart (sinful and in need of salvation) does not change—until it is transformed by the power of the Holy Spirit.

By all means, adapt the message as best you can to a rapidly-changing world, but don't get frustrated or anxious trying to keep up with all the fads in order to be relevant. And don't compromise the message so that you give a green light to sin. Instead of over-working your eyes to spot the latest trends, keep your eyes fixed on Jesus. The most important changes you can make do not involve your church's style of worship music, the lingo used in the sermon, the shape of your building, or the curricula used in your small groups. The most important changes you can make involve throwing off the sins that so easily entangle, so you can run the race of faith (see Hebrews 12:1-2).

Chasing down cultural changes can be like chasing after the wind. So let's change the subject and talk about what doesn't change. The grass withers, the flowers fall, but the Word of God endures forever (Isaiah 40:8). Technologies become obsolete, trends lose traction, the latest loses appeal, the fads fade, what's hot cools off, and what's contemporary becomes contemptible, but the Word of God endures forever. It's a Word that creates the only changes worth seeking.

Choices

We live in a time of unprecedented choices. Just going into a restaurant presents you with a myriad of options. Beef, chicken, fish for an entrée? Let's go with beef. Hamburger, taco, meat balls, steak? Hamburger. Rare, medium, well-done? Well done. Cheeseburger, barbecue burger, avocado burger, jalapeño? Cheeseburger. American, Swiss, cheddar, mozzarella? Cheddar. Pickles, relish, ketchup, onions, lettuce, mayo, mustard? On and on it goes, and you haven't even gotten to your two sides or what you want to drink. I know a man who got out of prison after a decade and the first thing his family did was take him to a restaurant. He was overwhelmed by the options.

We face many choices in life—most of which are pretty trivial in nature, but some of which are life-changing. But oddly enough, we also have a lot of addictive behaviors in this country that rob people of their choices. People choose to do something and like it enough to keep doing it until they lose the ability to not do it. Sometimes it's a case of a substance adding chemicals to the brain that cause a person to lose their ability to resist it. Think opioids, alcohol, cocaine, and other drugs. Sometimes it's a case of an activity causing the body to produce its own chemicals so that people lose their ability to resist it. Think video games, pornography, and exercise. It's almost like we don't know what to do with our freedom, and so we plunge into some activity that will take it away. We use our freedom to lose our freedom.

And then there are also elements of ourselves in which we feel like we had no choices at all. We don't remember making any choices to be a certain way or to like a certain thing. We just were that way. On the more trivial end of things, I have no idea why I like words, how they fit together into sentences, and their etymological origins. I even like the shapes of the letters in words (which explains my large font collection). I have no recollection of deciding to like words and letters. I just do. It probably has something to do with my environment growing up, but also with how my brain operates.

But on a more serious note, most of us do not remember ever choosing to be a certain way in terms of personality and temperament. Even from birth (or so our parents tell us) we already were quick-tempered or laid back. From early on we were cuddly or independent, fearful or brave, secure or insecure, grabby or generous. We didn't choose to be like that, but we were like that. Sometimes we've outgrown a certain way of being, or trained ourselves to overcome it, but most of us live out personal qualities and interests that we never chose (or at least don't remember choosing).

The *good* qualities we have, with no choices made on our part, we can count as blessings from God. I happen to be pretty even-keeled and slow-to-anger in times of conflict, but I take no credit for that whatsoever. I thank God that he blessed me in that way. The ongoing *bad* qualities we struggle with—with no awareness of ever choosing to have those qualities either—those we can call sin.

One important aspect of sin is its enslaving character. Without God's power, we are simply unable to resist it. As Jesus said in John 8:34, "Very truly, I tell you, everyone who commits sin is a slave to sin" (NRSV). Paul expressed his own sense of being a slave to sin in Romans 7:15-16, 18-19, 22-23, "For I do not understand my own actions. For I do not do what I want, but I do the very thing I hate...For I have the desire to do what is right, but not the ability to carry it out. For I do not do the good I want, but the evil I do not want is what I keep on doing...For I delight in the law of God, in my inner being, but I see in my members another law waging war against the law of my mind and making me captive to the law of sin that dwells in my members" (ESV). In other verses in this text, Paul's wording implies that sin is so much in charge of him that it doesn't even feel like it's the real him doing it (see Romans 7:20).

No one, of course, is a robot totally programmed by sin. Even as we function as slaves to sin, we make lots of little choices along the way. There's a complex matrix of choice and bondage at work in our hearts. The person addicted to alcohol makes a choice to call up a friend (who often likes to party). He makes a choice to go visit the friend. He later makes a choice to have his first can of beer, and the second, and...the tenth. He is conscious of what he is doing—to a point. Somewhere in the process, he is no longer choosing anything, but has become fully in bondage to the drink. Perhaps we could liken it to falling off a very tall cliff. While you're falling, you do have a few choices in how you're going to twist your body and what you'll think about on the way down. But none of those choices will keep you from hitting the bottom. You can have all kinds of options for the way in which you will sin—maybe in a party mode or maybe in a Pharisaical mode—but on your own you cannot "not sin."

Most people can identify with what Paul is saying. If we had our choice, we never would have done the things we did, but we did do them anyway. The sense of having no choice, and yet knowing we're responsible for what we did, is part of the sinful human condition. But Paul has hope in all this, for he looks to Jesus for deliverance and freedom (see Romans 7:24-25). This freedom starts to happen when we are united with Jesus in his death on the cross: "We know that our old self was crucified with him so that the body of sin might be destroyed, and we might no longer be enslaved to sin. For whoever has died is freed from sin" (Romans 6:6-7, NRSV). This doesn't mean Christians are now sinless; the battle still rages. But now we have received power and freedom to win at least some of the skirmishes—with final victory awaiting the day Jesus returns. But in the meantime, "thanks be to God that you, having once been slaves of sin, have become obedient from the heart to the form of teaching to which you were entrusted, and that you, having been set free from sin, have become slaves of righteousness" (Romans 6:17-18, NRSV).

It is through this lens that I view the issue of same-sex behavior. Many progressives will say that we need to affirm those involved in same-sex relations because they are only living out who they were made to be: "They did not choose to be same-sex attracted, and so how can we blame them for being themselves or expect them to act any differently?" They bring up this lack of choice with the hopes of stirring empathy. It's as if they were saying to me, "You would not like to be faulted for something you had no choice about, so don't fault these people for that."

Well, such words do stir up empathy in me, but not in the way they think. As a sinner myself, I know just what it's like to feel like I had no choice in some deed I had done. Apart from the work of the Holy Spirit, I am unable to choose for God or for the good. Apart from the work of the Holy Spirit, I am unable to choose against the sin in my heart. But I cannot use this as an excuse. I dare not say to God, "I did not choose to be sinful, so how can you blame me for it or expect me to act differently?" I am in bondage to the sin in my life, and I am responsible for it. But I am not in despair, because the Lord offers me forgiveness and the power to loosen—and even break—the chains of sin and live for him. When I am walking on the path of temptation, I have many small choices I can make to choose differently, and by the Spirit's power, I can. I don't always, but the Spirit is at work, and "we shall overcome."

I believe the LGBT community can find that same hope.

Circumcision

Progressives are probably less inclined than conservatives to look for an isolated verse here or there that seems to back their case for more acceptance of the LGBT community. Instead, they are looking for bigger picture patterns of how God might be at work in the world. One story many of them find helpful is the story found in Acts 10-15 of how the church moved from being a Jews-only group to being a group that included people from every nation of the world. And in this process the church had to figure out what to do with some Old Testament verses that created obstacles toward the full inclusion of non-Jews, especially verses about unclean food, and even more, the verses that commanded circumcision. If the Spirit of God could set aside these earlier requirements in order to include non-Jews, isn't it possible that the Spirit is doing the same today in order to include the LGBT community? At least that's their hope.

Here's what happened in Acts 10-15. In chapter 10, a Roman centurion named Cornelius was very interested in following the Jewish faith. One day God sent him a vision telling him to invite a man named Peter to come to his home with a message. Shortly after this, the apostle Peter had a vision as well in which a great sheet came down from heaven filled with unclean animals, and a voice told him to rise and eat. Peter was aghast because as a practicing Jewish Christian he did not eat unclean food. The vision, however, was repeated twice more with a heavenly voice saying each time, "What God has made clean, you must not call profane" (Acts 10:15, NRSV). Right after this, the invitation came to visit Cornelius. Peter was hesitant to go since he had never been in the home of a non-Jewish person before. But he went because of his vision and Cornelius' vision (which had been reported to him).

While sharing the gospel at Cornelius' home, the Spirit was poured upon all those assembled, and they began to speak in tongues (as Peter did at Pentecost). Peter and his companions interpreted this as a movement of God and saw no reason not to baptize them on the spot, even though none of them had been circumcised.

When news got back to other Jewish Christians, Peter was criticized for fellowshipping with uncircumcised men. But when Peter explained all that had happened, no one raised any objections. Perhaps they thought this was a one-time exception caused by God's Spirit (see Acts 11:1-18). Not long after this, however, persecution caused the Jewish Christians to scatter outside the boundaries of Israel, where the gospel was quickly accepted by many non-Jews. Paul was brought into this work by Barnabas (see Acts 11:19-26).

In Acts 13-14, we read that Paul and Barnabas were set apart by God to go on a mission journey, which took them to Cyprus and south-central Asia Minor. The Jews in those communities were fairly resistant, but many non-Jewish people were eager to follow Jesus.

The rapid growth of the non-Jewish sector of the church was of great concern to some of the Jewish Christians back in Judea. They sent representatives to Antioch to inform the church that they must all be circumcised and follow the law of Moses. To settle the controversy a meeting of leaders was called in Jerusalem (Acts 15). At this meeting both sides spoke—with Peter, Paul, and Barnabas arguing for not placing undue requirements on the non-Jewish converts. In the Jerusalem church, Jesus' own brother James had become an influential leader, so when he sided with Peter and Paul, the issue was decided. A message was sent to all the churches informing them that non-Jewish Christians would not be required to be circumcised, but they were asked to avoid food offered to idols, sexual immorality, meat from strangled animals, and meat with blood in it (see Acts 15:20). As you might expect, it did take a number of years for this decision to prevail (as evidenced in some of Paul's letters).

So let's consider more closely the dynamics found in this story to see whether they provide a model for full inclusion of the LGBT community today. [1]

The Spirit pushes us to cross boundaries.

For progressives, the idea here is that just as the Spirit caused the church to get out of its comfort zone and reach out to non-Jews, so the Spirit is pushing us to cross boundaries in reaching the LGBT community.

In the book of Acts we do indeed see the Spirit causing the church to cross geographic boundaries—from Jerusalem to Judea to Samaria and to the ends of the earth (as Jesus said in Acts 1:8). There is also a crossing of ethnic and racial boundaries, so that the church begins to include Ethiopi-

---

[1] Most of the dynamics observed in the next few pages in bold print were first observed by a friend of mine named Stephen Mathonnet-VanderWell in post he wrote for *The Reformed Journal's* daily blog called "The Twelve"—(blog.reformedjournal.com/2015/10/06/the-ever-bigger-welcome/). He did not explicitly connect his essay with the LGBT controversy, but that issue certainly seems to be in the background. I wrote my own responses to him in an email, much of which became part of this essay.

ans, Macedonians, Greeks, Romans, and barbarians. Each person from these various ethnic groups still belongs to that group, but since Christ has "broken down in his flesh the dividing wall of hostility" (Ephesians 2:14, ESV), they now fellowship with each other and no longer live in hostility toward each other.

The Spirit also worked in the church to cross other sociological boundaries that divided rich from poor, slave from free, men from women, and full-bodied from the disabled. In some cases, one's sociological position could not change (such as gender), while other aspects of one's sociological position might possibly change (as in the case of slaves who were freed or the disabled who were healed), but that certainly was not the case for everyone.

But there was also another kind of boundary that the church learned to cross, namely, moral boundaries. Although the instinct of Pharisees was to withdraw from evil-doers, it was the way of Jesus to reach out to prostitutes, extortionists, and partyers. The disciples followed Jesus in this, crossing moral boundaries to bring the gospel to adulterers, gossips, idolaters, hot-heads, murderers, and more. But here the boundary-crossing had a different result. People who encountered Jesus in the preaching of the gospel were transformed by that encounter. Whereas they had been adulterers and idolaters, now they were transformed so that they no longer were engaged in such activity.

And it is at this point that conservatives and progressives disagree about crossing boundaries toward the LGBT community. Both agree that the Spirit is prompting the church to reach out to the LGBT community, but they disagree on what should happen next. Is being gay or lesbian like being part of an ethnic group, so after they trust in Christ they can remain just as gay or lesbian as they were before they met Christ (as progressives might say)? Or is being gay or lesbian about a moral behavior that the Spirit intends to transform (as conservatives would contend)?

I side with the conservatives here. I do so because in 1 Corinthians 6:9-11 Paul talks about some of the moral boundaries that the gospel crossed in Corinth and how the Spirit then transformed those people. Paul's list not only includes idolaters, adulterers, the greedy, drunkards, slanderers, and thieves, but also those engaged in same-sex behaviors. Paul's message is not that these people needed to shape up before God would accept them, but that when God accepted them, they would be transformed in such a way as to live differently: "And such were some of you. But you were washed, you were sanctified, you were justified in the name of the Lord Jesus Christ and by the Spirit of our God" (1 Corinthians 6:11, ESV). [2]

---

[2] For more on this text, see the essay "Seven texts" on page 211, especially pages 220-223.

For the sake of mission, the Spirit sets aside some Old Testament laws.
For progressives, the idea here is that just as the Spirit set aside long-established Old Testament laws about unclean food and circumcision in order
that non-Jews could be more readily included in the people of God, so today
the Spirit is setting aside laws about same-sex behavior in order to welcome
people of the LGBT community into the church.

Sometimes people will refer to some of these laws as taboos. This is
rhetorically effective because most people do not regard the term "taboo" in
a positive way. A "taboo" is regarded as a humanly-constructed prohibition,
full of superstitious silliness. And if we are able to label any commandment
against same-sex behavior as nothing but a mere taboo, then no wonder the
Holy Spirit would want to get rid of it.

But the laws being set aside in Acts are not man-made taboos, but divine commands. In the story of Acts 10, the Spirit is calling Peter not just to
break a human taboo, but to break God's previous commands about food
and how to treat Gentiles. So the precedent is set for God to retract his own
commands about these matters, at least for non-Jews.

This does not, however, open up the door to throwing every divine
command into the mix, so that all that God has said before might eventually
be tossed out. The commands that are no longer to be enforced among non-
Jews are those very commands that were designed to make Israel distinct
from other nations (although other ethnic groups also did practice circumcision). Other commands that reflected God's will for all humanity, and not
just the Jews, appear to still be in place by the end of the New Testament
era. So while we do see the Spirit pushing the church to cross boundaries by
reaching out to adulterers, gossips, hot-headed people, and dishonest tax
collectors, we do not see the Spirit urging anyone to break commands
against adultery, gossip, rage, and dishonesty.

That's where the rub lies with the LGTB issue. All of us can conceive of
the Spirit breaking through to reach out to the LGTB community, but not all
of us believe the Spirit is urging anyone to break biblical commands against
same-sex behavior. If same-sex behavior was only spoken against in the Old
Testament, there might be a case for seeing how the coming of Christ has
subverted those commands. But if same-sex behavior is prohibited in both
testaments, it would be a misstep to set them aside. It often happens that
when a Bible verse meets head-on with a person's sexual drive, usually the
sex drive will find a way to prevail. God calls us to work against this human
tendency.

Visions from God can help the church see new possibilities.
For some progressives, sometimes the church gets so stuck in a certain way
of looking at biblical texts that God needs to intervene with visions and

dreams to get the church out of a rut to follow his will. Just as the Lord gave Peter a vision to get the church to move beyond old understandings of the circumcision laws, so perhaps God is giving a new vision to the church to help move them beyond old understandings of same-sex commands.

The church, of course, is called to embrace divine visions and dreams. God proclaimed in Joel 2:28 that a day was coming when "I will pour out my Spirit on all flesh; your sons and your daughters shall prophesy, your old men shall dream dreams, and your young men shall see visions" (ESV). And Peter declared this was fulfilled on the day of Pentecost (Acts 2:17-18).

We are to be a people of visions and dreams, but there is an ambiguity built into those terms. Some visions and dreams are purely of human origin, as Jeremiah declared (Jeremiah 14:14; 23:16). My own experiences in the charismatic movement have taught me to make a big distinction between human visions, dreams, and wishes, and the visions and dreams sent by the Spirit. Often it seems like vision-casting in the church is just a sneaky way to persuade people to commit to a human leader or a building project.

I would like to believe that if the Lord spoke to me in a fashion similar to what Peter experienced (dreams corroborated with a prophecy about who is coming to call, followed up with an outpouring of the Spirit similar to Pentecost), then I would lay down my previous biblical interpretations and yield to the Spirit. But maybe I don't know myself that well, and my cautious nature would rule the day. I know people who have said to me that they've had an Acts 10 experience and now believe that God is no longer calling same-sex behavior unclean, but I have yet to be convinced. It seems more like wish-fulfillment—they wish it to be true and thus recruit God to their cause.

God's Spirit is setting up a trajectory of welcoming more people.

For progressives, this means that God's Spirit is setting up a pattern of welcoming more and more people into God's kingdom. In recent years, we have seen the Spirit move us along the trajectory toward greater racial reconciliation and more acceptance of women in leadership. And so, they argue, a similar trajectory is pointing us in the direction of welcoming and celebrating the place of the LGBT community in God's kingdom.

We do indeed see a trajectory in Scripture that undermines slavery and frees women to be all that God made them to be. It's a trajectory that bore great fruit beyond the first century, even though some might think the trajectory moved much too slowly. But I fail to see any trajectory established in Scripture with regards to same-sex behaviors.

And we must remember, it's not just the establishment of God's will that moves in a trajectory; temptation and corruption also follow their own trajectories. So while some people might regard the movement toward affirmation of same-sex behavior as a *transformative* Spirit-led process, others of us see this is a *conformative* world-led process that is undermining the faith. Most people today would analyze the world as getting worse and worse with regards to violence, sexuality, greed, and deception. Thus it seems rather naïve to regard the affirmation of same-sex behavior as the one Spirit-led exception to the general immoral direction being taken by our declining society.

Our sense of what's "yucky" is not a good moral compass.

This is how some progressives have described what's happening in Acts 10. For his whole life Peter had been trained to experience revulsion about a set of animals regarded as unclean in the Old Testament. Just the thought of eating a fish with no scales (like an eel) would seem "yucky" to him. And we're familiar with that same kind of food revulsion. North American culture can hardly stomach the idea of eating a dog, but that's acceptable in other cultures. But Peter learns in his vision that just because some food seems revolting to him does not mean it's revolting to God: if God calls it clean, it is clean. Progressives then take this principle and apply it to same-sex behavior. Many of us learned to regard such behavior as disgusting and "yucky," but that response may not be God's response. If God has deemed it acceptable, who are we to say no?

Let's back up and first think about the "yuck" factor as a moral guide. Part of me agrees that just because something's different or odd or gross to me does not mean it's actually bad (whether talking about what you eat or how you have sex). But I'm not sure this point really affects this debate as much as it once did. Our society talks so frequently about same-sex behavior that I think, except for maybe the older generation, hardly any sexual action has the "yuck" factor anymore. Talk-shows, mainstream movies and pornography have all contributed toward a normalizing of what was at once time regarded as deviant and even "yucky."

Yet there's a part of me that laments this loss of the "yuck" factor. I know the term abomination used to be associated in the Bible with same-sex behavior, and that that term had the unfortunate consequence of making many view LGBT people themselves as abominable—beyond the pale of compassion and love, resulting in disdain, abuse, and even violence directed toward them. And that's not good. But on the other hand, is it good that we have lost all sense that various actions should be regarded as abhorrent, only to be replaced by other phrases like "interesting," "edgy," "pushing the envelope," "a diversity to be celebrated," or even just a shrug of the shoulder? The media may still promote various programs as "shocking," but one gets the impression that we're really not shocked or appalled by anything anymore. Something seems wrong with a society like that.[3]

But now let's return to the line about unclean animals now being clean because God has declared them to be so. Some read this line and ask, "If God can reverse his judgment on the cleanliness of animals to eat, then who are we to say God could not reverse his decision about sexual actions that he had earlier forbidden?" But has God actually made such a declaration about same-sex behavior? There are a number of people who would like him to do that, but wanting it to be so and it actually being so are not the same thing. As far as I can tell, God has not declared same-sex behaviors to be acceptable in his sight.

There is great power in a story.

Progressives take note of how Peter's story (as well as Paul's stories of his missionary journey) seem to have influenced the outcome of the council in Jerusalem. No big exegetical debates were recorded, but testimonies were given. Many progressives believe that the best way to change the church in a more LGBT-affirming direction is not by engaging in exegetical duels, but by telling stories from the LGBT community of how they have experienced life-changing transformation from Christ and yet have remained gay or lesbian in their way of life.

It cannot be denied that there *is* tremendous power in story. Peter's thrice-told story was very persuasive in the early church. So was Paul's thrice-told story of his calling on the Damascus Road. And at denominational gatherings designed to foster harmony, the emphasis is on telling our personal stories.

But both sides have stories. Those opposed to Peter at the Jerusalem Council likely had their stories too. So the stories duke it out, if you will, and the prevailing story continues. As someone once said, history is the story told by the winners; their story is the one that gets repeated, and the stories of others get ignored. That saying often gets used to criticize orthodox Christianity, so I feel ambiguous about it, but I do understand it.

Nonetheless, an awareness of the conflict of stories helps us realize that just because someone has a story does not validate what they have concluded from the story. I personally can tell the story of a same-sex attracted man who was transformed to the point of leaving his same-sex attraction behind. Others know stories of same-sex attracted people whose attempts to change only made them miserable. Stories must come into play, but we still must do the hard work of adjudicating stories.

---

[3] For more on this, see the essay "Abomination" on page 3.

Scripture plays only a small role in the Acts debate.
Progressives note that little appeal is made to Scripture in Acts 10-15 concerning why non-Jews are not bound by the commands about unclean animals and circumcision. We hear nothing from Peter or Paul about how we ought to interpret the relevant Old Testament texts, and James provides one Old Testament citation from Amos 9:11-12. So if the deciding factor at the council of Jerusalem was the movement of the Spirit, and not Scripture, why can't we follow the same line today? At least that's what some wonder.

It is notable that Scripture does not play a major role in the small portion of the Acts debate that was recorded. As some have said, the Pharisaical party in this debate probably would have won in a Scripture face-off (although, surprisingly, commands to be circumcised are few and far between in the Old Testament—much more frequent are the calls to be circumcised in a spiritual sense). This should give pause to those of us who are interested in Scriptural face-offs.

But even if Luke's very short summary of the council's discussion doesn't mention much Scripture, that doesn't mean that Scripture was unimportant in discerning the inclusion of the Gentiles. Later, Paul relies heavily on Scripture to make his case against requiring circumcision—especially in Romans, and Galatians. So we dare not make any decisions in the LGBT debate without closely examining Scripture.

As you can see, then, the setting aside of the commands to be circumcised in Acts 10-15 does not provide a model for setting aside biblical commands against same-sex behaviors. The latter commands still stand.

Common Ground

Jehovah's Witnesses have hardly ever come knocking on my door. I think it's because I've often lived in a parsonage next door to a church building. When the Witnesses figured out I was a pastor, they dismissed me as a hopeless case.

But I did have one brave young Jehovah's Witness try to convert me many decades ago. I didn't mind talking with him, but I didn't want to just go back and forth with opposing Bible verses. So I made this proposal to him: let's talk about what we believe in common.

So we proceeded, and we found a number of common beliefs, so much so that my young friend was beginning to crack. He assumed all my beliefs would be completely wrong, and when he saw how much we could agree on, he started to wonder if he was on the right path. So the third time we met, he brought along a "heavy," a more experienced Jehovah's Witness who only wanted to argue about my "wrong" beliefs. I never saw my friend again.

When I chaired our denomination's Commission on Theology, and we were at an impasse in talking about same-sex issues, I proposed that we follow a similar path by spending time looking for things we agree on that were relevant to the issue (we already knew that we agreed on things like the doctrine of the Trinity). Perhaps I didn't elaborate enough on why that might be helpful, but my suggestion garnered no interest, so we returned to our debate.

But I would like to use this essay to follow up on my suggestion. I think it's helpful for a couple reasons: (1) since so much of the debate is focused on points of disagreement, it might be helpful to step back, catch our breath, and shift into something a little more positive; (2) by presenting points of agreement, we might learn to resist the urge to lecture our opponents about something about which they already agree with us; and (3) by highlighting points of agreement, the parameters of the debate might become a little clearer.

But since I'm the only one writing this essay, I will be doing some guesswork about what the two sides might agree to. I'm positive that there are a few conservatives who might not even agree with the "points of agreement" that I present, and it's probable some progressives won't agree with my list of what they believe either. But it's a start, and I would welcome others to come up with their own lists.

You will notice, however, that I am not sticking only with the points of agreement, but also noting what we do not yet have a consensus on (and maybe never will).

1. **We agree that** there is such a thing as sexual sin which wreaks havoc in the lives of the people involved.
    But we do not have consensus on whether all same-sex behavior should be regarded as sexual sin.

2. **We agree that** *some* forms of same-sex behavior are sinful (such as promiscuity and rape).
    But we do not have consensus on whether *all* same-sex behavior should be regarded as sinful.

3. **We agree that** being gracious and compassionate sometimes means telling someone the truth about the wrongness of their actual or potential moral choices.
    But we do not have consensus on whether this is the kind of thing that should be said to those involved in or desiring to be involved in same-sex behavior

4. **We agree that** calling an action sinful—when it is not—is to speak a rejecting and condemning word to those involved in it, and only the increases the person's despair or anger, with the possibility of pushing that person away from Christ.
    But we do not have consensus on whether same-sex behavior is one of those actions which is wrongly labeled as sinful.

5. **We agree that** all people are sinners, whether they identify themselves as part of the LGBT community or not.
    But we do not have consensus on which same-sex behaviors are evidence of this sinfulness.

6. **We agree that** there is a kind of internal givenness in the self-understanding of those who are same-sex attracted.
    But we do not have consensus on whether this givenness is part of the bondage of sin or the good creative work of God, nor to what extent this givenness can be altered.

7. **We agree that** the LGBT community has been sinned against and therefore stands in need of justice.
    But we do not have consensus on whether justice also means affirming same-sex behavior.

8. **We agree that** the Bible verses which do mention same-sex behavior speak negatively against it.
    But we do not have consensus on whether these negative words apply to only some forms of same-sex behaviors.

9. **We agree that** self-deception, rationalization and the internal suppression of truth is a common component in the process by which people give in to sexual sin.
    But we do not have consensus on how this truth applies to same-sex behaviors.

10. **We agree that** a biblical response to same-sex behaviors must not only incorporate specific biblical texts, but also the larger theological picture of Scripture.
    But we do not have consensus on how the specific texts and larger picture speak to this issue.

11. **We agree that** heterosexual patriarchalism has played a role in the wrongful oppression of the LGBT community.
    But we do not have consensus on whether all opposition to same-sex behavior is based on heterosexual patriarchalism.

12. **We agree that** how we interpret biblical texts (about same-sex relations) is influenced by our life experience and/or what we want the text to say.
    But we do not have consensus on what conclusions are unduly influenced in this way.

13. **We agree that** some of the church's stances on various sexual issues in the past and how to respond pastorally have since come to be regarded as wrong-headed (for instance, the belief that sex is only for procreation).
    But we do not have consensus on whether the traditional stance against same-sex behavior might be another example such wrong-headedness.

14. **We agree that** the church's stand on sexual issues should be not be based on a general discomfort with the human body in general or sexuality in particular.
    But we do not have consensus on whether some people in this discussion (either affirming or not) are coming at these issues on that basis.

15. **We agree that** sexual desire and expression in themselves are good, life-affirming gifts from God, but are affected by sin.
    But we do not have consensus on the extent to which sin affects sexual desire and expression, especially with regards to same-sex relationships.

16. **We agree that** Jesus said nothing explicit about same-sex behaviors.
    But we do not have consensus on the significance of this.

17. **We agree that** God does have a will regarding sexual behavior.
    But we do not have consensus on what that will is with regards to same-sex behavior.

18. **We agree that** issues of social justice have often been neglected or downplayed by those who are concerned about sexual morality, and issues of sexual morality have been neglected or downplayed by those concerned about social justice.
    But we do not have consensus on what to do about that.

19. **We agree that** scientific findings must be included in our own understanding of same-sex behavior.
    But we do not have consensus on what weight current scientific understandings should have when it seems to counter Scripture.

20. **We agree that** a key element in the story of Sodom is the horror of homosexual rape.
    But we do not have consensus on whether that story also has something to say about non-coercive forms of same-sex behavior.

21. **We agree that** love and grace should be the key element in the church's response to the LGBT community.
    But we do not have consensus on whether love and grace must mean affirmation of at least some forms of same-sex relationships.

22. **We agree that** the church is called to unity, purity, and peace.
    But we do not have consensus on how those three elements should work together in the church's response to same-sex behaviors by church members.

23. **We agree that** the gospel brings transformation to those who trust in Jesus, including a transformation of sexual desire.
    But we do not have consensus on what the transformation of sexual desire for those who are same-sex attracted should look like.

24. **We agree that** the church in the past has argued about things that seem rather inconsequential today.
    But we do not have consensus on whether taking a moral position on same-sex behaviors will one day be seen as one of those inconsequential issues.

Is anything resolved by such a list? No, but it might help us discuss more clearly, so we don't make false assumptions about those who stand on the other side of same-sex issues.

Confronting

I have been a "general practitioner" kind of pastor for all of my 35+ years in the ministry. I never had a desire to be a specialist, such as a youth pastor or calling pastor, executive or preaching pastor. That's because I like the variety of the general practitioner position that comes with being in smaller to mid-sized churches.

I like to design bulletin covers, call on the elderly, teach young children, visit in the hospital when there's been a birth, attend committee meetings, take care of denominational business, and lead worship. There are also a few other jobs that are not "enjoyable," but they bring a sense of satisfaction. Those are the times when I walk with people through times of pain and sorrow: the difficult surgeries, the unexpected deaths, the prodigal child, the collapsing marriage, and such. It is rewarding to help people in times of distress.

But there's one job I dread. That's when I know someone needs to be confronted about a sin, and it's my responsibility to do it. I haven't had to do that very often, for which I'm grateful, but whenever it needs to happen, I am out of my comfort zone.

Occasionally it has gone well. I raise the issue and the person readily admits to it and wants to change their ways. A few times it has gone okay. I raise the issue, the person is willing to listen—guardedly. They might admit that what they're doing is sin, but don't seem ready to change their ways. But most often, it doesn't go well at all. I raise the issue, and the walls go up immediately. They don't usually throw a fit on the spot, because I approach them gently. But the look in their eyes tells me they think I have a lot of audacity to even bring it up. I will usually end our visit by saying, "If there's anything I've said that really bothers you, please let me know and we can talk about it some more." They usually don't do that; instead, they get all upset after I leave. It's no fun—not for me and, I assume, not for them either.

It's usually been two very different sins that I've had to confront: when someone is being a quarrelsome trouble-maker in the church and when someone has been involved in sexual sin. It's not that I think these are the worst of all sins, but they are the easiest to tell if they have occurred. I haven't called anyone out for idolatry or greed because I'm not sure I can tell when someone has committed these sins. I might suspect it, but have no proof. But if they've been quarrelsome with sharp words exchanged in social settings, then it becomes known to me, and it's my role to speak with those involved. Likewise, if there's sexual sin, usually there is some unusual sleeping arrangement, an unexpected pregnancy, or a devastated spouse to let you know what's happening.

Maybe as you read this, you are thinking that I must be some kind of professional critic, constantly telling people where they are in error. I don't think I am. I can only recall fewer than ten times I've had to personally confront someone about sin in my ministry, but each situation stuck in my mind as hard.

Confronting sin is uncomfortable enough for everyone involved, which explains why many pastors have just decided to say nothing about misbehavior. It hardly seems worth it. "Maybe," we think to justify ourselves, "what they're doing is not really a sin anyway. Just leave people alone and things will work out just fine, and they won't be resenting the church for sticking its nose into their business."

It's so tempting to take that route because we like to be liked (which is an occupational hazard for most pastors). Talking to someone about their sin often doesn't make us seem very likeable to them. And yet, it's our responsibility to help people become disciples who follow Jesus. That's why I keep doing it, but I have a harder time gearing up for it as I get older.

I bring this up in this book of essays about LGBT matters because I realize that my stance on same-sex behavior means that I have created more challenges for myself in this regard. It would be a lot easier to just cave in and affirm the LGBT community. I recently had a lesbian couple I knew ask by phone if they could use our church building for their wedding reception, which is against our church's policy. I tried to tell them gently, and offered to explain why in person; but I could tell that the few words I said were interpreted as rejection. They used to come to some worship services and fellowship events, where I thought they were warmly greeted. But I no longer see them at church. It would have been a lot easier to just say "sure" to their request, but it didn't seem right to participate in making something more permanent that I don't believe should happen at all. It's a pastoral care dilemma.

It's relatively easy to help members of the LGBT community feel welcomed at the church. The worship, the sermons, the fellowship events, the opportunities to serve—I don't think they'd find anything offensive (except the one time per pastorate that I have addressed same-sex matters). The rub comes when they want to request some formal, official recognition that overlooks their same-sex relationship, such as a wedding, baptism, or profession of faith. Then it feels like we need to have "that talk," that uncomfortable talk.

I feel slight jealousy toward those pastors who have no qualms about same-sex behaviors. They don't face these pastoral dilemmas—at least I don't think so. Although it's possible they face the same dilemmas when an LGBT parishioner has been acting in a promiscuous manner. I don't know.

I have often wondered if one reason some pastors move from a conservative position on this issue to a more progressive one is related to the issue of this essay. Did they change their opinion because they found a certain argument convincing, or was it because they just didn't have the heart anymore to tell someone that what they were doing was not God's will for their life? Did their opinions shift partly because they no longer cared to deal with the fallout when you question someone's lifestyle? Did they change their mind because they didn't like to see that look of rejection in the eyes of a person they genuinely like? I can't answer that question for others, but I can't help but wonder.

Conservative

Someone once wryly commented, "There are two kinds of people...those who say there are two kinds of people and those who don't." Americans tend to divide people into two camps. You're either Republican or Democrat; pro-life or pro-choice; evangelical or mainline; and of course, conservative or liberal. While these labels help us define ourselves and others, they also have their limits in usefulness. By lumping people together in big blocs, we often miss clear distinctions between individuals and positions. [1]

Most people who know me would probably label me as a theological or biblical conservative. That's partly because I come out on the conservative side of the progressive/conservative debate about same-sex behavior.

But in spite of my biblically conservative ways, I must confess that I am not always comfortable with others who call themselves conservatives. We may have the same opinion about a number of issues, but our styles are not always similar.[2] The more I reflected on this, the more aware I became that there's more than one way to be a conservative. I want to put the emphasis on being a *Christian* conservative, and I will be using some distinctive marks of the Protestant Reformation to explain what I mean.[3]

First, Protestant theology has always emphasized the centrality of the Bible. "Scripture alone" was a rallying cry of the Reformation. We do not base our thinking on what a good tradition says, but on what the Good Book says. A Christian conservative, then, will be someone who doesn't believe something just because it's the traditional belief of conservatives. We will want to be like the Jews of Berea, who after hearing Paul preach, "examined the Scriptures every day to see if what Paul said was true" (Acts 17:11, NIV11). The traditional conservative, for example, may tell us that all conservatives oppose taxes and gun control, but a Christian conservative won't go along with that agenda unless there's good biblical warrant for it. We are Christian conservatives, not *traditional* conservatives.

---

[1] For a different take on this, see the essay "Binary" on page 25.

[2] For more on this, see the essay "Allies" on page 10.

[3] I could have instead spoken of being a Reformed or Protestant conservative, but I didn't want to leave out conservatives of other Christian traditions.

Second, Protestant theology has taught us the principle of "Christ alone." We do not need other human mediators in order to know the Lord, for Christ is our only Mediator. There is no need for human priests to pave the way, for Christ is the one anointed High Priest, and in him we too are anointed as priests—able to approach the throne of grace. Because of the priesthood of all believers in Christ, a Christian conservative does not adopt a stance just because a prominent conservative spokesman has declared what we all must believe. We need to go to God ourselves and find the truth (in the Word)—not wait for a conservative leader to tell us what we should think. Our attitude should not be, "If those conservative leaders said it, I believe it." As much as we might appreciate them, they are not our popes. We are Christian conservatives, not *bandwagon* conservatives.

Third, Protestant theology has emphasized the principle of "faith alone." We are not saved through doing the works of the law, but through faith. Sometimes I get the impression from my fellow conservatives that if we could just get the right laws passed, then things would get better in our world. They speak as if our main goal is to make sure that righteous laws are enacted. While Christian conservatives certainly appreciate rulers and laws that follow biblical morality (and some of us are called to devote considerable time to advocating for these things), we also know that it is far more important for us to preach the gospel of faith in Jesus Christ. People and societies are not transformed by legislation, but by Jesus. The angels in heaven may nod their heads in approval when a righteous law is passed, but they reserve their celebrations for one sinner who repents (Luke 15:10). We are Christian conservatives, not *moralistic* conservatives.

Fourth, Protestant theology teaches the truth of "grace alone." We have experienced an undeserved love from God that can only be called "grace." And because we have been loved so lavishly in spite of our sins and errors, we want to love others in the same way. We love because God first loved us (1 John 4:19). Sometimes I cringe, however, when fellow conservatives use the language of mockery and hatred in making their case. Sarcastic venom, mud-slinging, threatening remarks—people saved by grace should have nothing to do with such things. Even if that makes us appear weak, we must be the model of graciousness to those we think are wrong, for the Lord has been gracious when we were wrong. We are Christian conservatives, not *hateful* conservatives.

Fifth, Protestant theology has always emphasized loving God with not only our heart and soul and strength, but also with our minds. Instead of giving free reign to our gut reactions, we stop and think through the best responses. We don't want to have knee-jerk reactions against what progressives say. They may actually have some valid points, but it will take brain power to listen fairly, instead of merely responding to red-flag words. We are Christian conservatives, not *unthinking* conservatives.

Sixth, the doctrine of total depravity has always loomed large in Protestant theology. Sin infects all of us, even the redeemed, even conservatives. Although we think we're right, as Christian conservatives we will also be aware of our own sin. In humility, we must recognize that we might be wrong, or that we might be expressing our right beliefs in the wrong way. And when we're wrong, we should be humble enough to confess it. We might hesitate to admit where we're wrong out of fear that it will give our opponents more weapons to use against our cause, but I think retractions and apologies, where appropriate, would actually strengthen our case. We are Christian conservatives, not *arrogant* conservatives.

Seventh, Protestant theologians never wanted to say that they had the last word. Their claim was that the church of Jesus Christ is "reformed and always being reformed" by the Word of God. This motto of an ongoing reformation means that we cannot in principle stand against change. Some changes may be for the worse, but some changes are for the better. We expect God to be continually changing and transforming the church. So unlike those conservatives who oppose change because they regard themselves as preservationists and guardians of the past, Christian conservatives welcome any and all changes which God brings through the Word. We are Christian conservatives, not *unchanging* conservatives.

Eighth, Christian conservatives also emphasize the truth of God's sovereignty. In spite of the mess that we are all making of this world, God is still on the throne. In an effort to defeat our foes, it's common for conservatives (and progressives) to increase the fear factor by painting worst-case scenarios of what would happen if the other side wins. For instance, some conservatives gave me the impression that losing our case against same-sex marriages will bring the end of civilization. But what about God in all this? Even when our legislatures and courts approve of immorality, it does not change the fact that God is working his purposes out in judgment or blessing. I believe that same-sex marriages will create lots of problems, but it doesn't change the fact that the Lord is in charge of human history. The end of 1950's morality, or the end of the United States, or even the end of the world, will not bring to an end the kingdom of God. And so we cannot be filled with fear. We are Christian conservatives, not *fearful* conservatives.

Lastly, and I owe this point to my friend Miguel Cruz, Protestants have also emphasized that all the glory goes to God alone. We speak the Word of God not to get our way, put our favored party into office, win a debate, or portray ourselves as God's favorites. When we talk about sin—same-sex sins or otherwise—it's not because we are against people, or that we want them to conform to our moral standards. We do it because we want God to be glorified in all things, and we don't want to see any belief or behavior stand that works against the glory of God. We are Christian conservatives, not *self-promoting* conservatives.

Yes, there are many kinds of conservatives—traditional, bandwagon, moralistic, hateful, unthinking, arrogant, unchanging, fearful, and self-promoting conservatives. But the Lord has not called us to be conservatives like that. Instead, we are to be Christian conservatives, following our unchanging Lord through the twists and turns of history.

Creation

If it had been up to me, I never would have invented sleep. When nighttime comes, I have to force myself to go to bed. I would much rather stay up and continue to use the time for all the things I like to do. Why should I waste a third of my life in bed, unconscious of what's going on around me?

If I lie awake at night (which is not that often), I'm not upset that I'm losing out on sleep time. Instead, I'm glad that I get to keep on thinking about life, and I might even get up to do something. When the opportunity arises to stay up all night for some reason, I like the challenge.

Recently, however, I had to stay up all night twice in three days, and it wasn't much fun. That's because even though I would rather do without it, God made me in such a way that I need sleep. If I have to, I can go about thirty hours without sleep, and then I hit a wall. My brain needs to be rejuvenated by a good night's rest. And that's true of everyone else too.

In a sense, my desire to go without sleep is a form of rebellion against God's creation. I am attempting (in vain) to ignore my body as it was created to be, and instead be something I am not.

The attempt to ignore or downgrade the good reality of creation has often created problems for the Christian church. It was common in first century Greek culture to think of the body as an impediment to life, a prison house of the soul. And that mentality continued to influence people even after they became Christians. Thus Paul had to deal with church members who argued against the resurrection of the body (1 Corinthians 15), thought that treating the body harshly was the best way to experience worship with the angels (Colossians 2:16-23), and believed Christians should not marry or eat certain foods (1 Timothy 4). To counter all this, Paul preached that Jesus created all things with the Father, was born in the flesh, and will someday bring a new creation with resurrected bodies. He would have agreed with C. S. Lewis, who said, "There is no good trying to be more spiritual than God. God never meant for man to be a purely spiritual being. That is why he uses material things like bread and wine to put the new life into us. We may think this rather rude and unspiritual. God does not: he invented eating. He likes matter. He invented it."[1]

But in spite of Paul's efforts, anti-creational false teaching continued to plague the church. In the second century a variety of heresies, now collectively referred to as Gnosticism, blossomed. One of the common ideas behind Gnosticism is a rejection of creation. They contrived strange notions of how the pure spirit of God could not possibly have been involved in creating a filthy world of blood, sweat, tears, semen, and urine. Nor could they accept that Jesus came in an actual physical body. Some of the Apostles' Creed can be read as an attempt to battle early Gnosticism, for it refers to the Father as the Creator; the Son being born, suffering, dying, and rising; and a future resurrection of the body for all.

Even today Gnostic anti-creational tendencies show up in many ways.[2] Although progressives would strenuously disagree with me here, there are some aspects of the case for LGBT acceptance that strike me as a refusal to accept God-given creational realities.

The first has to do with the biological reality of the human body and its sex organs. Men have penises; women have vaginas. And they were designed to fit together in sexual activity. Can men insert their penises in other body cavities, such as the mouth or the anus? Yes. Can something besides a penis be inserted into a vagina, such as a tongue or finger? Yes, again. And such actions are not necessarily wrong—although some actions may be more uncomfortable or less healthy than others. They have likely been a part of sexual play for as long as humanity has been created. But the primary sexual act involves the biological reality of a penis penetrating a vagina (or, alternately, a vagina enveloping a penis). And this gives us an obvious clue that the human body was created and designed by God for sexual activity between a man and a woman—not between two males or two females.

And yet, oddly enough, some seem to mock this idea. To talk of penises and vaginas seems vulgar and coarse to them. Why, they wonder, should we disturb the beauty of two men or two women enjoying the mutual pleasure of sexual intimacy by talking about how the "plumbing" doesn't fit together. Well, we don't intend to be vulgar or coarse, but we do intend to pay attention to creational reality.

But this raises the issue of appealing to creation to make moral decisions. My denomination recently took a look at a document called "The Great Lakes Catechism on Marriage and Sexuality." It was an attempt to use the question-and-answer method of catechisms to talk through some issues

---

[1] C. S. Lewis, *Mere Christianity* (New York: Macmillan Publishing, 1943), 65.
[2] See Philip Lee, *Against the Protestant Gnostics* (Oxford: Oxford University Press, 1987) for many examples of this.

about human sexuality from a positive perspective, and yet still speak against same-sex behaviors. One of the criticisms made by our Commission on Theology against this catechism was a reference to "creation orders." Here's what the Commission said:

> Historically, the appeal to creation orders has been a way of setting up an authority independent of Scripture, so that the church no longer needs to return to Scripture as the primary source of God's revelation. Given the reality of sin and its devastating effects on creation and human reason, it seems hard to imagine that we could ever ascertain the purposes of God in sexuality or marriage by seeking them in the "creation order" outside of the witness of Scripture. Further, appeals to "creation order" have been used to support things such as apartheid and misogyny. In appealing to a "creation order," the commission believes that this document distracts from its goal of "bearing witness to the kingdom of God."

Fair enough. Many have argued from the ordering of creation to justify all kinds of evil things, even Nazism. But the key problem, as the Commission notes, happens when creation is set up as "an authority independent of Scripture" or "outside of the witness of Scripture." This would indeed be problematic. And yet we find progressives doing this very thing when they appeal to the latest scientific study supposedly linking same-sex attraction to some study of chromosomes or the brain.

But while we would not want to set up creation as an authority *independent* of Scripture, there is nothing inherently wrong with declaring a creational reality that's *fully in line* with Scripture. Creational reality cannot legitimately be used to justify racism or misogyny, for Scripture declares the equal value of all races and genders. But creational reality does line up with the Bible when declares that God created two sexes—men and women—and one purpose for this creation of two sexes is that they would be fruitful and multiply: "So God created humankind in his image, in the image of God he created them; male and female he created them. God blessed them and said to them, 'Be fruitful and multiply; and fill the earth and subdue it'" (Genesis 1:27-28, NRSV). Jesus himself endorsed this idea when questioned about divorce, "'Haven't you read,' he replied, 'that at the beginning the Creator "made them male and female"'" (Matthew 19:4, NIV11; see also Mark 10:6).

While it's true that Genesis does not refer to penises or vaginas, the fact that God calls men and women to be fruitful and multiply demonstrates that they were designed for sex together. Does this mean sexual activity should only be engaged in if it's for a procreational purpose, as some have argued?

No, but it does mean that humanity is biologically designed by the Creator for sex to be between a man and a woman. Could God have designed it differently, so that we multiply asexually like amoebas or that sex would need three people for it to happen, or two people of the same gender? He could have, but creation and Scripture together show that he did not. To pretend otherwise is like me trying to be a human being without sleep.

The other way that creation seems to be ignored in LGBT matters has to do with transgender issues. I won't say much about this because I will readily admit that I know little about this from a scientific, psychological, or even pastoral standpoint. But it seems to me that no matter what the spiritual and emotional challenges of feeling transgendered are, the creational reality of a male or female body cannot be ignored. Some surgical procedures could give one the illusion of having a body of the opposite sex, but it's an uphill battle against the creational reality of the body.

Indeed, there seems to be no major moral problem with trying to shape the body in some way, such as tanning for darker skin, going to the gym to develop firmer abs, getting a tattoo, or getting a hair transplant to cover baldness (though some of these can still create problems). These are developmental adjustments in creational reality. But the bedrock foundation of having a male or female body is something God set in place from the beginning. And to wish it wasn't so is to set ourselves against creation.

In many settings, where a person's biological body does not matter (as is true of many occupations), being transgendered may be a non-factor with others. But there are other settings where the body plays a key role (such as athletics) where we should definitely acknowledge creational reality. Again, at the risk of sounding crude to some people, the woman who believes she is a man still has a body that will fool no one in the gym locker room. And the man who believes he is a woman will likely have an advantage when he tries out for the women's track team. Those involved in transgender issues and policies clearly need to keep sight of the creational reality of the body. A person with a male body may want to be a woman, and may feel like a woman trapped in a man's body, yet the reality of that body cannot be denied.

I would expect that those who feel differently on this transgender issue might argue back and say there is more to created reality than large body parts. How the brain is wired is also part of creational reality. Could it not be, they ask, that a person is created with a male body, but has also been created with a brain that is wired to be a female? I am not prepared to totally deny the possibility, for we also have in our world other anomalies like people born with ambiguous male and female sexual organs. But I am skeptical, for it seems to me that other than the reality of the body, what it means to be male and female can vary tremendously from culture to culture. For a man to say the he thinks and feels like a female may only mean that he doesn't fit his culture's message about what it means to be male, and instead he is enamored with his culture's message about what it means to be a female. So if a boy enjoys dolls and cooking and dressing up in frilly things—that doesn't mean he is actually a female. It only means he is a male who likes things that the majority of his own culture has deemed to be feminine. Perhaps cultures should not have tight and rigid ideas about what men and women should be like. But cultures would be foolish to move beyond the reality of the male or female body. Rather than disassociating one's gender from one's body, it would be better to make allowance for different expressions of what those with a male or female body should like or do—with the notable exception (because of Scripture and the created reality of the body) of engaging in same-sex behavior.

I'm still not a big fan of having my body prevent me from being the never-have-to-sleep person I want to be. And I'm guessing others are not a big fan of having a body that doesn't match their gender preference, or a body that isn't built for same-sex relations. But we are children of the Creator who made us and knows us best. It becomes us to gladly be who God has made us to be, body and all. For as the psalmist confessed to the Lord, "Your hands have made and fashioned me; give me understanding that I may learn your commands" (Psalm 119:73, ESV). Notice the link between God's creation of the human body and obedience. The best way to praise God for our created bodies happens when we obey God's commands for our bodies.

Debating [1]

I once taught a video Sunday School class that made me uncomfortable. Each week we would watch a short video clip of a debate between a Christian and a non-Christian over significant questions, such as "Is Jesus really God?" "Is the Bible reliable?" "Are there many ways to find salvation?" and "Did Jesus really rise from the dead?"

What made me uncomfortable is not that these questions were being asked. Since 1985 I have been raising many difficult questions myself in my "Discussion Questions" column in the weekly *Sunday School Guide.* Nor does it make me uncomfortable when non-believers articulate opinions that differ from Scripture.

What made me uncomfortable was watching the styles which some of the Christians used in the debate, styles which undercut their case for the gospel. One believing scholar, for instance, could not listen to his unbelieving opponent without a smirk on his face, as if he were thinking, "Yeah, yeah, yeah, this guy doesn't have a clue." The next Christian debater got all flushed in the face and let loose a torrent of words as if he could overcome his foe by having a higher word count in his sentences. Then there was the Christian who couldn't help but interrupt the non-Christian at every possible chance to point out flaws in the latter's argument. Another Christian adopted a very cold attitude as he precisely and accurately dismantled everything the unbeliever had just said.

It's hard to watch these believers contend for the faith. The content of what they say is excellent, but the way in which they say it undermines their case. One can see why many in the church are losing their taste for debates. While the world still tunes in to debates on talk shows and in elections (most of which are nothing more than verbal versions of professional wrestling), many believers today think we should do a lot less debating and a lot more dialoging instead.

But I'm not convinced. Even though I'm very aware of how debating styles can turn ugly, I'm not ready to give up on debating. Nor am I ready to

---

[1] Based on an editorial entitled "The Debate Over Debating," which I wrote for *The Sunday School Guide,* Vol 85, January 14, 2007, 15, 26-27. Used by permission.

embrace dialogue as the way forward, for dialogue also has its share of problems. While it's easy for debate to slip into disrespectful sarcasm, dialoguing can slip into problems on the other side of the ditch.

The main problem often afflicting dialogue, especially as practiced today, is its undercurrent of relativism. In many dialogues, it's regarded as bad manners to make any truth claim. People who like dialogue rather than debate are appalled when someone says, "I know...," or "the Bible says..." Instead, it is common to hear the following phrases in dialogue: "Nobody knows for sure, so let's just accept each other"; "I'm not saying 'you're wrong,' for we can each be right in our own way"; "Instead of looking for answers, let's just live with the questions"; "I think we can all agree that no one has the answer."

On the surface, these kinds of comments sound laudable. They give the impression that the speaker is humble about his or her own beliefs and respectful toward the beliefs of others. But if we look a little closer, these comments can often cover up an arrogance and disrespect which is characteristic of relativism. These comments actually make outrageous claims, which should be tested in debate. After all, those who say, "No one has the answer," are obviously excluding themselves from that assessment, for they make the absolute claim to *know* that no one has the answer. But if you raise an objection then you're reminded that this is a dialogue, not a debate.

That's why I'm often not in favor of dialogue. The rules are stacked against anyone who believes that specific truth can be known. Their claim that no one knows the truth for sure often becomes the ground rule in dialogue. So if you don't agree with the ground rule, you're not allowed to fully participate. If you believe God has revealed certain truths which can be known and which stand in opposition to other ideas...well, you have to keep that to yourself.

There has to be a better approach, a way that borrows the best from debate and dialogue, and rejects the worst. There has to be a way to debate truth claims without being disrespectful. There has to be a way to dialogue without caving into relativism. Maybe we could call it a debatalogue.

Here are a few characteristics from James 1:19, 21 (NIV11) of how debataloguing should be practiced among Christians and with non-believers.

(1) "Everyone should be quick to listen." In watching the videos I mentioned earlier, what really stood out is how often believers will interrupt their theological opponent. But the Lord calls us to listen to others. We cannot really make an adequate response, if we don't actually know what they said. Too often we hear a certain phrase spoken by another person, and we have a knee-jerk reaction. We quickly make assumptions and stick them with a progressive label or put them in a conservative category, rather than

hearing what they have really said. And we must not only listen to what others say, but also what they mean. It's easy to read the worst possible interpretation into an opponent's words, but we need to be charitable in our listening. If we listen, we might just discover we're not as far apart as we thought; we just use words differently to mean the same thing.

(2) "Slow to speak." We cannot be quick to listen unless we are slow to speak. Although some might interpret the slowness of our response to mean that they've got us stumped and they're winning the debate, we must run that risk by carefully measuring our response. Words chosen wisely can be influential. Our words should not come off the top of our heads, but from the depths of our soul. What is initially admired as quick-witted can often turn into what is quite-wicked.

(3) "Slow to become angry." When we are quick to let our tongue go, where it often goes is to the land of anger. It is said that the word "debate" is rooted in the idea of "beating down." Too many debaters want to use words to humiliate and vanquish their foe with insults and one-upmanship. Yes, we want to defeat lies, but we are not to be about the business of beating other people in an argument. We want to win them over, not defeat them. When Jesus told us to love our enemies and call God's blessings upon them, I believe he even meant for us to love our theological foes.

(4) "Humbly accept the word planted in you." The first three points all can be found in James 1:19, and taken by themselves they seem to promote dialogue, instead of debate. But in verse 21 of that same chapter and paragraph, James also issues a command that opposes the relativism so common in dialogue. He calls us to continue faithfully in the Word of God, the very Word that gave us new birth (James 1:18). Being quick to listen does not mean that every opinion we hear is equally valid. Being slow to speak does not mean we keep the truth of God's Word to ourselves as just one opinion among many. Being slow to anger does not mean that we give an accepting smile whenever someone speaks what's against God's Word. Whether we are debating or dialoging, we are called to continually measure everything by the Word of God—including our own currently-held beliefs—and never let go of that standard. We hold the truth of Scripture *humbly* (which is what verse 19 is all about), but we also hold the truth of Scripture *firmly* without budging an inch.

So let debates and dialogues continue, but not with the nastiness of the former or the relativism of the latter. Instead let us speak the truth—in love.

Erring on the side of grace [1]

The editorial section in most local newspapers not only features nationally syndicated columnists from the right and the left, but also some colorful local writers who seem to enjoy provoking the public on "hot button" issues. One such writer once attempted to justify and affirm same-sex behavior in my local paper. None of his arguments struck me as particularly truthful, but it was his conclusion that caught my eye. He confessed that it's possible that his positive assessment of same-sex behavior was wrong, but he was willing to run that risk because he would rather "err on the side of grace."

This is a line I've heard before. And on the face of it, there's something that seems compelling about it. Since God is a God of grace, doesn't it make sense for God's people, when faced with a controversial issue, to choose whatever response seems to be the most gracious? And if it turns out to be the wrong response, well, at least we responded in a manner that deals with others as God deals with us.

I want to affirm the importance of being on the side of grace, but I also want to examine more thoroughly this whole notion of "erring" on the side of grace. My hunch is that it's a line which betrays a profound misunderstanding of what grace is, and that the local columnist's use of the slogan takes us down the wrong path.

First, we need to recognize that grace simply does not err. It is always right and holy to show grace. God's will is always that we respond to others in a gracious way. When people sin against us, we forgive. When people hurt us, we bless. When people persecute us, we pray for them. When people fall into sin, we lift them up. Even if we have to admonish someone, we always do so with gentleness and respect—well aware that we too are only sinners saved by grace. There may be a number of different ways to show God's grace—ranging from forgiveness and welcome to encouragement and admonition—but they are all gracious responses. If we act in these ways,

---

[1] Based on an editorial entitled "Erring on the Side of Grace?" which I wrote for *The Sunday School Guide,* Vol. 83, July 10, 2005, 15, 26. Used by permission.

we are not "erring on the side of grace," but doing what grace always does: righteously following God in loving a sinful world.

Second, we need to be aware that truth and grace are partners, not competitors. The columnist was hoping they were on the same side, but he was actually driving a wedge between them by talking about "erring on the side of grace." He admitted the possibility that the truth about same-sex behaviors may be different from what he believed, but it was hard to tell he cared. He wanted to side with grace, even if that meant leaving truth behind. It may seem like a small thing, but if the slogan's little distinction between truth and grace is hammered enough, it creates a large wedge that pits truth and grace against each other. But we have nothing in Scripture to suggest that we must choose a fork in the road between the two. Grace and truth are found together in Jesus Christ (John 1:17).

In fact, grace can only flourish in the context of truth. If I'm lying to myself about my sin, I rob myself of experiencing God's grace. God may still love me and act graciously toward me, but I am unable to experience it because I am still living the lie of justifying myself. I cannot know God's grace apart from the truth about my sinfulness. Grace and truth go together.

That's also the case with how we deal with others. Some would tell us—like the local columnist—that I can only act graciously toward others if I believe that what they do is not sinful. They say that as long as I regard the behavior of others as sinful, then I cannot act in a gracious way toward them. But that's a lie. If they ask us what we think of same-sex behavior, and we keep quiet, letting them lie to themselves by redefining their sin as non-sin, we are not showing them grace, but indulgence. The only way I can truly demonstrate grace toward others is by recognizing that what they do is sinful (just as what I do is sinful), helping them to see that truth (if they ask), and always showing them the love of God. That's amazing grace. Knowing the truth about sin and showing grace toward sinners—these are partners that I dare not drive apart.

But there's one more problem with the idea of "erring on the side of grace": as the phrase is often used, many imply by it that God not only extends grace to errant people, but God also extends grace to error, as if God is not all that bothered by false teaching as long as people experience love. But this is wrong. God's grace is extended to people, even errant people, but God's grace is not extended to the error itself. Grace and truth stand together *against* error and sin. For many people, grace is a mushy kind of tolerance that doesn't stand against anything. But biblical grace stands up *for* people by standing *against* the errors which bring them down.

Therefore, unlike the columnist, I cannot be as casual about whether one's position on an issue is true or not. If my aim is to be as gracious as possible, it matters immensely whether or not I am informed by God's truth in how I respond to people. If I speak lies to them, even unwittingly, I am not dealing graciously with them, but making their situation worse. It is necessary for me to discern as best I can what the mind of God is concerning issues relevant to our relationship. I am not being gracious if I tell a teenager that abusing opioids is perfectly acceptable to God. I am not being gracious if I tell a worried businesswoman that God doesn't mind her violating the tax code in order to increase the bottom line. I am not being gracious if I tell a man tempted to engage in same-sex behavior that the Lord celebrates his sexual identity. I must speak the truth with grace, yes. But I can only speak with grace if I tell the truth.

So instead of being willing to "err on the side of grace," I would rather hear the columnist say that he wants to speak truth on the side of grace, and speak grace on the side of truth. We don't want to drive grace and truth apart. For we find them together in Jesus Christ. And if we abide in Christ, grace and truth will come together in our lives as well.

Eunuchs

Old Testament laws had an interest in the bodily perfection of sacrificial animals. Again and again we hear how only those animals that were unblemished and whole were to be brought to the tabernacle or temple as an offering (see Exodus 12:5; Leviticus 1:3; Numbers 6:14; Deuteronomy 15:21; Ezekiel 43:22; Malachi 1:14, for just a few of many examples).

The idea behind this seems to be three-fold: One, usually animals with blemishes—perhaps blind or lame—were less valuable than other animals. So if you sacrificed a defective animal, you were not offering up your "best to the Master," but only giving him what was of little worth. The poor quality of your gift reflected the poor quality of your faith and your poor view of God (see Malachi 1:14).

Secondly, animal sacrifices indicated some kind of transfer was going on. By laying your hands on a perfect animal about to be slaughtered, you were transferring your moral imperfections to a perfect animal (see Leviticus 1:3-4). If the animal was already imperfect before the sacrifice was made, it would not serve as a very good symbol of being able to take on your imperfection.

But thirdly, there also seems to be in the background the idea that only the best—unblemished—creatures can be brought near to God. Imperfect creatures seem to serve as evidence that creation has been marred by humanity's fall into sin (perhaps under the curse of Genesis 3 or, as Romans 8:20-21 says, subjected to futility and in bondage to corruption). Creatures without blemishes, however, reflect in a better way the created world as God originally made and pronounced good.

This latter reason for not bringing blemished creatures for sacrifice probably lies behind some Old Testament laws that we regard as unloving and unfair. Some laws barred priests with defects from coming before the Lord's presence in the sanctuary or eating the consecrated food (Leviticus 21:17, 21, 23). This prohibition included priests who were blind, lame, hunchbacked, dwarves, as well as those with a mutilated face, a limb too long, an injured hand or foot, or an itching disease. Also barred from entering the assembly of the Lord were those with crushed testicles. And this last rule not only applied to priests, but also to anyone whose testicles were crushed or whose male organ was cut off (Deuteronomy 23:1). We should not allow such verses to shape our current views about people with disabilities, but the main idea is that in the Old Testament, the worship of the Creator was not a time for being reminded of sin's effect on God's created world.

Thus eunuchs, whose testicles had been crushed or removed, were not allowed into the assembly of the Lord. Some of these men had become eunuchs because of an accident. More commonly, however, men who served in the royal court were purposely castrated so there would be no sexual misconduct on their part with the royal wives and daughters. For example, the man placed in charge of the Persian concubines was a eunuch (Esther 2:3, 14-15; see also Daniel 1:3).

But there is hope for eunuchs, even in the Old Testament. For example, Jeremiah 38:7-13 and 39:15-18 blesses an Ethiopian eunuch, Ebed-melech, who was responsible for rescuing Jeremiah after he was thrown into a cistern. But an even better sign of hope is spoken in Isaiah 56:3-5, "Let not the foreigner who has joined himself to the LORD say, 'The LORD will surely separate me from his people'; and let not the eunuch say, 'Behold, I am a dry tree.' For thus says the LORD: 'To the eunuchs who keep my Sabbaths, who choose the things that please me and hold fast my covenant, I will give in my house and within my walls a monument and a name better than sons and daughters; I will give them an everlasting name that shall not be cut off'" (ESV). We begin to see this prophecy fulfilled when Philip leads the Ethiopian eunuch to the Lord and baptizes him in Acts 8:26-39.

Some progressives interpret this verse as a sign of hope for the LGBT community as well. The story of the Ethiopian eunuch, they say, shows us that those who are sexually different may have at one time been excluded from God's presence, but now the Lord has opened the doors to all those who are sexually different (and mutilated and disabled for that matter). Some will even take this a step further and point out the eunuchs were often involved in same-sex behavior as the so-called "penetrated" partner, since they were incapable of opposite-sex behavior, and that they were often oppressed by the heterosexual majority for being different. So it's significant, according to this interpretation, that Philip offers salvation to this sexually different eunuch, without a word of him needing to repent of some sin first. The moral of the story, for progressives, is that the Spirit is leading the church (as he led Philip) to be at the forefront of welcoming those who are oppressed because they are sexually different (like gays and lesbians), without first demanding some kind of repentance.

It's important to notice the flaws in this argument. First, the welcome of the eunuch does not mean that God is indifferent to any and all sexual "differences." There's a great deal of difference between being a man who has no sexual drive because he has been castrated (probably against his will) and being a man involved in same-sex behaviors.

Second, historians tell us that when eunuchs were engaged in same-sex behaviors, the main reason was that many of them were slaves and were raped by their masters (in fact, all slaves were in danger of being treated this way). This may not have been the case of the eunuch in Acts 8, because he was a high-ranking official (although probably still a slave). But the main thing to note is that eunuchs were not living out some kind of same-sex orientation; rather, many of them were victims of homosexual rape. The most common form of oppression for eunuchs, then, was not that of heterosexuals mocking these people who were sexually different, but that of being raped by their masters.

Third, although Philip issues no specific call to repentance here, that does not mean, as some new interpreters imply, that God is no longer concerned about unusual sexual behaviors. The Isaiah text is full of references to Jesus bearing our sin. In order for Philip and the eunuch to talk about atonement and baptismal cleansing, they would have talked about sin. This eunuch would still have to repent of his particular sins, but those sins probably did not include homosexual behavior (because of his status). And if he had been homosexually raped in the past, he would have no need to repent of that either, because there's no need to repent of being sinned against. This story does not open the door to affirmation of same-sex behavior, but it does offer hope to those who may have been abused in a same-sex situation.

Fear [1]

T he same-sex issue had just come up for debate at the denominational meeting. Conservatives and progressives quickly drew their microphones to do battle. A warrior for the progressive cause fired the first shot, urging the delegates to reject the anticipated conservative arguments because they were dictated by fear instead of faith.

Fear? How did fear get in this debate? Is it true that our theological positions are not based purely on the thoughtful consideration of biblical texts, but also on something as emotional as fear? I'm afraid so. Like it or not, fear is part of the theological process.

The role of fear in theologizing is not by my choice, however. I'm part of a world that proudly displayed the Nike slogan "No Fear" on its tee-shirts, baseball caps, and sports cars. And even after the ad campaign was over, the sentiment remained. Fear is for wimps, wusses, and gutless wonders. For me, terms like "healthy fears" and "rational fears" are in the same oxymoronic category as "jumbo shrimp." I know that "fear" is used in a positive way in the Bible, but my world view gravitates toward the negative references to fear, especially the one in 1 John 4:18, "There is no fear in love. But perfect love drives out fear, because fear has to do with punishment. The one who fears is not made perfect in love" (NIV11).

Because of that verse I have always desired to be orthodox in a fearless way. Faith should be joyfully confessed with big-hearted trust instead of fearful finger-pointing. Fearless orthodoxy welcomes needed changes to a sinful status quo. Fearless orthodoxy has no interest in bolstering human traditions. Fearless orthodoxy will listen to any and all perspectives. Fearless orthodoxy knows the reality of God's absolute truth, but doesn't assume that any one person or group absolutely knows that truth. Fearless orthodoxy seeks to serve, not to retain power. Fearless orthodoxy is characterized by grace for all. Fearless orthodoxy would rather wrestle with principalities and powers than posture for political battles in the church. Fear-

---

[1] Based on an editorial entitled "The Role of Fear in Theology" which I wrote for *The Sunday School Guide,* Vol. 85, October 8, 2006, 15, 26-27. Used by permission.

less orthodoxy finds victory at the foot of the cross, not at the feet of the corpse of the divided body of Christ.

But ironically, even in my desire to theologize fearlessly, I'm still afraid. I'm afraid of theologies constructed out of fear. As much as we might want a fearless theology, the fear-factor lurks behind the theologies of both conservatives and progressives. Unfortunately, we are more adept at recognizing fear in our opponents than in ourselves.

Progressives, for instance, dismiss conservatives as embattled people who fear change and any disruption to the status quo. They suspect that conservatives fear the loss of power and influence. Indeed, many conservatives are afraid that the faith will disappear if progressives win the day. They fear the loss of certainty in the face of difficult questions. They are afraid to even consider the merits of other perspectives, lest they displease their constituents and allies. They are afraid that God's kingdom will fall unless the world follows their agenda. And they might be afraid of people who are too different from themselves, which is why (at least for a time) it was common to label conservatives as homophobes.

But fears also lurk among progressives, as any conservative could tell you. Progressives are afraid of being irrelevant in a rapidly-changing culture. They are afraid that the faith will be discredited if the conservatives win the day. They fear that grace will disappear and all questions will be ruled out of order. They fear a return to exclusivism, legalism, patriarchalism, ethnocentrism, and a host of other unjust isms.

Yes, fears can fuel the progressive cause as much as the conservative cause. So it doesn't really mean a lot to accuse the other side of fear-mongering. In a fallen world, where truth can be so easily twisted, we all have our fears about the faith.

So even though I would love to propose a theological method that helps people find truth without being influenced by fear, I'm afraid that we will have to settle for something more modest. The division is not between fearful theologies and fearless theologies. Instead we need to distinguish between theologies influenced by foolish fears and those influenced by wise fears. Two wise fears that our theologies should heed are fearing the Lord and fearing for the well-being of others.

Fearing the Lord

The most important wise fear is the fear of God. Although this aspect of faith is widely neglected in today's pulpits and Sunday Schools, it is lauded throughout the Scriptures. According to Proverbs 1:7 (and many parallels), the fear of the Lord is the beginning of knowledge. Fearing God is job one in the theological process. We can't practice theology well without it.

Fearing the Lord is especially associated in the Bible with obedient attention to God's Word. It was the fear of the Lord that empowered Abraham to obey God's difficult command to sacrifice his son (Genesis 22:12). According to Exodus 20:20, the reason that God appeared on Mt. Sinai in such a terrifying form was "so that the fear of God will be with you to keep you from sinning" (NIV11). Deuteronomy 6:2 notes that we fear the Lord by keeping all his decrees and commands.

The connection between fearing God and being obedient to God's Word is also found in the Psalms. In Psalm 112:1, "those who fear the LORD," are equivalent to those "who find great delight in his commands" (NIV11). Likewise, Psalm 128:1 pronounces a blessing on "all who fear the Lord, who walk in his ways" (NIV11)

The language of fearing God is less frequent in the New Testament, but still present. Jesus commanded his disciples, "Do not be afraid of those who kill the body, but cannot kill the soul. Rather, be afraid of the one who can destroy both soul and body in hell" (Matthew 10:28, NIV11). Paul wrote, "Therefore, my dear friends, as you have always obeyed...continue to work out your salvation with fear and trembling" (Philippians 2:12, NIV11).

Although we might prefer a fearless theology, we don't have that option. Any theology worthy of the name must be informed by a fear of the Lord which is obediently attentive to God's Word. Here are four ways that the fear of the Lord can shape our theologizing:

1)   To truly fear God we must pay close attention to the living voice of God's written Word. We can't respectfully obey God unless we truly seek to know what God has spoken. The devil is not in the details of God's Word; the Spirit is. The fear of God prompts us to study these details. There is no fear of God in us if we twist Bible verses into "proof texts" that back our ideological cause. Putting a conservative or progressive "spin" on a Bible verse shows great disrespect for the Word of God.

Conversely, there is also no fear of God in us if we dismiss scriptural input as "nothing but proof texts." When someone has quoted Scripture in a debate, I have seen others roll their eyes as if to say, "Oh, that tired old verse again. Can't we ever get past that?" No, we cannot get past those verses. God continually speaks them as a living word of truth we would rather ignore. Even though the Bible has been subjected to so many diverse interpretations, we must not despair of finding its truth. Without the wisdom of God's Word, our only other option is to be wise in our own eyes, which is just the opposite of fearing God: "Do not be wise in your own eyes; fear the LORD and shun evil" (Proverbs 3:7, NIV11).

2)   Fearing God not only leads us to pay attention to God's Word, but it also leads us to *obedient* attention to that Word. We should avoid pontificating about truth that we're not living out. Nothing is sillier than two peo-

ple debating about whether more or less government involvement is better for the poor, if neither are doing anything for the poor. God's call is not for us to have the right opinion about various issues, but to actually minister by the Spirit's power in those areas. It is when we obey the Word that we are best qualified to theologize in that area.

3) Fearing God also helps us theologize, because it frees us from fearing other things that keep us from hearing the truth. When we fear God, we don't have to fear anything else. We don't have to be afraid of angering a right-wing coalition, an LGBT lobbyist, a potential donor, a denominational executive, a conservative militia, a feminist pressure group, a congregational power-broker, or a dangerous trend. As Isaiah 8:12-13 says, "Do not call conspiracy everything this people calls a conspiracy; do not fear what they fear, and do not dread it. The LORD Almighty is the one you are to regard as holy, he is the one you are to fear, he is the one you are to dread" (NIV11).

When we fear God instead of others, then we are able to give a fair hearing to all sides in theological disputes. When Jehoshaphat appointed judges in the cities of Judah, he told them, "Consider carefully what you do, because you are not judging for man but for the LORD, who is with you whenever you give a verdict. Now let the fear of the LORD be upon you. Judge carefully, for with the LORD our God there is no injustice or partiality or bribery" (2 Chronicles 19:6-7, NIV). These are good words to remember when opposing sides are using pressure tactics to get their way.

Peter once succumbed to pressure tactics when he was in Antioch. He had been eating with the Gentiles, but when more conservative believers from Jerusalem arrived, Peter "began to draw back and separate himself from the Gentiles because he was afraid of those who belonged to the circumcision group" (Galatians 2:12, NIV11). Peter bowed to ideological pressures because he had forgotten that when we fear God, we don't have to fear anyone else. According to the word picture of Jeremiah 10:5, ideologies are just scarecrows—idols that cannot speak or move. "Do not fear them; they can do no harm nor can they do any good" (NIV11).

4) Fearing the Lord not only helps us *pursue* God's truth, but it also frees us to *share* that truth, unafraid of our listeners' response. God-fearers are bold in speaking the truth. As Paul said in 2 Corinthians 5:11, "Since, then, we know what it is to fear the Lord, we try to persuade others" (NIV11).

The fear of the Lord is the beginning of wisdom and properly shapes all theological understanding.

Fearing for the well-being of others

Wise Christians know that theology is not done in a vacuum. For good or ill, theology affects individual Christians, congregations, denominations, the catholic church, and the world that has yet to respond to the church's evangelistic mission. Knowing that a misstep could mislead present and future generations, wise Christians will do their theological work with fear and trembling. They do not want future generations to look back on them as the great misleaders of the church. Nor do they want to sit back and let others mislead the church.

Fearing for the well-being of others is not a fear *of* other people; it's a fear we take up *on their behalf.* Anyone given responsibility for the safety and well-being of a loved one knows this fear. Because of this fear, mothers put their babies in car seats. Fathers place curfews on their teenagers. Parents give cell phones to their children. Little old ladies check on their shut-in friends each day. Fear of bad consequences causes us to care for those we love, instead of endangering them.

Paul knew this kind of fear in his rocky relationships with the churches he founded and nurtured. When false teachers were luring his churches away from Jesus, Paul would write theological letters motivated by a fear of what heresy was doing to his spiritual children.

To the Galatians Paul wrote, "I *fear* for you, that somehow I have wasted my efforts on you" (Galatians 4:11, NIV11). To the Thessalonians Paul said, "I was *afraid* that somehow the tempter had tempted you and that our labor had been in vain" (1 Thessalonians 3:5b, NRSV). Paul said similar words to the Corinthians, "But I am *afraid* that just as Eve was deceived by the serpent's cunning, your minds may somehow be led astray from your sincere and pure devotion to Christ...I *fear* that there may be discord, jealousy, fits of rage, selfish ambition, slander, gossip, arrogance and disorder" (2 Corinthians 11:3; 12:20b, NIV11, all italics mine in this paragraph).

Some might dismiss Paul as a theological worry-wart, but his love-shaped fear is what distinguished him from his opponents. False teachers do not truly care about the spiritual well-being of individual believers or churches. They do not care if their words are dividing churches over non-essentials, trapping Christians in sinful legalisms or addictions, or diverting attention away from Jesus. Such theologians practice theology as an intellectual or political game, to see whose side will win. They might think of themselves as fearless, "going where no one has gone before," but they are only being foolish.

So when progressives accuse conservatives of being homophobes— well, maybe some of them are. Some conservatives are ridiculously nervous around gays and lesbians. They don't know what to say or do when they meet one. They wonder if they're being "hit on." They get all "creeped out" just thinking about these people. But I seriously doubt there are many Christian "homophobes" like this. Most conservatives I know have fears for the sake of others. Their fears run in two directions. Concerning the LGBT community itself, conservatives have a fear concerning their eternal destiny. Some may laugh at that, or be insulted by it, but the fear is nonetheless real because they take Scripture seriously. And concerning society as a whole, conservatives often fear for the sake of future generations that a "normalizing" of same-sex behavior will push society in a bad direction.

But let's return to the general role of fear in theology. Motivated by a fear for the well-being of others, Christians doing theology should ask themselves questions like these:

- Will this teaching help Christians focus on the central truths of the gospel, or does it divert their attention to peripheral matters?
- Will this teaching strengthen or undermine the mission of the church to the world?
- Does this teaching create unnecessary conflict in the body of Christ?
- Does this teaching build up the body of Christ, or does it simply allow me to vent my personal frustrations?
- Will this teaching create changes that will make things better or worse for future generations?
- Does this teaching create an atmosphere in which the voice of the Lord in Scripture is preeminent?
- How will this teaching impact people who are vulnerable in the church and society?
- Since subtle nuances are usually lost whenever a theological position is popularized, how will this teaching sound when it trickles down to children's Sunday School classes?

Fearing for the well-being of others is a necessary ingredient in any theology worthy of the name "true." There is always a danger, of course, that we will become overbearing in our fear, assuming that we always know better than others what is good for them. We might use our profession of love as a pretext for imposing a wrong-headed theological agenda on future generations. But this possibility does not blot out the truth that fear for the well-being of others is necessary for theologizing.

Fearing the Lord and fearing for the well-being of others—these are two proper fears in the theological enterprise. Although understanding this will not settle any theological disputes, it does mean two things:

1)   It proves nothing to accuse a theological opponent of being motivated by fear. Even if true, it may be that they are motivated by a wise fear,

not a foolish one. Everyone engaged in theological debate should be more cautious in leveling this charge.

2) Both progressives and conservatives need to examine their own fears. If they would weed out the foolish fears and cultivate the wise ones, both sides just might find more reasons to agree.

Paradoxically, it is only by cultivating wise fears that we can become fearless in our faith. It's much like what Moses said to the trembling Israelites at the foot of Mount Sinai, "Do not be afraid. God has come to test you, so that the fear of God will be with you to keep you from sinning" (Exodus 20:20, NIV11). Notice in that verse that fearing God makes it possible to be unafraid. Wise fears draw us near to God and others; foolish fears teach us to keep our distance. Wise fears free us, liberating us with God's truth; foolish fears freeze us, hardening our divisions and immobilizing us for mission.

Fifty shades of grace

N ot that long ago, there was a best-selling pornographic book, followed by a movie, called *50 Shades of Grey.* Since my mind likes to take popular culture and think of how, with just a few word changes, you could have something profoundly God-honoring, I immediately thought of the phrase "50 shades of grace."

So that got me looking in the Bible for the different nuances of grace in the Scriptures to see if I could come up with 50 of them. I did this with a belief that for many people grace has been wrongly confined to only a few definitions.

The most secular meaning of grace (and quite well-known in the world) has to do with the beauty of moving in a smooth and flowing manner. In this sense, it is usually found as an adjective (graceful) or adverb (gracefully). With this definition, we might speak of a graceful ballerina or ice-skater. Or of a klutzy, clumsy person as being ungraceful.

The second meaning of grace is disappearing from North American culture, but it used to be defined as a prayer said before a meal. With this definition, a parent might say, "Before we eat, we need to say grace."

The last common definition of grace has become virtually equivalent to the phrase "unconditional love."[1] This is the definition most often used by Christians to mean that God loves us even though we fail him. A popular line puts it this way, "There's nothing you can do to make God love you more, and nothing you can do to make God love you less." We are simply loved. This is the reason why "Amazing Grace" is often sung at funerals, even of those who rejected God their whole life long. This understanding of grace especially grew under the influence of Protestants, who highlighted the words of Ephesians 2:8-9, which says that we are not saved by our own righteous works, but by grace alone. And by extension, Christians urge each other to treat people with this same unconditional kind of grace.

The issue of grace enters into the picture in the debates over LGBT matters. Progressives call on conservatives to show more grace. If God loves the LGBT community unconditionally (which is the most common perception of

---

[1] For more on this, see the essay "Unconditional love" on page 255.

grace), then why can't conservative Christians do the same? From their perspective, to keep calling on the LGBT community to repent seems decidedly to be acting without grace, with more than a hint that these people can only be saved by works of heterosexual behavior.

Conservatives feel misunderstood on this issue. They believe that the widely-popular understanding of grace is not the whole picture. So let's consider 50 shades of grace in the Bible, looking at every verse in the New Testament that uses the Greek noun *charis*.

1.   Grace expresses God's favor. This does not mean that a person is God's favorite, but only that he or she receives favor from God. Gabriel announced that Mary had found favor [*charis*] with the Lord (Luke 1:30), and Jesus himself found favor with God and others (Luke 2:40, 52). Stephen reports that God gave Joseph grace before Pharaoh and that David found favor from the Lord (Acts 7:10, 46). This is the most common meaning of *charis* in the Septuagint, the Greek translation of the Old Testament.

2.   Grace comes from God. While grace can characterize human behavior, it is not a man-made thing. Rather, most references to grace indicate that it comes from God the Father.

3.   Grace comes from God the Father through Jesus the Son. This is especially seen in the opening words of all the letters from Paul and Peter. A typical example would be: "Grace to you and peace from God our Father and the Lord Jesus Christ" (1 Corinthians 1:3, ESV). In the same vein Paul said, "For if many died through one man's trespass, much more have the grace of God and the free gift by the grace of that one man Jesus Christ abounded for many" (Romans 5:15, ESV). Notice how grace now comes from both God and Jesus. Any concept of grace cut apart from God working through Jesus is just a free-floating illusion—not really grace at all.

4.   We can bless one another with God's grace. That's what Paul and Peter are doing in the opening lines of their letters. Although they cannot convey grace themselves, they can serve as conduits for God's grace to be poured out. These words of blessing are not just wishful thinking on their part, but express their confidence that God truly blesses others through their words.

5.   Grace and peace are connected. When Peter and Paul bless others in the opening lines of their letters, they speak of grace and peace together. Some might dismiss this as just a customary greeting—the Roman world used *chara* (meaning greetings, which sounds a lot like *charis*) and the Jewish world used the Hebrew *shalom* or Greek *eirēnē* (both meaning peace). But there is more than just custom at work. When God pours out grace, we also experience peace with God and peace with others.

6. Jesus is filled with grace. Not only does grace come from Jesus, but he is able to share it because he himself is filled with grace: "And the Word became flesh and dwelt among us, and we have seen his glory, glory as of the only Son from the Father, full of grace and truth" (John 1:14, ESV). Jesus is filled with all the fullness of God (Colossians 2:9), and so God's grace fills him as well.

7. Jesus is filled with grace so that he can fill us with that same grace. John 1:16 declared, "For from his fullness we have all received, grace upon grace" (ESV). Paul would add that God showed "the immeasurable riches of his grace in kindness toward us in Christ Jesus" (Ephesians 2:7, NRSV).

8. Jesus fills us with grace by emptying himself. "For you know the grace of our Lord Jesus Christ, that though he was rich, yet for your sake he became poor, so that you by his poverty might become rich" (2 Corinthians 8:9, ESV). Jesus does not hoard the grace he has freely received from the Father, but empties himself so that we too can receive fullness (Colossians 2:10).

9. Jesus could be thought of as grace personified. Paul said in Titus 2:11, "For the grace of God has appeared, bringing salvation for all people" (ESV). And what is this grace that appeared, or rather, *who* is this grace that appeared? Paul answers that question just two verses later. It's none other than "the appearing of the glory of our great God and Savior Jesus Christ," whom we expect to return for us (Titus 2:13, ESV). When you meet Jesus, you meet the grace of God.

10. Grace and truth are connected. John 1:14 (just quoted under #6) not only said that Jesus was filled with grace, but also that he was filled with grace *and truth*. John repeats this in John 1:17, "For the law was given through Moses; grace and truth came through Jesus Christ" (ESV). Paul also calls the gospel the "grace of God in truth" (Colossians 1:6, ESV). Truth would include both a propositional expression of God's reality and a relational expression of God being true to the promises he made to us. While some might pit truth and grace against each other—thinking that it's gracious to overlook certain truths, and even saying that we should "err on the side of grace,"[2]—grace and truth belong together.

---

[2] For more on this, see the essay "Erring on the side of grace" on page 73.

11. Truthful grace is conveyed to us through the word. Those on the receiving end of both the words *of* Jesus (Luke 4:22) and the words *about* Jesus (the gospel) will experience grace. Paul believed it was his calling "to testify to the gospel of the grace of God" (Acts 20:24, ESV). He commended believers "to God and to the word of his grace" (Acts 20:32, ESV).

12. Grace is not only found in what we speak, but how we speak it. "Let no corrupting talk come out of your mouths, but only such as is good for building up, as fits the occasion, that it may give grace to those who hear" (Ephesians 4:29, ESV). Paul added in Colossians 4:6, "Let your speech always be gracious, seasoned with salt, so that you may know how you ought to answer each person" (ESV). If we speak about the grace of God in a harsh, unloving manner, we are not speaking aright.

13. The way of grace stands in contrast to the way of law. This came out in John 1:17's contrast: "For the law was given through Moses; grace and truth came through Jesus Christ" (ESV). Paul painted the contrast more starkly when he said to those who thought they needed to be circumcised, "I testify again to every man who accepts circumcision that he is obligated to keep the whole law. You are severed from Christ, you who would be justified by the law; you have fallen away from grace" (Galatians 5:3-4, ESV). We are saved by grace and not by keeping the law. Paul knew that if he lived by the law, he would nullify the grace of God; but as it is he lives through Christ, and thus by grace (Galatians 2:20-21).

14. Salvation by grace stands in contrast to salvation by works. Working only gets you wages, not grace (as Paul noted in Romans 4:4), but the only wage we'll get as sinners is death (Romans 6:23). The truth that salvation is by grace and not works is stated most plainly in the well-known Ephesians 2:8-9: "For by grace you have been saved through faith. And this is not your own doing; it is the gift of God, not a result of works, so that no one may boast" (ESV). If we think we can act righteously enough to merit salvation, we will be disappointed. This truth is probably behind the popular understanding of grace as unconditional love.

15. Grace comes through faith in Christ, not works. Even though God pours his grace in our direction, it is not experienced fully until we respond to it. This response to God is called faith. Ephesians 2:8-9 (just quoted in the previous point) did not just say we are saved by grace, but that we are saved by grace *through faith.* As Paul said in Romans 4:16, "Therefore, the promise comes by faith, so that it may be by grace" (NIV); and a few verses later he said, "Through [Christ] we have also obtained access by faith into this grace in which we stand" (Romans 5:2, ESV). Speaking personally, Paul declares that when he became a follower of Jesus, "the grace of our Lord overflowed for me with the faith and love that are in Christ Jesus" (1 Timothy 1:14, ESV). Non-Christians might receive God's abundant *common* grace apart from faith (like sunshine and rain), but no one receives *saving* grace apart from faith.

16. Faith itself is a gift of grace. Since a human response is part of what salvation is all about, it might be tempting to think saving faith is a human work. But even this faith comes to us by grace (as stated in Ephesians 2:8-9, just cited in #15). Acts 18:27 tells us that when Apollos came to Achaia, "he greatly helped those who through grace had believed" (ESV).

17. Grace means that God initiates salvation and ministry. While many like to think that it is their human response that brings salvation, it is always the prior gracious work of God that truly makes it happen. Without getting into all the mechanics of predestination (as if that were even possible), we should note the following: (a) God "saved us and called us to a holy calling, not because of our works but because of his own purpose and grace, which he gave us in Christ Jesus before the ages began" (2 Timothy 1:9, ESV); (b) the prophets foretold that grace that would be ours (1 Peter 1:10); (c) before we even knew what was going on, Jesus tasted death for everyone by the grace of God (Hebrews 2:9); (d) Paul knew he was called by God's grace even before he was born (Galatians 1:15); and (e) the believing remnant among the Jews only followed God because they were chosen by grace (Romans 11:5).

18. Both Jews and non-Jews can only be saved by grace. When addressing the Jerusalem Council, Peter said, "But we believe that we [Jewish Christians] will be saved through the grace of the Lord Jesus, just as they [the non-Jewish believers] will" (Acts 15:11, ESV).

19. God's grace is especially for dealing with sin. In spite of the wickedness in our hearts and our world, God pours out his grace to deal with it: "But where sin increased, grace abounded all the more" (Romans 5:20, ESV).

20. God's grace forgives sinners. The Lord no longer counts our sins against us: "In [Christ] we have redemption through his blood, the forgiveness of our trespasses, according to the riches of his grace" (Ephesians 1:7, ESV).

21. God's grace justifies sinners. God not only forgives sins by grace, so that the bad is wiped away, he also looks on us in a new way. At the cross, the Lord swapped his righteousness for our sin, so that now God looks at us in Christ as if we had never sinned (see 2 Corinthians 5:21). We now stand in Jesus' righteousness, a truth which is called "justification." We may have sinned and fallen short of what God expected, but now we "are justified by his grace as a gift, through the redemption that is in Christ Jesus" (Romans 3:24, ESV), who provided an atoning sacrifice for us (Romans 3:24). Jesus saved us "so that, having been justified by his grace, we might become heirs having the hope of eternal life" (Titus 3:7, NIV11). As Paul said in Romans 5:17, Christians are "those who receive the abundance of grace and the free gift of righteousness" (ESV).

22. Some pervert the message of grace into a license for sin. If our understanding of grace stopped at the previous point, we might think that, as someone once said, we can enjoy sinning because God enjoys forgiving. But this is a perversion of grace. As Jude 4 noted, "For certain men whose condemnation was written about long ago have secretly slipped in among you. They are godless men, who change the grace of our God into a license for immorality and deny Jesus Christ our only Sovereign and Lord" (NIV). Paul must have encountered this same attitude, because he asked the rhetorical question in Romans 6:1-2, "What shall we say then? Are we to continue in sin that grace may abound? By no means!" (ESV).

23. God's grace reigns in our lives. When God's grace shows up, it doesn't just change our standing and wash away our past sins. It also comes to reign in our lives: "...grace abounded all the more, so that, as sin reigned in death, grace also might reign through righteousness leading to eternal life through Jesus Christ our Lord" (Romans 5:20-21, ESV).

24. God's grace conquers sin in our hearts. When grace is reigning in a person's life, then sin has no more dominion over us: "For sin will have no dominion over you, since you are not under law but under grace. What then? Are we to sin because we are not under law but under grace? By no means!" (Romans 6:14-15, ESV). Does that mean we never sin anymore? No, but we now have the power of grace to resist it.

25. God's grace raises us to new life. "But God, being rich in mercy, because of the great love with which he loved us, even when we were dead in our trespasses, made us alive together with Christ—by grace you have been saved—and raised us up with him" (Ephesians 2:4-6a, ESV).

26. God's grace gives us eternal comfort and hope for the future. "Now may our Lord Jesus Christ himself, and God our Father, who loved us and gave us eternal comfort and good hope through grace, comfort your hearts and establish them in every good work and word" (2 Thessalonians 2:16-17, ESV). Peter likewise said, "Set your hope fully on the grace that will be brought to you at the revelation of Jesus Christ" (1 Peter 1:13, ESV). It's for this reason we—especially husbands and wives together, as Peter pointed out—can be heirs of the grace of life (1 Peter 3:7).

27. God's grace teaches us to live holy lives. "For the grace of God that brings salvation has appeared to all men. It teaches us to say 'No' to ungodliness and worldly passions, and to live self-controlled, upright and godly lives in this present age" (Titus 2:11-12, ESV).

28. God's grace puts us to work in ministry. God's grace does not come upon us, and then nothing happens. If that were so, God would be acting in vain. Rather, we can each operate like Paul, who wrote, "But by the grace of God I am what I am, and his grace toward me was not in vain. On the contrary, I worked harder than any of them, though it was not I, but the grace of God that is with me" (1 Corinthians 15:10, ESV). Paul also noted, "By the grace God has given me, I laid a foundation as an expert builder, and someone else is building on it" (1 Corinthians 3:10, NIV). And when we fulfill our ministry, as Paul prayed would happen among the Thessalonians, then Jesus is glorified in us and us in him—and it all happens "according to the grace of our God and the Lord Jesus Christ" (2 Thessalonians 1:11-12, ESV).

29. God's grace gives us the spiritual gifts we need to build up the church. "Having gifts that differ according to the grace given to us, let us use them" (Romans 12:6, ESV). Romans 12 provides a few examples of such grace-gifts: prophecy, service, teaching, exhorting, contributing, leading, doing acts of mercy. Paul also noted in Ephesians 4:7 that "grace was given to each one of us according to the measure of Christ's gift" and then he listed apostles, prophets, evangelists, shepherds, and teachers (ESV). See also 1 Peter 4:10 for more on being graced with spiritual gifts. 1 Corinthians 12 lists even more gifts, which are called *charismata* (a word related to *charis*/grace).

30. God's grace empowers people to work miracles. Some of these more miraculous gifts are highlighted in 1 Corinthians 12, including healing and speaking in tongues. The Corinthians were noted for having received "surpassing grace" upon them, which may be due in part to receiving these miraculous gifts (2 Corinthians 9:14). Acts 6:8 tells us that "Stephen, a man full of God's grace and power, did great wonders and miraculous signs among the people" (NIV).

31. God's grace empowers our witness to the world. God did not give his grace only so that we could enjoy it in the church. His grace empowers our witness to the world. "Through [Christ] we have received grace and apostleship to bring about the obedience of faith for the sake of his name among all the nations, including you who are called to belong to Jesus Christ" (Romans 1:5, ESV). Paul speaks later of "the grace given me by God to be a minister of Christ Jesus to the Gentiles in the priestly service of the gospel of God, so that the offering of the Gentiles may be acceptable, sanctified by the Holy Spirit" (Romans 15:15-16, ESV). Paul's ministry is a stewardship of God's grace to preach to the nations (Ephesians 3:2, 7-8). Other apostles also perceived the grace given to Paul to be an apostle (Galatians 2:9). And before leaving on their first missionary journey, Paul and Barnabas were commended to the grace of God by the church in Antioch (Acts 14:26). Paul knew that it was only by the grace of God he was able to evangelize in a godly way (2 Corinthians 1:12).

32. Through God's grace, all Christians are called to be partners in sharing the gospel with the lost. Paul tells the Philippians that they share in a partnership with him in his ministry (Philippians 1:5), "for you are all partakers with me of grace, both in my imprisonment and in the defense and confirmation of the gospel" (Philippians 1:7, ESV).

33. God's grace empowers us for good works. Although Paul stated strongly that we are saved by grace and not works, he also insisted that grace will empower us to do good works. Right after he said his famous words about being saved by grace through faith and not by works (Ephesians 2:8-9), he added, "For we are his workmanship, created in Christ Jesus for good works, which God prepared beforehand, that we should walk in them" (Ephesians 2:10, ESV). In 2 Corinthians 9:8, Paul states, "And God is able to make all grace abound to you, so that having all sufficiency in all things at all times, you may abound in every good work" (ESV).

34. God's grace empowers us to do good to those who cannot repay us. This brings us to one of the few times that Jesus used the word *charis*, although it's hidden by most translations. It's found in Luke 6:32-34, when Jesus is talking about loving your enemies: "If you love those who love you, what *benefit* [*charis*] is that to you? For even sinners love those who love them. And if you do good to those who do good to you, what *benefit* [*charis*] is that to you? For even sinners do the same. And if you lend to those from whom you expect to receive, what *credit* [*charis*] is that to you? Even sinners lend to sinners, to get back the same amount" (ESV). It's an odd way of using the word for "grace" in the English language, and so the translators are on the right track. But we could perhaps get at the gist of Jesus' words by saying, "If you only love people who love you and help people who can help you back—what is grace to you? You obviously don't know the first thing about grace." When we truly experience grace, we help those in need, even our foes.

35. God's grace empowers us to give monetary gifts. According to 2 Corinthians 8:1-2, God's grace had empowered the Macedonian Christians to contribute toward the needy in Jerusalem: "We want you to know, brothers, about the grace of God that has been given among the churches of Macedonia, for in a severe test of affliction, their abundance of joy and their extreme poverty have overflowed in a wealth of generosity on their part" (ESV). They would count just the privilege of being able to participate as grace from God: "they urgently pleaded with us for the privilege [*charis*] of sharing in this service to the saints" (2 Corinthians 8:4, NIV).

36. The act of giving is itself a form of grace. Paul sent Titus to the Corinthian church so that they could complete their giving to Paul's fundraising project for the church in Jerusalem. He urged them to excel in this giving. Paul's wording is unusual enough to tempt translations to add extra words. Thus, the NRSV calls this giving a "generous undertaking"; the NIV and ESV call it an "act of grace." But the Greek only says *charis*, grace. Paul wants the church to complete this grace and excel in this grace. Giving itself is a form of grace.

37. The monetary gift given is a form of grace. Paul is so intent on associating grace with his fundraising project that even the funds themselves are called grace (*charis*)—which is usually hidden in the translations (1 Corinthians 16:3 and 2 Corinthians 8:19). Paul believes that the recipients of the gift will regard it as God's grace shown to them.

38. God's grace is given to strengthen his people. While we might associate grace with God's willingness to welcome and accept us, grace is also a power given for strengthening us. As Paul says to Timothy, "You then, my child, be strengthened by the grace that is in Christ Jesus" (2 Timothy 2:1, ESV). It is not following Jewish food laws that will strengthen us, but the grace of God: "It is good for our hearts to be strengthened by grace, not by ceremonial foods, which are of no value to those who eat them" (Hebrews 13:9, ESV).

39. God's grace strengthens us to endure suffering. Paul prayed for the Lord to relieve him of some kind of "thorn in the flesh," which was likely a physical condition. But the Lord did not do this miracle, but instead said to Paul, "My grace is sufficient for you, for my power is made perfect in weakness" (2 Corinthians 12:9, ESV).

40. God's grace strengthens us to endure *unjust* suffering. Peter said to Christian slaves who were mistreated by their masters, "For this is grace if, through consciousness of God, someone endures sorrows, while suffering unjustly...But if suffering for doing good and you endure, this is grace before God (1 Peter 2:19-20, my translation—other translations obscure the word "grace"). Peter probably had unjust suffering in mind later when he said, "And after you have suffered a little while, the God of all grace, who has called you to his eternal glory in Christ, will himself restore, confirm, strengthen, and establish you" (1 Peter 5:10, ESV).

41. God's grace is closely connected to the giving of thanks. The usual Greek noun, verb, and adjective concerning gratitude all contain the word *charis* in them. It's unfortunate that this linguistic connection between grace and thanks is not strong in the English language. The connection still shows itself, but barely, in words like gratitude, grateful, and gratis, and in the phrase "saying grace" to describe a thankful prayer given before a meal (see 1 Corinthians 10:30). The Spanish word for "thanks," *gracias*, more readily reminds us of grace. *Gracias* is the fitting response to grace. Paul sees God's grace at work, and so he says *gracias* to God. This is behind an odd idiom in Greek used for expressing thanks to God. When Paul wanted to say "Thanks be to God," he would actually write, "Grace/*charis* be to God" (see Romans 6:17; 7:25; 1 Corinthians 15:57; 2 Corinthians 2:14; 8:16; 9:15; Hebrews 12:28).[3] We can thank God for grace (1 Corinthians 1:4).

42. God's grace (*charis*) increases thanksgiving (*eucharistia*) to God. Paul sees this especially happening in evangelism: "For it is all for your sake, so that as grace extends to more and more people it may increase thanksgiving, to the glory of God" (2 Corinthians 4:15, ESV). Thus Paul sees

---

[3] Although Jesus himself likely spoke Aramaic, when the gospel writers translated his words into Greek, they only had Jesus speak of *charis* in two texts: Luke 6:32-34 (cited earlier in #34 to speak of doing good to those who cannot repay you) and Luke 17:9 (where Jesus tells a parable in which a master does not say *charis*/thanks to a servant who only does as he is commanded). Neither text is about an unconditional love sort of grace.

Jesus acting for the praise of God's glorious grace (Ephesians 1:6). And though the translation is debatable, it's even possible that Paul is saying in Colossians 3:16 that we sing praise to God by grace.

43. God's grace remains continually with God's people. Paul follows a consistent pattern at the beginning and end of his letters. At the beginning of all his letters he says "grace *to* you," and at the end he says "may God's grace be *with* you." This movement from "grace *to* you" in the beginning to "grace *with* you" in the end is so consistent that it's as if Paul is visually portraying the movement of grace. When Paul "appears" at the beginning of the letter, he brings the Lord's grace with him and extends it to those who are gathered: *grace to you.* Then when he "takes leave" at the end of the letter, he doesn't take the Lord's grace back with him, but instead leaves it behind to remain with his listeners: *grace with you.*[4] That's important because we do not live by occasional encounters with Jesus' grace. Rather, we are sustained by this grace that goes "with us" on our journey of faith. (Hebrews and Revelation also end with "grace be with you" benedictions.)

44. We can grow in grace. Although God's grace abides with his people, we should not think of it like a substance that remains in a constant, inert state. Rather, God's grace happens in our relationship with God, and thus it ebbs and flows. While we always have God's grace upon us, it is possible to grow in that grace: "But grow in the grace and knowledge of our Lord and Savior Jesus Christ" (2 Peter 3:18, ESV). Along the same lines, Acts 4:33 reports that the church experienced "great grace" when the apostles were testifying to Jesus' resurrection with great power.

45. We can have multiple experiences of God's grace. In 2 Corinthians 1:15, Paul wrote, "Because I was sure of this [a mutual boasting of one another on judgment day], I wanted to come to you first, so that you might have a second experience of grace" (ESV). Literally, Paul said "that you might have a second grace." Some groups talk about a second grace as if it were a formulaic thing: first you have the grace of salvation, and then later the grace of the baptism of the Spirit. Paul is not talking about that. He's only saying that we can have multiple experiences of God's grace, and in this case, one of them would have been a visit from him.

46. We are invited to ask God for grace. We not only ask for grace in becoming Christians, but in continuing our walk of faith: "Let us then with

---

[4] See Romans 16:20; 1 Corinthians 16:23; 2 Corinthians 13:14; Galatians 6:18; Ephesians 6:24; Philippians 4:23; Colossians 4:18; 1 Thessalonians 5:28; 2 Thessalonians 3:18; 1 Timothy 6:21; 2 Timothy 4:22; Titus 3:15; and Philemon 25.

confidence draw near to the throne of grace, that we may receive mercy and find grace to help in time of need" (Hebrews 4:16, ESV).

47. God especially gives grace to those who are humble. Both James 4:6 and 1 Peter 5:5 quote from Proverbs 3:34, saying, "God opposes the proud but gives grace to the humble" (ESV). As Paul notes, "For by the grace given to me I say to everyone among you not to think of himself more highly than he ought to think" (Romans 12:3, ESV).

48. It's possible to receive the grace of God in vain. Paul wrote in 2 Corinthians 6:1, "As we work together with him, we urge you also not to accept the grace of God in vain" (NRSV). While this raises lots of issues about the possibility of losing one's salvation and the doctrine of irresistible grace, what needs to be said at a minimum is that accepting God's grace in vain is enough of a possibility that people need to be warned of it. In a similar vein, Paul expressed to the Galatians, "I am astonished that you are so quickly deserting him who called you in the grace of Christ and are turning to a different gospel" (Galatians 1:6, ESV).

49. It's possible to fall from grace and to jeopardize one's salvation. Paul warned that those who get circumcised as a way to please God have "fallen away from grace" (Galatians 5:4). Hebrews 12:15 warns us to make sure that "no one fails to obtain the grace of God" and lists bitterness, sexual immorality and unholiness as roots of this possibility (ESV). We might think that because God is gracious, we will have some automatic guarantees of safety, but Hebrews 10:29 warns of a fearful future if we outrage this gracious God: "How much worse punishment do you think will be deserved by those who have spurned the Son of God, profaned the blood of the covenant by which they were sanctified, and outraged the Spirit of grace?" (NRSV).

50. We are called to stand fast in grace. Although warnings are given about falling away from grace, Peter calls on Christians to continue to stand in it: "This is the true grace of God. Stand fast in it" (1 Peter 5:12, NIV11). Along the same lines, when passing through Antioch of Pisidia the second time, Paul and Barnabas "urged [the new Christians] to continue in the grace of God" (Acts 13:43, ESV). Earlier when Barnabas saw the grace of God at work among the new converts in Antioch in Syria, he exhorted them to remain faithful to the Lord (Acts 11:23).

As you can see from these 50 items, grace includes an acceptance and love for sinners, but that's only a part of it. God's grace cannot be reduced to a general acceptance of others based on a vague and sentimental unconditional love. Rather, God's grace is intimately tied to Jesus Christ and his death and resurrection for sinners. God's grace has gospel power to accept, forgive, and transform sinners, sending and equipping them on a mission for the Lord. If we're going to talk about grace in our discussions about same-sex behavior, then we need the fullness of grace. Anything less than that, as Bonhoeffer famously stated, can only be called "cheap grace."

For or against [1]

S ometimes Bible verses appear to be contradictory. The most famous example of this is Proverbs 26: 4-5: "Do not answer a fool according to his folly, or you will be like him yourself. Answer a fool according to his folly, or he will be wise in his own eyes" (NIV). Verse 4 says *not* to answer a fool in a foolish way, but verse 5 says we *should* answer a fool foolishly. So which one is right?

If those verses had been separated by many chapters, we might think of them as a mistake on the part of Solomon who had compiled the proverbs. But because they're placed right next to each other, we know it's no accident that both proverbs are included. Solomon knows that in certain situations, one must *not* answer a fool as a fool. For example, if a fool is in a fit of rage, you'll only make things worse if you imitate their anger. But in other situations, it might help to imitate a fool, because they might see just how foolish they have been.

So both proverbs are true, but students of the Bible need the wisdom to discern when is the right time to apply each one. That's because wisdom is not just knowing truth from falsehood. Wisdom also includes good timing in applying the truth.

Another seemingly contradictory pair of verses is found in the gospel of Luke where Jesus said, "Whoever is not with me is against me" (Luke 11:23), and, "Whoever is not against you is for you" (Luke 9:50; both NIV11). The first verse has a narrow sound to it (as if to say, "anyone not on my side is my enemy"), while the second has a much broader ring to it (as if to say, "as long as you haven't taken a stand against me, you're my friend"). Yet both are right, and we need the wisdom to see how each is right in different situations.

---

[1] Based on an editorial entitled "For or Against" which I wrote for *The Sunday School Guide,* Vol. 89, August 14, 2011, 15, 26-27. Used by permission.

He who is not with me is against me.
Jesus spoke this line in Luke 11 shortly after he was accused of being in league with the devil. Skeptics accused him of using devilish power to cast out demons. Jesus, of course, defended himself, for he knew that his exorcisms meant that God was at work in him. It's at this point that Jesus says, "Whoever is not with me is against me."

Jesus is not speaking to his accusers when he says this. Both he and they already know they're against him. No, these words are for the bystanders listening to the debate. If you put yourself in their place for a minute, you'll realize that many of them were sitting on the fence. They were trying to figure out if Jesus was of God or the devil. Yes, he spoke powerful words, but he also said outrageous things, like claiming the power to forgive and claiming to be alive before Abraham was born. And yes, he did powerful deeds, but some of his actions were outrageous too, like eating with sinners and healing on the sabbath. So it would be easy to sit on the fence and wait to decide about Jesus.

But then Jesus drops the bombshell: He turns to the fence-sitters and says, "Whoever is not with me is against me." With that one sentence, Jesus trips the switch, and the fence that many had been sitting on turns into an electric fence, and they've got to jump off—either toward Jesus or away from him. The message is clear; there is no neutrality with Christ. You're either for him or against him. If anyone imagines themselves neutral or undecided, that's only a figment of their imagination. To be undecided means to be decided against Jesus. When it comes to believing in and following Jesus, it's either yes or no, black or white. There are no shades of grey.

There are many things you can be undecided about, but you can't be undecided about Jesus. You can be undecided about moral issues, like capital punishment, but you can't be undecided about Christ. You can be undecided about some doctrinal issues, such as the baptism of the Spirit or the millennium, but you cannot be undecided about Jesus. Or you can be undecided about what church to attend—whether traditional or contemporary, governed by bishops or elders—but you cannot be undecided about Christ.

Jesus does not give us the luxury of time to sit and weigh our options. Shall I follow Jesus or should I wait a while? When Jesus calls, we must decide; if you're not with Jesus, you're against him. And Jesus is not just talking about taking a stand for him once, as happens in making profession of faith or in praying "the sinner's prayer." Being on Jesus' side is not just settled once, for he is always on the move to expand the kingdom. And if Jesus is on the move, then in order to be "with" him, we must "move with" him. Jesus not only wants us *for* him, but *with* him, going where he goes.

So if your faith has not moved for a while, it's not because Jesus is standing still. It may be because you haven't been moving with him, and then Jesus would say, "He who is not with me, that is, not moving with me, is against me." Fence-sitting is not an option for the Christian, nor is standing still. Not to decide is to decide against him.

But now we need to look at Jesus' other statement.

Whoever is not against you is for you.

Unfortunately, Christians sometimes take Jesus' question, "Are you with me or not?" and twist it just a bit. Instead of the legitimate question of "Do you belong to Jesus or not?" we shift the question to "Do you belong to our group or not?" It's a slight change, but it has a great impact. For when the question changes from "Do you belong to the Savior?" to "Do you belong to our saved group?" the focus is no longer on Christ. Instead, we adopt an "us *versus* them" mentality in which we reject anyone different from our group.

That's what was happening in Luke 9. The fuller context of this is, "'Master,' said John, 'we saw a man driving out demons in your name and we tried to stop him, because he is not one of us.' 'Do not stop him,' Jesus said, 'for whoever is not against you is for you.'" (Luke 9:49-50, NIV).

For John, the question was not "Do you belong to our Savior?" but, "Do you belong to our saved group?" So when he saw an exorcist working in Jesus' name, even though not a part of the Twelve, he was upset. It didn't help that earlier in the chapter, the Twelve had failed at an exorcism. So it made John a little angry to see a stranger exorcising demons successfully. That's when Jesus must say a different word, "Whoever is not against you is for you." For John, being a Christian meant belonging to the right saved group, but for Jesus it meant belonging to the right Savior. Even though the exorcist was not one of with Twelve, the fact that he works in Jesus' name means that spiritually he does belong with them.

This is a good lesson for all who stand for Christ. While we must insist that there's only one way of salvation, we must be clear on what that one way is. The one way is not our church or denomination. The one way is Jesus Christ, and he works through many different groups and churches. John Fischer once put it this way in a song: "Jesus is the only way, but there's more than one way to Jesus." No group of Christians should claim, "We alone are right." Rather we confess, "Christ alone is right." We're on the side of anyone who belongs to Christ.

Why then does Jesus say both, "Whoever is not with me is against me" and "Whoever is not against you is for you"? It's because God's kingdom is both narrow and broad. When Jesus faces *indifference*—people refusing to take a stand for him—then he makes things narrow. "If you're not with me, you're against me." But when Jesus faces *differences*—people following Jesus, but in different ways—then he broadens things, "If you're not against us, you're with us."

Indifference to Christ is not tolerated, but *differences* among Christians are to be celebrated. We want to get off the fence and stand for Christ, but in a way that works with other Christians, even if they're not part of our group or denomination.

But now, how does what we see here fit our approach to LGBT matters? Progressives will say that being LGBT is just a difference among Christians that needs to be celebrated. Conservatives will see the continued same-sex practices in the LGBT community and conclude that these people are indifferent, and even defiant, toward Jesus—no matter what their pro-Jesus words might say.

So how do we view other Christians whom we regard as clearly in the wrong, and yet they claim to be followers of Jesus Christ? I can see only four main possibilities:

(1) Come to the conclusion that they are not Christians at all.

(2) Accept them as Christians, but view them as so flawed in their perspective that we will not be able to be close partners in ministry (such as within the same congregation or denomination).

(3) Accept them as Christians, but even though we regard them as flawed in their perspective, we can still work closely together in ministry (as within the same congregation or denomination).

(4) Celebrate the differences found between all those who name the name of Jesus as their Savior.

Option 1 closely aligns with the mood of "Whoever is not with me is against me" (Luke 11:23). Option 4 more closely corresponds to "Whoever is not against you is for you" (Luke 9:50). I have tried, but been unable to come up with similar pithy statements to match options 2 and 3.

I imagine that a progressive might use any of those *four* options as their perspective from which to view conservatives in general, relying most often on option 3. Some progressives might claim to adopt option 4, but I wonder if they truly celebrate the conservatives who regard same-sex behavior as sinful.

A conservative, on the other hand, might use the first *three* options as a perspective from which to view progressives in general. Conservatives would never adopt option 4 because they could not celebrate the belief that same-sex behaviors were a good thing. Even those who followed option 3 would be more likely regarded as moderates and not true conservatives.

I find myself in option 2. If progressives or those in the LGBT community are naming Jesus as their Savior, it's not my role to say they are not Christians—though I must confess that the judgmental side of me wonders about some of the more extreme ideologists in the progressive camp.

But to work closely with them would feel to me like I was aiding and abetting them in their defiance of God. I would have to oppose their actions, and thus it would not work to minister closely with them, even though they still might belong to the larger body of Christ. In saying that, I'm completely aware that they may feel the same way toward me. If they are true to their beliefs, they should in some sense be against me, or at least against what I preach and practice.

I wonder how Jesus would have responded if the disciples said, "There's a man out there who is casting out demons in your name, and he's also a mean-spirited bigot and an adulterous philanderer"?

Genetics

L ady Gaga, a pop singer, not long ago had a hit called "Born This Way." The gist of it was that we should never be ashamed of who we are, and especially of our genetic heritage, because that's the way God made us.

According to the song, when Lady Gaga's mother was helping her young daughter put on makeup, she said to her that we are all born to be superstars. "'There's nothing wrong with loving who you are,' she said, 'cause he made you perfect, babe. So hold your head up and you'll go far'...I'm beautiful in my way 'cause God makes no mistakes. I'm on the right track, baby, I was born this way." The song goes on to celebrate all those who are "born this way," including black, white, beige, Lebanese, disabled, gay, straight, bi, lesbian, and transgendered. The melody of the song is very fun with a catchy hook, so it's easy to absorb the message along with the music.

It's a message that resonates with people. In a world that focuses media attention on celebrities, it's nice to think of ourselves as superstars. In a world full of bullies, who knock us down, it's great to think of ourselves as people to be celebrated. In a world filled with bigotry against people who are different, especially different in skin color, it's wonderful to know God made us the way we are.

But it's not clear to me that matters of sexuality belong in this song about God-caused genetic givens. To begin with, not everything we're born with should be considered a good gift from God. As the Bible tells us, we are all born with a sinful nature, an inborn propensity to pull away from the very relationships we want—undermining them through sins of commission and omission. David confessed truly, "Behold, I was brought forth in iniquity,and in sin did my mother conceive me" (Psalm 51:5, ESV). And lest we think David was exaggerating to make a point of how evil he felt, Paul noted that we all have sinned (Romans 3:23), because sin came into the world through Adam (Romans 5:12). To be born a sinner is not a mistake on God's part, but it is our fate that traces back to Adam and Eve's rebellion in Eden.

That means that not everything we are born with is to be celebrated. We find much that is God-given and glorious in the human body and spirit, but there is also a sinful nature that is part of our genetic makeup. The exact form that sinful nature will take in any given life varies from person to person. Some are born with a propensity to throw a temper tantrum. Others are born with a tendency to be jealous or extremely self-centered. Still others have a life-long struggle with lying or rebelliousness toward authority. And then there's a genetic predisposition toward addictive substances like alcohol. In the sexual realm, most men have a propensity toward lust and promiscuity (and many women do, too). We're all sinners, but each of us struggles with some particular sins more than others. We usually learn from our environment how to develop these ingrown sinful tendencies, but it was in us from the start. "Baby, we were born this way."

And this is no excuse for us. We wouldn't think much of the person who yelled obscenities at us in fit of rage, and then instead of apologizing they said, "Hey, I was born this way. I'm just living out who I was created to be. Hot-headed people like myself have been mistreated by society and shunned by others. But it's just not right to suppress our God-given nature, so I have learned to embrace who I am, and I expect you to do the same. After all, I didn't choose to be hot-headed, as if one day I just woke up and said, 'I'm going to be an angry young man.' No, I was born this way."

We would not go along with a person who talked like that. for even if people have had a propensity toward rage since birth, we still expect them to learn to control their tempers. It would have helped if they had been trained in self-control when young, but it's never too late to learn ways to keep it somewhat in check. And of course, for real change inside and out— but not always complete change in this life—Christians look to Jesus to transform their hearts, replacing rage with love.

And the same applies to those who deal with same-sex attraction. It's quite likely there is some genetic predisposition toward same-sex attraction, but that offers no excuse for giving in to it. Rather, the Lord calls on that person—and can empower that person—to keep those desires under control. To say they were born that way and thus should give in to it is like telling a person predisposed toward alcoholism to take a drink or a person predisposed toward rage to throw a tantrum.

Every so often someone will haul up an old study of twins raised in different homes. Decades ago *Newsweek* ran it as a cover story called "Is This Child Gay?" In the study, if one of the twins had come out as gay, there was a high likelihood that their sibling was also gay, even though they grew up in different environments. The popular conclusion drawn from this is that same-sex attraction is completely genetic. But if that were true, then there would not have been just a high correlation, but 100% correlation: if one twin was gay, the other one should have been also—in *every* case. The man who did the original study later refuted his earlier findings, but that didn't make any headlines. The lesson here is that even if you are genetically predisposed toward certain sins over others, it's not a foregone conclusion that you will give in to that sin. For all I know, I could be genetically predisposed toward alcoholism, but I'll never find out because I've never imbibed.

Surely, scientists are barely scratching the surface concerning how our genes affect our behavior. But unless we are prepared to say we are nothing but genetic robots, no one should be able to excuse their behavior, including same-sex behavior, by claiming, "I was born this way."

Others, of course, see this differently. They do not look on same-sex attraction as a genetic predisposition toward a certain behavior, but rather they see it as similar to being dark-skinned or hazel-eyed. For them, it's not a genetic factor that entered in *after* the Fall (which we are called to resist), but a genetic factor purely tied to God's creative power (which we are called to celebrate).

I'm not convinced. I'm a subscriber to *Games* magazine, and that magazine used to rate new games on a spectrum ranging from all luck to all skill. No game was purely one or the other, but there was an obvious difference between Candyland (mostly luck—the only skill you needed was to actually move your marker to the correct color) and crossword puzzles (mostly skill). Nearly all games could be placed somewhere on the spectrum, with skill often consisting of what you did with whatever "hand you were dealt" (to use a phrase from the world of card games).

There's a similar spectrum happening in genetics, but instead of luck and skill, we could talk about genetic givens (luck) and genetically-influenced behaviors (skill). Toward the "givens" end of the spectrum we would not talk about sin or responsibility, but toward the "behaviors" end of the spectrum, we would.

Let's look at that spectrum a little more closely, starting on the end of purely genetic givens, things which would be true of you even if you were born in a "vegetative state." A good example would be the color of your eyes. No behavior of yours could change or alter your eye color, except covering them with colored contacts. And it will never be a sin to have hazel-colored eyes.

A little further along, but still toward the genetic givens end of the spectrum, you would run into skin color. Again, if you were born in a "vegetative state," people might be able to discern something of your racial heritage by your skin color. Nothing you do can completely alter your skin color, except perhaps getting a dark tan or undergoing some kind of dying procedure. Even though some ignorant bigots have thought so, reasonable people know it is no sin to be red or yellow, black or white. Sin, however, can enter in, when we allow skin color to shape our moral decisions, as happens when white supremacists wrongly assume that their skin color makes them superior to others.

A little further along we might come across body size and shape. Here there are many genetic givens that will affect a person's height and weight, but now we start to see how behaviors can affect them (but not completely determine them). A nutritious diet can help a person become taller, but only to a point. A non-nutritious diet can affect a person's weight for the worse. It's not a sin to be short or tall, thin or fat, but we do bear responsibility for our eating behaviors (at least if food choices are available), and poor choices in this matter point us toward sins like gluttony.

Closer toward the behavioral end of the spectrum, we might see things like a predisposition to alcoholism. There's no sin in being born with genes that make you more likely to become an alcoholic, but now we see that moral decisions are needed to avoid letting the genetic givens turn into a fate. There's a tragic element here because a person who becomes an alcoholic may not have been drinking any more than the next person, but their genetic givens have made their decisions about drinking more consequential.

Further along the spectrum, we see that many men (and maybe more women than we might think) are genetically predisposed toward promiscuous sexual behavior. But now we have come a long way toward the behavioral end of the genetic spectrum. If they would be people who follow Jesus Christ and love others, these men must resist their genetic predisposition and be faithful to their wives.

I suppose progressives could argue that same-sex attraction is more on the "givens" end of the spectrum, but to me it seems a lot closer to the behavioral end. If a child was born in a vegetative state, lived to age 30, (even though they were unable to engage in any behaviors), you'd be hard-pressed to argue that the child was gay. Being same-sex attracted is closely tied to behavior, and behavior always lands us in the realm of responsibility, morality, and faith. I have contended in other essays that this means no matter how a person is genetically predisposed, they should call on the Lord to empower them to refrain from same-sex behaviors.

Gratitude

In Colossians 2 Paul launches an attack on some in the church who had been distorting the truth. But right before he begins to expose this false teaching, he writes this: "Therefore, as you received Christ Jesus the Lord, so walk in him, rooted and built up in him and established in the faith, just as you were taught, abounding in thanksgiving" (Colossians 2:6-7, ESV).

It's that last phrase that intrigues me—"abounding in thanksgiving." Although Paul will soon enter into debate against the Colossian distortion, he is not approaching the issue with an irritable, grouchy spirit. Nor does he want the Colossians to do so. Rather, he encourages all those who walk in Jesus and his truth to be overflowing with thanksgiving.

Having a grateful heart surely affects how we deal with those who promote a distorted message. We might be serious and stern in opposing them, but we do not approach them full of anger or with the desire to prove we know better than they do. In that case, we would be planting ourselves squarely in the arena of self-justification. Rather, we come overflowing with gratitude for the grace of God.

So even though this book is filled with objections to what I regard as false teaching about human sexuality, I do so with a spirit of gratitude. Maybe you haven't picked up on that as you have been reading this book. Perhaps if you disagree with much of what I've written, you might think I sound ornery and crabby. I hope not, but I can't control how you hear me.

But what I can do is what I was taught in a hymn long ago, "Count your blessings, name them one by one." So I would like to count twelve of my blessings concerning the subject of this book:

1.   I am grateful for my progressive brothers and sisters who are not pushing some ideological agenda, but are simply working hard to reach out to the LGBT community. While we might disagree on how best to do that, I am thankful for their loving heart.

2.   I am grateful for progressive brothers and sisters and members of the LGBT community who have been willing to have frank and respectful discussions with me about same-sex issues. They could have turned away

from me and rolled their eyes, but instead they stuck it out and we had a good time talking.

3.   I am grateful that the Lord has used this debate to make me (and the whole church) more sensitive to those who deal with same-sex attraction.

4.   I am grateful for like-minded brothers and sisters who have been faithful in helping the denomination I serve to hold fast to the Word of God.

5.   I am grateful for God's Word that provides a clear light in dark times.

6.   I am grateful that the church I currently serve was kind enough to give me a sabbatical to work on this book.

7.   I am grateful that Jesus gave his life for me, welcomed me as I was into his kingdom, and keeps on transforming me by his Spirit.

8.   I am grateful for opportunities I have had to attend General Synod meetings, participate in a Diversity Retreat, serve on the Commission on Theology, be a part of a Special Council concerning same-sex issues, and serve on our denomination's General Synod Council. It was at these meetings especially that I was able to participate in discussions about same-sex matters.

9.   I am grateful for the many teachers, theologians, and biblical scholars—both conservatives and progressives—who have helped me think through the biblical and doctrinal issues involved.

10. I am grateful for parents who modeled for me what it means to live according to both the grace and truth found in Jesus.

11. I am grateful that no matter where my denomination lands on same-sex issues that Jesus is still on the throne as the head of the church.

12. I am grateful that even though same-sex issues seem to consume denominational life, so much good ministry continues to happen throughout the church of Jesus Christ.

Hate

One of the standard lines that conservatives use in the discussion about same-sex behavior is one that is almost guaranteed to rile the LGBT community: love the sinner, hate the sin. To them, it doesn't mean much to love a person if you hate their actions, because they are the one doing that hated action. As a rejoinder, I've heard a few members of the LGBT community respond with, "Love the sinner, and hate your own sin."

In the last few years, the role of hate has also gotten wrapped up in the current jargon of referring to some people as haters. I'm not sure, but I believe this use of the term "hater" first became prominent in debates about race. The idea is that if you do or say anything that expresses disdain or obstructs justice for a racial or ethnic minority, then you are a hater. The term quickly began to be used against those who do not express full support for the LGBT community.

So what do we do with all this hate? I would like to explore what it means to hate sin, and what it means to call others haters.

Hating sin

When we look for words about hatred in the Bible, most of the references are to the experience of being hated by evildoers, even though you did nothing to deserve that hatred (Proverbs 29:10). This happened to individuals like David (Psalm 89:23; 118:7), Solomon (2 Chronicles 1:11) prophets like Micaiah (1 Kings 22:8), and psalmists (Psalm 9:13; 18:17). But it was also the experience of Israel as a nation (Esther 9:1; Isaiah 60:15) and the followers of Jesus (Matthew 10:22; 24:9; Mark 13:13; Luke 21:17; John 15:18-19; 17:14; 1 John 3:15; 4:20). Jesus said, however, that his disciples would be blessed for being hated (Luke 6:22).

Evildoers not only hate righteous *people*, but they also hate their righteous *qualities and actions*, such as justice (Job 34:17), discipline (Psalm 50:17; Proverbs 5:12), peace (Psalm 120:6), knowledge (Proverbs 1:22, 29), reproof (Proverbs 9:8; 12:1; 15:10), and the truth (Amos 5:10). They hate what is good (Micah 3:2) and the light (John 3:20). They also hate God, who will bring judgment upon them for their hatred (Exodus 20:5; Deuteronomy 5:9; Psalm 68:1; Romans 1:30). Their hatred is extended to God's Son as well (John 7:7; 15:23-25).

But the wicked are not the only ones who hate. God is also said to hate evildoers (Psalm 5:5; 11:5). Sometimes God's people think he hates them too (see Deuteronomy 1:27; 9:28; Job 16:9), and sometimes their behavior is so bad, he does hate them (see Hosea 9:15; Jeremiah 12:8)—a truth that is hard for us to swallow. But what God really hates are not so much evil *people*, but evil *actions*. He hates:

- the abomination of idolatry (Deuteronomy 12:31; 16:22; Jeremiah 44:4)
- meaningless worship by those who practice injustice (Isaiah 1:14; Amos 5:21)
- haughty eyes, lying tongues, murderous hands, scheming hearts, feet that run to evil, a false witness, and those who spread discord (Proverbs 16:16-19)
- robbery and injustice (Isaiah 61:8)
- Israel's pride in its strongholds (Amos 6:8)
- scheming and false oaths (Zechariah 8:17)

Since God hates evildoers and their evil actions, it's no surprise to find in Scripture that the people of God also hate both evildoers and their actions. But all the references to God's people hating evil-doers are found in the book of psalms. The psalmists hate the assembly of evildoers (Psalm 26:5), the idolaters (Psalm 31:6), the double-minded (Psalm 119:113), and those who hate God (Psalm 139:21-22). This last reference is especially stark in its expression of hatred: "Do I not hate those who hate you, O LORD? And do I not loathe those who rise up against you? I hate them with complete hatred; I count them my enemies" (ESV).

Much more commonly the people of God are not hating *evildoers*, but they are hating their *evil deeds*. God's people are even commanded to do this in Psalm 97:10 and Amos 5:15. God's people do hate wickedness and evil in general (Psalm 45:7; 101:3; Proverbs 8:13), and in particular they hate:

- unjust gain (Exodus 18:21; Proverbs 28:16)
- bribes (Proverbs 15:27)
- every false way (Psalm 119:104, 128)
- falsehood (Psalm 119:163; Proverbs 13:5)
- arrogance, pride, the way of evil, and perverted speech (Proverbs 8:13)
- bloodshed (Ezekiel 35:6)

Thus far we have not looked at what the *New* Testament says about hating evildoers or their evil actions. It's notable that in the New Testament, unlike the Old, nothing is said about either God or his people hating evildoers (with the possible exception of Paul quoting from Malachi 1:3 about God hating Esau (Romans 9:13). Instead, we find grace and mercy extended to sinners through Jesus Christ: "but God shows his love for us in that while we were still sinners, Christ died for us" (Romans 5:8, ESV). Jesus himself was known as the friend of sinners (Matthew 11:19; Luke 7:34). And Paul testified that he had experienced God's grace, even though he had been a violent persecutor of God's people. His conclusion: "The saying is trustworthy and deserving of full acceptance, that Christ Jesus came into the world to save sinners, of whom I am the foremost. But I received mercy for this reason, that in me, as the foremost, Jesus Christ might display his perfect patience as an example to those who were to believe in him for eternal life" (1 Timothy 1:15-16, ESV).

Jesus himself taught his disciples to love those who hate them (Matthew 5:44; Luke 6:27). And he lived this out by forgiving those who crucified him and bearing the sins of the whole world. Love for sinners is so important that John added that if you have hatred in your heart toward a brother, you are not in the light no matter what you claim (1 John 2:9, 11).

So there is nothing in the New Testament about hating evildoers. There is still a strong message of judgment and a call to repentance, but nothing is said about God or God's people hating evildoers. That's not because God has had a change of heart from the Old Testament to the New Testament. Rather, it's because the sacrifice of Jesus on the cross not only revealed God's eternal heart of love for sinners, but it also dealt with all that evil by nailing it to the cross with Jesus (Colossians 2:14). In the New Testament God did not decide to merely overlook sin by shrugging his shoulders over it; instead, he conquered sin by placing it on the shoulders of Jesus on the cross. So there is no hatred for evildoers in the New Testament.

There is, however, some space in the New Testament left for hating evil actions, but it plays a minor role. Paul expressed in Romans 7:15 that when he sinned, he was doing what he hated. And even though words related to "hate" are not used, we do hear a call to respond to God's action of crucifying us with Christ by putting our own particular sins to death, just as you would do to a hated enemy: "Put to death therefore what is earthly in you: sexual immorality, impurity, passion, evil desire, and covetousness, which is idolatry" (Col 3:5, ESV; see also Romans 6:11-14). Jesus also called on us to drastically lop off body parts if they prevent us from following the will of God (Matthew 18:8-9). So if we do hate sin, then the LGBT comeback is correct: job number one is hating our own sin.

But there are a few other New Testament verses about hating sin we need to explore. The first one to notice is Hebrews 1:9, which is a quotation of Psalm 45:6-7. The writer is using quotes from the Old Testament to establish that Jesus is the Son of God who is more exalted than the angels. The quote points out that the Anointed Son loves righteousness and hates wickedness. We do see Jesus' hatred of wickedness in the Gospels (although that word is not used). But his hatred is not directed toward the usual suspects (prostitution and extortion), but toward the sinful hypocrisies and legalisms of the religious leaders. So while some of us conservatives might glibly say that they love sinners, but not their sins, it should give us pause to realize that that's what Jesus would say about us: he loves us conservatives, but he hates our sins.

Another example of hating sinful deeds is in Revelation 2:6 where the church in Ephesus is commended—in spite of their flaws—for hating the works of the Nicolaitans. It's unclear what these works are, but it's likely they are similar to the idolatry and sexually immoral practices of those who followed Balaam-like or Jezebel-like leaders in other regional churches (see Revelation 2:14-15, 20).

Probably the verse most akin to the line "love the sinner; hate the sin" is found in Jude 22-23: "And have mercy on those who doubt; save others by snatching them out of the fire; to others *show mercy* with fear, *hating* even the garment stained by the flesh" (ESV, italics mine). Jude is counseling his readers on how to deal with those who are in danger of condemnation, probably the false brothers who have crept into the church (Jude 4) and their followers. *Loving the sinner* is seen in how Jude counsels his readers to show mercy to evildoers who live on the edge of hell. *Hating the sin* is seen in how Christians are still called to be "hating even the garment stained by the flesh." It's not exactly clear what he means by this, but in his own mind he sees a distinction between the person and their actions. Just as a person is distinct from their clothes, even though few people see them apart from those clothes, so a person is distinct from their actions, even though we really don't see people apart from their actions. While some might argue that "clothes make the man," they're really not the same thing. Thus, says Jude, it's possible, to love a person even if you hate their actions—and even if their identity is closely tied to those actions.

So there is New Testament precedent for the idea that we can love evildoers, even though we hate their actions.

Part of me wants to argue for the continued use of this phrase, because I would hope that progressives would feel this way toward me. Even though they might regard my perspectives on same-sex behavior as hurtful, and maybe even evil, I would hope they could look at me and say, "That Dave, I hate his book, and I hate his thoughts and actions, which I regard as so harmful to the LGBT community; but I still love him."

But another part of me says it may be time to refrain from using the phrase, even though I believe the thought behind it is right. But it has become a slogan that doesn't seem to be too helpful. The problem is that many in the LGBT community do not make a big distinction between their own identity and their actions. Many do not perceive themselves as people who engage in gay or lesbian behavior; rather many of them regard themselves as gay or lesbian to the core. So when conservatives say, "We love you, but not your same-sex actions," I get the impression that this hardly makes any sense to them. They so identify themselves by those attractions and behaviors that, to them, to reject the action is to reject them. To hate the action is to hate them.

I'm hard-pressed to think of this dynamic happening in the same way with others and their actions. How would murderers, alcoholics, gossips, or hot-tempered people respond to someone saying, "I love you, but I hate what you are doing"? They might not like to hear it—no one likes to hear that their actions are hated by others—but it seems to me their reactions would not be the same as that of the LGBT community in general. There is more of a distinction in their minds between who they are and what they do. But I would gladly welcome disagreement on this. I'm just trying to explore my own perceptions of how the LGBT people respond to "love the sinner; hate the sin." And because of this reaction, it may be time to refrain from using this phrase, especially if it is only used as a glib slogan.

Haters

But let's consider another topic that revolves around the topic of hatred, namely, the use of the term "hater." Are there haters in the world? Of course. Without the kindness of the Lord in our lives, we were "passing our days in malice and envy, hated by others and hating one another" (Titus 3:3, ESV). And unfortunately, even after we experience God's kindness, many of us still hate others (see 1 John 2:9, 11). Sometimes this hatred is based on sibling rivalry, being rebuked by another in public, or just persistent rudeness done to us by another. But much of the hatred on display today is a malice against others simply because they are different: they have a different colored skin, speak a different language, or practice a different religion. And some of this hatred is directed against the LGBT community because their sexual identity and practices are different from the majority of people. Hate crimes against all of these so-called "different" people are on the rise, and it's important for the church to stand against it.

So it's understandable why those who either perpetrate hate crimes, downplay hate crimes, or ignore hate crimes might be called "haters." And even if no actual crime takes place, those who are involved in perpetuating a system in which minorities are oppressed or disadvantaged, whether through legislation, negative remarks, or neglect—they also seem to deserve being called "haters."

But maybe a little caution is needed here. For one thing, a person who too readily labels others as "haters" might be acting with hatred as well. Oppressors do not have a corner on the market of hate. The oppressed also might have hatred growing in their hearts as well. Two wrongs don't make a right, and two hatreds don't make love.

Secondly, some issues are complicated enough that it's difficult to tell what is actually a form of oppression. It's pretty clear that if you "beat up" a transgendered male, then you are acting like a hater. But it's not as clear—even if it seems that way to a given person—that it's an act of hatred to ban those who are anatomically men from using the women's restroom. Nor is it clear to me that regarding same-sex behavior as a sin means you are acting as a hater. If you disagree with someone who is advocating passionately for a position or a law that you believe is helpful for a minority group, that doesn't automatically make you a hater. If disagreeing is enough to earn the label of hater, then both parties are haters because they both disagree. Disagreeing is not the same thing as hating. There may be many different paths toward promoting justice in our society.

I can understand why some in the LGBT community might regard people like me as haters, because we seem to be standing in the way of their full affirmation in the church (and perhaps society). Still, I ask for them to give us the benefit of love. At least some of us are opposing same-sex behavior because we love: we want God's best for the LGBT community in this life and the next, and we don't think same-sex behavior will take them in that direction. I fully expect them not to agree with how we conservatives live out this love (and some of us are really bad at it), but we don't think we are haters.

But it does place us all in a dilemma. If the way conservatives show love makes the LGBT community feel hated, we conservatives have a lot of work to do. Still, it's not very helpful to anyone if we are just dismissed as haters.

Hell

I f you talk long enough with a progressive person in explaining your position on same-sex behavior, the following question frequently arises: "So you think they're [or I'm] going to hell?" And if they don't voice it, I suspect that many of them are thinking it. This question comes up even if "hell" had never been mentioned earlier in the conversation.

The verse that raises this issue the most is 1 Corinthians 6:9-10, "Or do you not know that the unrighteous will not inherit the kingdom of God? Do not be deceived: neither the sexually immoral, nor idolaters, nor adulterers, nor men who practice homosexuality,[1] nor thieves, nor the greedy, nor drunkards, nor revilers, nor swindlers will inherit the kingdom of God" (ESV). The implication is pretty strong that those who continually engage in at least some forms (if not all forms) of same-sex behavior will not spend eternity with the Lord.

The people who ask, "So you think they're [or I'm] going to hell?" don't seem to be asking me this because they are suddenly afraid for their LGBT friends or themselves. Rather, they ask me this because they are appalled I would even think God might do that, and they're hoping that's not what I'm really saying. They are giving me a chance to correct myself.

What I say is something like, "I have no interest in passing final judgment on any individual or group of people. All I can do is testify to what the Scriptures themselves say, as uncomfortable as that might be for us both." And it is uncomfortable for me. I'm not a fan of the doctrine of hell. If it were up to me I would eliminate it. But I must resist constructing my own god and instead remain faithful to what God has revealed about himself in the Scriptures. God is displeased with evil and passionately resists every will which is set against his. For me to undercut the judgment of God with my own ideas means that I'm actually passing judgment on God.

But who is most in danger of going to hell? We all might be surprised by Jesus' answer. We often assume that those most in danger of hell are atheists, murderers, Satanists, child abusers, etc., and the book of Revelation

---

[1] This translation is contested by some. For more on this text and how it has been translated and interpreted, see the essay "Seven texts" on page 211, especially pages 220-223.

does indeed talk about hell as the destiny for obvious evildoers. But Jesus warned an entirely different group about hell. According to Jesus, especially in the gospel of Matthew, it is conservative religious people who are most in danger of hell—the very ones who take their religion seriously, who try to do their religious duty, who attempt to live morally better than most. Hell is the destiny of religious people, at least the ones who have the form of godliness, but not the power, who have the trappings of Christianity, but not the reality of Christ.

Consider the following warnings about hell from the gospel of Matthew. John the Baptist said about Jesus, "I baptize you with water for repentance. But after me will come one who is more powerful than I, whose sandals I am not worthy to carry. He will baptize you with the Holy Spirit and with fire. His winnowing fork is in his hand, and he will clear his threshing floor, gathering his wheat into the barn and burning up the chaff with unquenchable fire" (Matthew 3:11-12, NIV11). Some have said this may be John the Baptist's mistaken idea of Jesus' mission, for Jesus did not come to judge, but to speak of mercy and love. It's true that John the Baptist did not fully understand what Jesus was about, but this he had right. Although Jesus spoke of mercy, he also spoke often of God's wrath and the fires of hell. If you'd check it out, you'd discover that no one else in the Bible spoke of hell more than Jesus. He brings redemption, yes, but also the fires of judgment to burn the chaff. And these words were not spoken to pagans or backslidden Jews, but to the religious cream of the crop. They are like unproductive fruit trees which the Lord is ready to chop up and throw into the fire.

Then when Jesus began his ministry, he said to his disciples in the Sermon on the Mount, "You have heard that it was said to the people long ago, 'Do not murder, and anyone who murders will be subject to judgment.' But I tell you that anyone who is angry with his brother will be subject to judgment. Again, anyone who says to his brother, 'Raca,' is answerable to the Sanhedrin. But anyone who says, 'You fool!' will be in danger of the fire of hell" (Matthew 5:21-22, NIV). Now we don't have space to talk about legitimate and illegitimate anger. Some forms of anger are clearly allowable in God's kingdom, but not the anger that leads to insults and curses. That kind of anger ultimately leads to hell. In effect, if you tell someone to go to hell, that's a good way to end up there yourself.

Jesus also comes with fire for religious people who disobey. They may do all sorts of things for God—giving, teaching, witnessing, and miracles—but if they fail to simply obey, it's worthless. It's even deserving of hell: "Not everyone who says to me, 'Lord, Lord,' will enter the kingdom of heaven, but only the one who does the will of my Father who is in heaven. Many will say to me on that day, 'Lord, Lord, did we not prophesy in your name and in your name drive out demons and in your name perform many miracles?'

Then I will tell them plainly, 'I never knew you. Away from me, you evildoers!'" (Matthew 7:21-23, NIV11). You would think that those who called Jesus "Lord," and who did mighty works in his name were doing good things, but Jesus dismisses them as evildoers. God has no time for religious folks who are all talk, but no show. He simply wants obedient servants.

Then there are the religious people who have little faith. In Matthew 8 a hated Roman centurion asked Jesus to heal his servant. He even trusted Jesus to heal from a distance, which was in contrast to the skeptical religious leaders standing nearby. "When Jesus heard this, he was astonished and said to those following him, 'I tell you the truth, I have not found anyone in Israel with such great faith. I say to you that many will come from the east and the west, and will take their places at the feast with Abraham, Isaac and Jacob in the kingdom of heaven. But the subjects of the kingdom will be thrown outside, into the darkness, where there will be weeping and gnashing of teeth'" (Matthew 8:10-12, NIV). It seems that the outsiders will enter the kingdom, while the insiders (those raised in religious homes) will be cast out into the darkness of hell. Judgment Day will contain many surprises.

Jesus also comes with fire for religious cowards. In Matthew 10 Jesus encouraged his disciples to share the gospel with others in spite of persecution, for fear can sometimes silence us. But Jesus offers a counter-motive to speak: "Do not be afraid of those who kill the body but cannot kill the soul. Rather, be afraid of the One who can destroy both soul and body in hell" (Matthew 10:28, NIV11). The threat of hell motivates us to witness in two ways. For one, when we realize that by *not* witnessing we are partly responsible for others going to hell, then we'll get moving with the good news. Secondly, we're also motivated when we realize that by not witnessing we ourselves may end up in hell. That may sound like a poor reason to witness. Of course, it's better to witness out of love for God and others, but Jesus knows that we're motivated more by rewards and punishments than we'd care to admit. And he will use those motivators to get his gospel out. We may be fearful of possible persecution or torture or simple rejection; those are natural human fears. But we should be more fearful of disobeying God when he commands us to bring the good news of Jesus to a lost world.

Religious people also expose themselves to the dangers of hell when they get so complacent about sin in their lives that they allow it to be a stumbling block. We hear Jesus says this to his disciples in Matthew 18:8-9, "If your hand or your foot causes you to sin, cut it off and throw it away. It is better for you to enter life maimed or crippled than to have two hands or two feet and be thrown into eternal fire. And if your eye causes you to sin, gouge it out and throw it away. It is better for you to enter life with one eye than to have two eyes and be thrown into the fire of hell" (NIV). Whatever we conclude about literalness here—the literalness of cutting off hands and the fires of hell—one thing is clear, if they are symbols, they are not *just* symbols. They stand for an even more powerful reality. To say the fires of hell is symbolic doesn't make it nicer. No, the fires stand for something far worse. And if the cutting off of limbs and the gouging of eyes are symbols, they are symbols of something far more serious. Jesus is telling us to get as drastic with sin as we can. For if we don't, if we easily accept sin as a part of our life, hell becomes a very real danger.

In the parable about the wedding banquet in Matthew 22, Jesus again warns about hell. A king (God) hosts a wedding for his Son (Jesus). When the first guests made excuses and killed the inviters, God destroys them and invites common folk. But since it is a royal banquet, even the commoners need to be rightly dressed, so God furnishes garments for all. But then we read in verses 11-13, "But when the king came in to see the guests, he noticed a man there who was not wearing wedding clothes. 'Friend,' he asked, 'how did you get in here without wedding clothes?' The man was speechless. Then the king told the attendants, 'Tie him hand and foot, and throw him outside, into the darkness, where there will be weeping and gnashing of teeth'" (NIV). What's going on here? The problem with this last man is that he's there in his own clothes, his own righteousness, if you will. But anyone who thinks their righteousness qualifies them for the kingdom is a religious person heading for hell. We need to be clothed in the righteousness of Christ.

In Matthew 23 Jesus gives an extended warning to religious people. In verse after verse, Jesus exposes the sins of the most pious. For one thing, they don't practice what they preach. Secondly, they put money before God. Then there's the matter of getting picky about little things and forgetting the major things. Add to that, they are clean on the outside, but filthy on the inside. They are hypocrites, and the fate of hypocrites is hell: "You snakes! You brood of vipers! How will you escape being condemned to hell?" (Matthew 23:33, NIV11).

Toward the end of Matthew 24, Jesus tells his disciples to be ready for his return, for even a religious person can act like a servant who misbehaves when the master is away—perhaps abusing fellow disciples, or getting caught up in partying. "The master of that servant will come on a day when he does not expect him and at an hour he is not aware of. He will cut him to pieces and assign him a place with the hypocrites, where there will be weeping and gnashing of teeth" (Matthew 24:50-51, NIV11). God has prepared hell for the unprepared.

And finally, Jesus warns the religious ones who may have avoided doing what's bad, but they also managed to avoid doing what's good. In particular, they failed to help the needy. On Judgment Day Jesus will say to them, "'Depart from me, you who are cursed, into the eternal fire prepared for the devil and his angels. For I was hungry and you gave me nothing to eat, I was thirsty and you gave me nothing to drink, I was a stranger and you did not invite me in, I needed clothes and you did not clothe me, I was sick and in prison and you did not look after me.' They also will answer, 'Lord, when did we see you hungry or thirsty or a stranger or needing clothes or sick or in prison, and did not help you?' He will reply, 'Truly I tell you, whatever you did not do for one of the least of these, you did not do for me.' Then they will go away to eternal punishment, but the righteous to eternal life" (Matthew 25:41-46, NIV11). These people would not have been known as terrible sinners. They sound as if they would have gladly helped Jesus, had they known he was in need. But because they focused on personal piety, and yet did nothing for the needy, the fires of hell await them.

These verses alone paint a very ominous, even hopeless, picture of the future. But these verses do not stand alone. They are located in the Gospels, the message of good news about Jesus. For Jesus did not just come to warn people of hell. He came to experience hell on our behalf, to experience separation from God on the cross, so that he could bear our punishment for sin. It's in him that we find our only hope, for in Christ Jesus there is now no condemnation. Whether we're religious or irreligious, same-sex attracted or opposite-sex attracted—we all stand under the same threat of hell, and our only hope in life and in death is Jesus Christ.

Without Jesus, the LGBT community is going to hell. And without Jesus, the pious, conservatively moral people are going to hell, too. Yes, without Jesus, we are all going to hell. But we need not be without Jesus. The main factor to consider about who goes to hell is not whether we did this or that sin, or how often we did it. The main factor is whether we live a life of turning to Jesus in faith—not to the Jesus that we want him to be, but to the Jesus who has revealed himself to us in the Scriptures. He's the Jesus who preached hell and underwent hell for us.

Identifying sins

Denominations occasionally have furious debates over whether or not a certain action should be identified as a sin. Is it a sin to belong to the Masons or drink alcohol? Is it a sin to gamble at the casino or gambol at the dance club? Is it a sin to promote communism or capitalism? Is it a sin to stockpile nuclear weapons or clone human beings? Is it a sin to hire a physician to give you an abortion or help you commit suicide? For many years, denominations have also been debating whether same-sex activity is a sin.

We should pause to consider some aspects of this ministry of identifying sins.

Identifying sins is an important ministry of the church

According to 2 Timothy 3:16, one of the main reasons God breathed out the Scriptures was to help us identify and avoid sins—to teach, rebuke, correct, and train us in righteousness. But the Bible is not a manual that supplies the ethical answers to every possible situation. Because of changes in technology, culture, and knowledge, we continually confront new ethical issues not specifically covered in the Scriptures. For example, the Bible does not explicitly address abortion, nuclear weapons, communism, capitalism, cloning, or doctor-assisted suicide. And even where the Bible does address a certain activity (such as same-sex activity, gambling, or alcohol), the current situation often introduces new dynamics into the discussion.

Because the Bible is the living voice of God and not a moral how-to manual, God has given to the church the ministry of prayerfully reading, studying, discussing, and debating the written Word in order to hear God's living voice speak to the contemporary situation. As the church is faithful in this, the Lord guides the church in determining whether an action is sinful or not. Jesus promised his disciples in Matthew 18:18, "Truly I tell you, whatever you bind on earth will be bound in heaven, and whatever you loose on earth will be loosed in heaven."

Of course, it is always possible for the church to misidentify an act, a possibility which stirs up fear on all sides. Both progressives and conservatives are afraid that what they regard as sinful acts might be misidentified as not being sinful. They are afraid that such a decision would encourage people either to go ahead and do the action or to lackadaisically ignore the plight of those hurt by it. Both progressives and conservatives also fear that what they regard as non-sinful acts will be misidentified as being sinful. They fear that the imposition of man-made rules will create obstacles that prevent people from coming to Jesus in faith.

It's because of the possibility of misidentification that debates are so furious. The stakes are high. No one wants to permit sin or impose man-made rules. We need to call on the Lord in prayer to work through these difficult discussions.

We also need to remind ourselves, however, that in spite of the importance of identifying sins, this ministry is not our ultimate one. For if we learn the knowledge of good and evil, but do not learn to know God himself, we do no better than Adam and Eve who ate from the Tree of the Knowledge of Good and Evil. If we can identify sins, but still live under the power of sin, we have missed the mark. The Lord does not call us only to distinguish good from evil, but more importantly to love the Lord with all our heart, soul, mind, and strength, and to love our neighbors as ourselves. When Paul was a Pharisee, he excelled at identifying sin, but that was rubbish compared to pressing on to "know Christ and the power of his resurrection and the fellowship of sharing in his sufferings" (Philippians 3:10, NIV). Our mission of identifying sins is important, but only as it builds faith and love.

Identifying sins is not the same thing as identifying sinners

When the church identifies some act as a sin, it does not mean that we can now place a new label of "sinner" on those who act in that way. That's because they already had that label—as does everyone else. All drinkers are sinners, but so are all teetotalers. All communists and capitalists are sinners. Both abortionists and abortion protesters are sinners. Everyone involved in same-sex behavior is a sinner and so is everyone involved in opposite-sex behavior. We are all sinners in need of God's grace. The purpose of identifying sin is not so that we can determine who needs forgiveness. We all need forgiveness.

This truth puts the ministry of identifying sins in perspective. Even if the church temporarily errs in identifying sins—perhaps castigating recreational dancing or condoning sex-selection abortions—all would be not be lost as long as the church continues to identify sinners (which is all of us) and minister the gospel of new life in Christ.

Too often, however, we don't think it's enough to view people as sinners in need of grace. We want to affix an additional label on them that specifies what sins they commit. We want to define people as thieves, materialists, baby-killers, adulterers, gays, or lesbians. But we are not consistent with this labeling. If a person commits only one murder in their lifetime, we call them a murderer. But if another person gossips only once in their whole life, we would be reluctant to call them a gossip.

This tendency to describe sinners by their specific sins will always be with us. Even God's Word uses labels like homosexual offender, thief, drunkard, slanderer, and swindler (see 1 Corinthians 6: 9-10, NIV). In part, this is because it's a lot handier to say "thief" than to say "person who steals or has stolen." We all prefer to use verbal shorthand to aid in communication.

But even as we continue to use sin-specific labels, we must be cautious. Sin-specific labels tempt us to rank them according to degrees of vilification. Many consider a gossip to be better than an adulterer, and the adulterer to be better than a murderer. But observe how easy it is to create rankings that work in our favor. We might all be sinners, but sin-specific labels allow us to think that some of us are "better" sinners than others.

Sin-specific labels also push us toward treating people as nothing but stereotypes and case studies instead of flesh-and-blood human beings with a unique name and history. When we define people by a specific sin, we forget that God has the last word in defining who they are. God identifies them as people made in his image. God identifies them as people he loves. God identifies them as people for whom Jesus died. God identifies them as people in need of transformation. Although a drunk may organize his life around the consumption of alcohol (and seemingly deserve the label "alcoholic"), God knows there is more to his life than his sin. God wants us to know that, too.

Sometimes these labels even backfire on us. Although we might have given a sin-specific label to vilify someone, they might embrace the label as a term that defines the sum total of who they are. Mary Stewart Van Leeuwen noted how this happened with the term, homosexual. "When Victorian doctors shifted attention from individual homosexual *acts* to the concept of homosexuality as a *pervasive personality structure*...the homosexual was now a species." And then quoting Michael Foucault's *Sexual Chaos*, she added, "The category Victorians invented to stigmatize homosexuality has now become the basis for celebrating it."[1]

When people embrace the sin-specific labels we pin on them, they come to believe that that's just the way they are. They don't believe God can change them, nor do they necessarily want to change. This reaction should make all believers reluctant to affix sin-specific labels.

---

[1] Mary Stewart Van Leeuwen, "Asking Better Questions in the Homosexuality Debates," *Perspectives: a Journal of Reformed Thought* 12 (April, 1997), 12.

Identifying sins is an act of compassion

Although some may think that identifying sins is just a tool of hatred and fear, our actual purpose in identifying sins is to show compassion.

For one thing, identifying an action as sinful can be a compassionate word of warning to those who have not committed that sin, but are tempted to do so. Our cautionary words can help people avoid that sin and the misery it brings in its train.

This doesn't always work, of course. Some people are even more attracted to something when they learn that it is wrong. But we cannot blame the warning for the sin. And even if we avoid one sin, there will always be other sins that bring heartache into our lives. But at least a warning about a certain sin might prevent us from compounding our problems.

Identifying an action as sinful can also help those who have already committed that sin. When a person presses on in sinful behavior, unknowingly bringing more misery on themselves, it is an act of compassion to tell them the truth. The truth about sin can set them free. No one comes to Jesus for mercy until they first recognize their problem with sin. That's why it is an act of compassion for the church to tell the truth about sins.

A number of people, however, are not convinced that identifying sins is a compassionate act. From their perspective, the identification of sins results in less compassion for sinners, not more. They are afraid that once an action is identified as a sin, then Christians will use that label as an excuse to judge, reject, and hate those who commit these sins.

Unfortunately, some Christians do actually respond in this negative way. For instance, many Christians who think of same-sex behavior as a sin have an intense distaste, and even hatred, for those who act in those ways. Some, therefore, believe that the only way to call Christians back to loving those in the LGBT community is by persuading the church to re-classify same-sex behaviors as non-sinful.

But the problem of Christians rejecting and hating sinners is not solved by defining sin away. What's needed is a recovery of the meaning and practice of grace. Grace is God's love for sinners. "But God demonstrates his own love for us in this: While we were still sinners, Christ died for us" (Romans 5:8, NIV11).

Those who call an action a sin, and then hate those who do this sin are not yet living in grace. But we could also say, those who are able to love people only by redefining sin as non-sin—they are not yet living in grace either. Their position implies that no one is really capable of loving a sinner, and so we must remove the label of "sinful." Those who live by grace, however, know how to love sinners. When a certain action is identified as sin, those who live by grace become more compassionate, not less, toward those who are trapped by that sin. As we learn about the Old Testament priests and Jesus our great High Priest: "Every high priest is...able to deal gently with those who are ignorant and are going astray, since he himself is subject to weakness... [And in Christ] we do not have a high priest who is unable to sympathize with our weaknesses, but we have one who has been tempted in every way, just as we are—yet was without sin. Let us then approach the throne of grace with confidence, so that we may receive mercy and find grace to help us in our time of need" (Hebrews 5:1-2, 4:15-16).

But even if identifying sins is an act of compassion, the world does not always perceive it that way. The world understands the word "sin" in the same way that many in the church do: as a rejecting word instead of a compassion-inducing word. In part, this is because the world does not *understand* grace. But even more, this is because the world has not *experienced* grace from Christians. The ministry of identifying sins will fail unless the church also lives out its ministry of extending God's grace.

Debates will continue on the question, "Is it a sin?" But there's no debate about another question that we should also be asking, "Is this an opportunity to love?" Behind every debate is an opportunity to love the opposition. Behind every action that could be regarded as sinful are people who need the love of Christ.

Identity

I am a pastor, a preacher, a writer, and a theologian. I am a husband, a father, a grandpa, a son, a brother, an uncle, a nephew, and a cousin. I am a Lego fanatic, a lyricist, a font-lover, and a tenor. I am a white male, a Dutchman, a South Dakotan, and an American. I am a Northwestern College alum and Minnesota Vikings fan. I am a sinner, a competitor, a mediocre pray-er. I am a Mountain Dew drinker, a tee-totaler, a chocoholic, and a night owl. I am a CVID patient (Common Variable Immune Deficiency). I'm a Jesus freak, a pacifist, a kid at heart, and an old hippie. I am God's well-loved child, and a follower of Christ.

Some of these identities I wear as a badge of honor and some as a mark of shame. Some of these identities have been with me my whole life long, and some I've newly-acquired. Some of these are based on what I do and others on who I am. Some identities I have chosen (although I can't always remember how that happened), and some seem to have chosen me. Some I live out energetically, and others I hardly pay attention to. Some identities happened because of relationships, both human and divine. And I am more than any one label can say.

The issue of identity is especially important for those who identify as gay, lesbian, bi-sexual, or transgender—who identify themselves as part of the LGBT community. But what kind of identity is this?

Honorable or shameful. As noted above, we embrace some identities and find a sense of pride in them, while other identities cause us shame. For many years, because of the social stigma involved—and because many of them thought their own actions and thoughts were wrong—many in the LGBT community would hide their identity. But in the past few decades, more and more they have been embracing that identity, "coming out of the closet," as the saying goes, and participating in what are often called "Gay Pride" parades.

Life-long or of more recent vintage. From what I hear, many in the LGBT community have lived with this identity for as long as they can remember (even if they did not admit it to others at an earlier time). But for some, they applied this identity to themselves later in life—perhaps after their first same-sex encounter in college or after a failed opposite-sex marriage.

Doing or being. Many who are not part of the LGBT community, especially conservatives, tend to think of same-sex sexual identity as based on something they do, namely, engage in same-sex activities, either in reality or fantasy. But for most progressives and nearly all in the LGBT community, they believe this identity is not just about what they do (like most people, they are not involved in sexual activity that often), but rather, it's about who they are.

By choice or a given in life. While some conservatives might insist that members of the LGBT community chose their lifestyle, most of the LGBT community itself do not believe that's the case. In their minds, their LGBT identity was set from the start and was never chosen by them. [1]

Major or minor. While some of our identities don't influence us much (the fact that I'm a cousin, for instance, only comes to mind at a reunion), other identities live at the forefront of our minds. I'm guessing that most members of the LGBT community see that identity as huge in what it means to be themselves. This doesn't mean at all that they're constantly thinking about "getting it on" with someone of the same sex, but it does mean they have an ongoing awareness that this is who they are.

Relational. While there may have been a time when many members of the LGBT community were loners, who only engaged in same-sex activity with relative strangers, increasingly it's about being in relationships with others. They have circles of friends and acquaintances in the LGBT community; they may have regular partners, or just one partner. And these relationships reinforce their identity as gay, lesbian, bisexual, or transgender.

And of course, LGBT identities alone do not completely define anyone in that community. They are also wives, grandchildren, video gamers, bankers, factory workers, sopranos, Native American, Italian, coffee snobs, cancer survivors, patriots, and complainers.

And this leads us to the question of how one's relationship with God through Jesus Christ might also be a formative part of an LGBT person's identity. If a gay or lesbian person wants nothing to do with Jesus—perhaps because of how they've been treated by Christians—then their identity will only be minimally shaped by Christ, if at all. But let's take the case of an LGBT person who was raised in church, who believed and still believes that Jesus loves them, died for their sins and has granted them eternal life. Being a Christian is part of their identity. They see themselves as a child of God, adopted into God's family through what Jesus Christ did for them.

The gut reaction of many conservative Christians is, "How can that be? How can they identify themselves as Christians and yet also identify them-

---

[1] For more on this, see the essay "Choices" on page 42.

selves as gay?" For conservatives, that would be like being a Christian atheist, or a Christian torturer, or a Christian pedophile. The two identities can't belong in the same body for long—something has to give.

Of course, at this point, many LGBT people who identify as Christians do not see a problem, because they do not regard same-sex behavior as sinful—at least not in how they live it out. To them, just as you can be a husband (of a wife) and a Christian at the same time, so you can be a husband (of a husband) and a Christian at the same time. If the progressives are right on this, there is nothing more to be said.

But what if they're wrong? What if all forms of same-sex behavior are against God's will? What then do we say to the person who identifies as both gay and Christian simultaneously? Do we say, "You're wrong. You must not be a Christian, even though you think you are"? That doesn't seem to be the right response either (although that is a possibility and only God would know the answer to that one).

Instead, we conservatives should remind ourselves that we are in a very similar situation to the person who identifies as both gay and Christian. We know what it's like to identify as a Christian and also to identify ourselves as a sinner—at one and the same time. And many of us don't just identify ourselves as some kind of generic sinner, but a certain kind of sinner. We are gossips; we are drunks; we are slanderers; we are hot-heads; we are grudge-holders; we are failures at prayer or witnessing. It's not like we just did these things once and got over it, but we are chronic sinners in these areas—and yet we identify ourselves as Christians at the same time. Other people might look at us and wonder, "How can they call themselves a Christian and be like that?" but we know it's possible, because that's the way we are.

So if the Christian who's also a chronic gossip is in the same boat as the Christian who's also gay, then the main thing conservatives should be saying to the LGBT community (if we have earned the right to say anything at all) is the same thing we need to be saying to ourselves. Here's what I say to myself:

(1) "Remember who you are and whose you are." I may have many components in my sense of identity, but the primary source of my identity is in Christ. Yes, I am a sinner, but ultimately that doesn't really define me. I am a child of God, whose sins have been washed away in the blood of the Lamb, and the power of Christ through the Holy Spirit is transforming me to be more and more conformed to his image. And because Christ is my primary source of identity, then all my other sources of identity need to align with him. It will be a life-long adventure, with plenty of slips, but it needs to happen if who I am is primarily who I am in Christ.

(2) "Because of the incredible power of self-deception, I need to pray that the Lord would help me discern—through prayer, Scripture, and the input of godly believers—any way in which I am defining myself by some sinful behavior or sinful priority." Just because I don't think something is wrong doesn't mean it's not. If I'm defining some behavior of mine as non-sinful when a lot of other Christians see it otherwise, I should be very open to the possibility that I have deceived myself.

(3) If I see that something I have been regarding as part of my identity clashes with my identity in Christ, then I should only speak of that aspect of my identity in a mode of confession and repentance, not a mode of self-assertion. The man who identifies himself as an alcoholic at a recovery meeting does so in confessional mode. He is recognizing and admitting his sin before God and others with the hope that he will not live out that sin-based identity. This is very different from the man who boastfully identifies himself as a ladies' man when out partying with the boys. This is no confession of sin, for he doesn't believe what he's doing is sinful at all, and he hopes to live out that identity fully. This contrast sheds light on the issue of identifying oneself as same-sex attracted. The Christian man who says, "I'm same-sex attracted" is called to speak those words in a confessional mode of an identity they are resisting, instead of in an assertive mode of what they intend to live out.

A middle-aged single man once confessed to me that he was gay. He had been suspecting this his whole life long, but didn't want to admit it to himself—nor to anyone else—because he was frightened by his expectation of how people would treat him if they knew. But the internal tension was driving him crazy. So he finally talked to a few people he knew well, including myself, and he was amazed that no one spurned him or rejected him. We simply showed him a lot of love and acceptance of where he was at this point in his journey in life. I'm not sure what the other people said to him, but I told him that as he began exploring the gay world that he needed to remember who he was in Christ and that there was a lot more to him than the identity of being "gay." I should not have been amazed, but within a month of this conversation, he experienced transformation from the Lord, turned away from same-sex experiences, and never looked back. I know his story is just his story, but I believe it shows the transforming power of finding your primary identity in Christ.

Interpreting experiences[1]

To be a human being is to be an interpreting creature. Our five senses not only take in data about what is happening around us and to us, but our mind is also trying to find meaning behind our experiences. We want to interpret what's happening in our world and in our hearts.

That's one reason why the news media moves beyond simple reporting of events, and instead tries to explain the meaning of what's happening. When we agree with their interpretation, we don't make any comments about how the media should quit giving us their opinions. But when we don't like their interpretation, then we grumble about how the media should simply stick to the facts.

But if the media did that—simply reported facts—we would not like that either. Let's say the newspaper simply stated that sixteen people were killed by a car bomb in Dallas, naming who died, what kind of car was used, how quickly the ambulance arrived, and...that's all. It would give us the facts and nothing but the facts, but we would be profoundly shaken. We'd want to know the meaning of the event. Why did this happen? Who's behind it? What is the President likely to do about it? Can we expect this kind of thing to happen again any time soon? What do the majority of Americans think about this turn of events? As interpreting creatures, we'd have lots of questions about the meaning of the event.

Which is why the media steps in to provide some meaning. Sometimes they formulate meanings too soon, or approach the issue with an obvious bias, even distorting facts in order to bolster their interpretation, and that's wrong. But nonetheless, we cannot fault them for giving us more than the facts. As people in search of meaning, we want (and need) more than facts.

We face a similar issue when it comes to our own experiences of faith. God moves in our life, and then we need to figure out what it means. Something is missing if we just report on the facts of our experiences with God.

Let's imagine, for example, that we are seated with a crowd on a hillside in Galilee 2,000 years ago. Our five senses are in good working order. We

---

[1] Based on an editorial entitled "Interpreting Encounters with God" which I wrote for *The Sunday School Guide,* Vol. 84, February 12, 2006, 17, 30-31. Used by permission.

hear Jesus speaking to us. We feel our stomach rumble. We see Jesus take five loaves of bread and two fish, breaking them and putting them in baskets. We smell baked bread in the air. As the basket comes our way, we take a piece and taste the fish. We observe how this large crowd is fed by such a small amount. And then we go home. If we only stick with what our senses have told us that day, we have learned very little. But this event cries out to be interpreted. What does it mean that Jesus can feed 5,000 people with just bits of food? If we don't move beyond sensory data to meaning, we're missing the main point.

Although few people have experienced such a mighty miracle as the feeding of the 5,000, many people have had powerful spiritual encounters with Jesus—even non-Christians. It could be a vivid dream, an inner prompting, an unusual "coincidence," a healing, a sermon that seemed directed right at them, a vision, a near-miss encounter with death, a Bible verse that took on life, and more. Often people are reluctant to share these experiences, lest others think they're going crazy. When people tell me about these experiences, they often preface it with words like, "You probably won't believe this, but one time..."

The fact that these spiritual experiences happen is beyond our control. They simply come as gifts from God, and we cannot force them to happen any more than we can make ourselves fall in love. But once we have a vivid encounter with God like this, it begs for us to interpret it.

One of the most important things to remember is to rely on the Word of God to help you interpret your own experiences with God. I have talked with a number of widows through the years who have had vivid dreams of their loved one appearing to them to assure them they'd be okay. They have found great comfort in this dream, but they wanted to know what I think it means. I tell them that they need to interpret this experience in light of Scripture. Because of Scripture, we know that this dream is not an invitation for the widow to seek more contact with their loved one through séances or other forms of contacting the dead. The Bible strictly forbids such activity (Deuteronomy 18:9-13). Instead it's more helpful to interpret such dreams as gracious signs from God that the widow and their loved one are both safe within the hands of God. Thank the Lord for such a comforting vision, but don't go seeking to repeat it.

But even with the help of Scripture, sometimes it's hard to interpret our experiences of God. When John Wesley, the unintentional founder of the Methodist Church, was a young man, he was very devout. He spent long hours in prayer, was daily involved in a small group Bible study, dedicated himself to obedient living, went on mission trips, and preached the gospel. Yet he had an inner sense of something not yet right in his heart. But after nearly a decade of living for Jesus, he read a biblical text in a small group meeting that caused his heart to become "strangely warmed." He inter-preted that to be his real moment of conversion. Prior to that he had not yet been saved, or so he thought. I have wondered if he learned to interpret that differently when he actually arrived in heaven. Maybe in heaven he learned that he had been saved well before that, and the strange warming of his heart was simply another touch of assuring grace.

I have had to change my interpretation of my own experiences as well. I spent a lot of time with Pentecostals when I was in high school, and they talked a lot about a necessary second step in the life of faith, which they called the baptism of the Holy Spirit. It's important to get saved, they said, but then you need to also be baptized with the Spirit, which in Pentecostal theology usually happens later than salvation. According to them, we need this baptism of the Spirit so that we can be empowered to be witnesses for Jesus (as found in Acts 1:8). At that point in my young life, this all made sense to me. So I looked at my own past experiences with God and found one which I figured must have been my baptism in the Spirit.

It happened a year after I became a Christian. I was set to go to Chris-tian camp again. But I had always been so shy and uncomfortable with un-familiar people. When I was praying about this one night, I sensed the Lord saying to me that I would be his witness and that I needed to forget about my shyness and just meet people. My heart was strangely warmed, and I became more extroverted from that point on. It sure seemed to me that that was my baptism of the Holy Spirit, and that's what I called it while running with the Pentecostals.

Later, however, I came to believe from Scripture that there are not two classes of Christians (those who have been baptized with the Spirit and those who have not), but that the baptism of the Spirit happens already when a person first becomes a Christian. Any later work of God in our heart is a fresh filling of the Spirit, but is not a distinct baptism that sets us apart from other Christians. So I had to re-interpret my experience with God once again. The experience remained the same throughout and still has changed me to this day, but how I interpreted it has changed to align itself better with what the Bible teaches. All of us should spend some time pondering our spiritual experiences with God—interpreting those experiences in the light of God's Word.

I once had a conversation with a Christian who regards himself as gay. He testified of a powerful experience of God's presence and grace, which is always wonderful to receive. But I could tell that he had interpreted this ex-perience to mean that God approved of his same-sex relationship. I had just met him and never met him again, but if I had had time to develop a rela-tionship of trust, I would have noted that it's always best to interpret the meaning of our encounters with God in the light of Scripture.

But let me add one more thing. Even though I have found vivid encounters with God to be such a blessing in my own life, I also know that ultimately faith is not about our own experiences. It's about God. I know a young man who, when he was about ten years old, was sitting at an evangelistic rally directly in front of me. When an altar call was given, this boy got up and went forward. I was thankful because he had always been a handful for his Sunday School teachers. This touch of God, however, didn't immediately transform him. In fact, he went through a period of adolescent rebellion and became even harder to handle. In high school, however, God really got a hold of him and turned him into a dynamic leader of his peers, and he now has a doctorate in spiritual formation.

One day I ran across the exact date of that earlier altar call and wrote him an email about it. He replied that he had no memory of that event at all, but obviously God was moving even when he didn't realize it. And that's true for all of us. Spiritual experiences are wonderful, but God is moving in our lives even when we are not aware of it. And what God is doing is more important than what we're consciously experiencing. In the end, it's God's interpretation that counts more than our own.

It's different now

Peple are people wherever you go. No matter what age you are, what historical era you lived in, or what culture you grew up in, there are still many constants about the human condition and the human heart. Certainly there are differences in terms of technology, priorities, assumptions, and options. And yet, every human has to deal with love and loneliness, joy and sorrow, sin and deliverance, fears and faith, worries and wonder.

It's because of this I don't put a huge stock in so-called generational differences. The great generation, the forgotten generation, baby boomers, Gen-X, Millennials...on and on it goes—always giving someone a reason to sell books and promote seminars. Undoubtedly there are some differences between generations, but the similarities are even more abundant. All generations have the same human heart.

Because of my gut feeling on this matter, I have a hard time with an argument that I often hear in same-sex discussion. The argument goes like this: While the Bible does speak against same-sex behaviors, same-sex relationships back then were different than they are now. Back then it was more like abuse, especially with older men taking advantage of younger guys. But today same-sex relationships are more about mutuality and equality. Therefore, goes the argument, the Bible's prohibition of same-sex relationships does not apply to the kind of relationships that happen today.

I would like to point out four things about this. First, this argument contains a classic case of what could be called "generational exceptionalism," the idea that "our generation is different and so doesn't have to follow the rules of the older generations." Every child uses this argument on their parents whenever they're trying to get their way. My generation used this argument to advocate for free love—sexual activity with "no strings attached." Are some old rules worth tossing? Of course, but you need a better reason than "because they're old." There's also a lot of wisdom in old rules.

Second, while some might paint all ancient same-sex relationships as bad as possible in order to form a contrast with today, it's likely that at least some of the ancient relationships were long-term, "monogamous," caring, and between equals. And yet the biblical commands stand against same-sex relationships, whether those qualities were present or not. Maybe I suffer from a lack of imagination, but I can't imagine Paul saying in Romans 1, "Those who refused to acknowledge God were given over to short-term, unfaithful, abusive same-sex relationships, while those who *did* acknowledge God were able to enjoy long-term, monogamous, caring same-sex relationships."

Third, while some might paint many of today's same-sex relationships as good as possible in order to form a contrast with the past, it's likely that a lot of today's relationships are just as plagued with promiscuity and taking advantage of people as was true long ago. There is a lot of sordid activity happening in today's LGBT community—and in today's heterosexual community too. The human heart is just as sinful today as it was in Bible times. The argument that same-sex relationships are different today doesn't work because the contrast between then and now is not that great.

Fourth, the whole argument hinges on the idea that sexual activities and marriages should be permitted for today's same-sex couples, because their love measures up to a certain level of goodness that couples in the ancient world never attained. But if that were true, then the implication is also true, namely, that when the love in a same-sex relationship is *not* of higher quality than in the ancient world, then the same-sex relationship should be disallowed, and I don't think that's what progressives want to argue for.

There are two other problems with using this line of argument to create space for same-sex relations. First, if the moral validity of a marriage is dependent on the quality of the love in that marriage, then no one's marriage would be valid. Even those in opposite-sex marriages are tainted by self-centered desires and less than perfect faithfulness and love. But that does not invalidate the marriage (although if the quality of love is really bad, the marriage may not survive). The *quality* of the love in a marriage, while very important and desirable, is not what makes a marriage morally valid.

Secondly, if we were to say that the moral validity of a marriage *is* dependent on the quality of the love in that marriage, who would be qualified to discern that? Nearly everyone will say that their love is pure and good. So this approach actually creates all kinds of room here for self-deception in which people will think that the quality of their love is good enough to ignore biblical commands.

Let me give a concrete example here. Let's say a gay couple asks a pastor to perform their wedding. One is aged 35 and the other is 26. They've been together for five years, and they met at work when the older one was a supervisor. How is this really any different from a first century situation in which a commander takes on a younger soldier as his lover, a relationship that lasts for decades? Since Paul would not condone the latter, why would we think he'd condone its modern equivalent?

So I'm skeptical that today's same-sex relationships are really all that different from long ago. If God's Word spoke against it in the first century, he'd speak the same today. Our failure to see this only means that everyone will be doing what is right in their own eyes, which Judges 21:25 suggests is a recipe for moral and spiritual disaster on a personal and cultural level.

It's no worse than...

In a less democratic time, people did not believe all sins were equal. Some sins were mortal; others were venial. Some were understandable; others made people ask, "How could they do that?" Some sins were scandalous, while others were ordinary. Unfortunately, when sins are seen as unequal and ranked in order of perversity, everyone devises a scale of sins to work in their favor. The sins of other people are always worse than one's own sins, especially sexual sins.

Today, however, people are more democratically-minded. They try to believe all sins are created equal. But the human heart is wicked enough to turn the notion of equal sins into yet another strategy for tipping the scales in its own favor. When people say, "Adultery is not any worse than gossip," they are not saying that adultery and gossip are equally horrifying to the Lord. Rather, the actual wording of the phrase "is not any worse than" implies that adultery is as socially acceptable as gossip. Similarly when someone confronts them for dishonesty, they might retort, "Well, what about your judgmentalism?" The implication is that since we are all equally imperfect, we are all equally immune from prosecution. The democratization of sin leads us to a lowest common denominator morality in which all sins are equally acceptable.

Even worse, this democratization eventually creates a new pecking order among sins. In a devilish version of "the first shall be last," the sins that used to be regarded as scandalous get dismissed as minor infractions (or even celebrated as evidence of freedom), while those that used to be overlooked get treated as heinous crimes.

Since the equality of sin and the inequality of sin can both be twisted to justify our own sin, we need to be more careful in defining the relationship between sin and the concept of equality. There are some respects in which sins are equal and others in which they are not equal.

Sins are equal
Sins are equal in earning the same wage of death (Romans 6:23). Every sin hurts our relationship with God (Psalm 51:4). Every sin is equally reprehensible in the sight of our holy God (Habakkuk 1:13). Every sin makes us a

lawbreaker, "For whoever keeps the whole law and yet stumbles at just one point is guilty of breaking all of it" (James 2:10, NIV11).

One point of near equality is that all sins, but one, are equally covered by the blood of Jesus. All sins but one can be forgiven. We are not sure exactly what this one sin is, but it has something to do with blaspheming the Holy Spirit (Luke 12:10), re-crucifying Jesus by turning away from salvation (Hebrews 6: 4-6), and deliberately sinning after having received the knowledge of the truth (Hebrews 10: 26-31). This is the sin that leads to death (1 John 5:16-17). But even though this one sin cannot be forgiven, we can rejoice that all other sins can be equally forgiven.

Sins are unequal

In some other respects, however, sins are unequal. For instance, every sin stirs up unequal consequences for others and ourselves. Adultery has different consequences than lust. Murder has different consequences than hatred.

In addition, every sin is done with different levels of awareness. With some sins we consciously know what we are doing. With other sins we suppress our awareness, so that we don't admit to ourselves what we are doing. Still other sins, especially sins of omission, are often done without any awareness on our part.

Another difference between sins is how they affect who we are in our wholeness as body and soul. Paul points this out in 1 Corinthians 6:18, "Flee from sexual immorality. All other sins a person commits are outside the body, but whoever sins sexually sins against their own body" (NIV11). Same-sex behavior would come under this rubric, because Paul had just mentioned same-sex sin (and some others) earlier in the same chapter (1 Corinthians 6:9-10).

This verse suggests that those ancestors of the faith who treated sexual sins as worse than other sins were not completely off track. Even if they lost track of grace and the heinousness of other sins, their spiritual instincts correctly told them that sexual sins are a different breed of sin. Sexual sins affect the whole person in a way that other sins do not. We are not just souls living inside of bodies. We are our bodies. And what we do with our bodies and sexual organs (and what is done to our sexual organs) has a profound impact on the kind of person we are and are becoming.

Those who would treat sexual activity as nothing but a recreational sport have lost sight of how self-defining sexual activity is. All the studies which show the disturbing impact of rape and childhood sexual abuse indicate the power of sexual activity to shape the whole person—body and soul.

Because all sins are equal in some respects and unequal in other respects, it might be better if we didn't view sin through the lens of equality at all. God's Word never uses the concept of equality to describe sin, anyway, but it does talk about a different kind of equality. According to 1 Corinthians 12:25, we are the body of Christ so that all parts "should have *equal* concern for each other" (NIV11, italics mine). Whether sins are equal or not, we must emphasize our equal concern for each other as we wrestle with various temptations and seek release from diverse transgressions. That's an equality that can't go wrong.

Judging

Judgment and judging have fallen on hard times. Our immediate gut reaction to these words is negative. Judging is regarded as a bad thing that no one should do. To some people there are no sins anymore, except this terrible sin of judging.

You can curse, get drunk, cheat on your spouse, lie to your boss, poke fun of another race, skip church, pursue money at all costs, and hate your in-laws—hardly anyone will bat an eye. But if you dare judge, you are an evil person. The first and greatest commandment for many today is no longer loving God with your whole being or loving your neighbor as yourself. Instead, these have been displaced by Jesus' words in the Sermon on the Mount: "Judge not that ye be not judged" (Matthew 7:1, KJV). This is the only Bible verse that some people know.

And this attitude has infiltrated the thinking of Christians as well. When talking with someone about a moral issue (such as gambling, drunkenness, adultery, same-sex behavior, etc.) and we even agree about what the Bible says, I quite commonly hear words like these added to the discussion: "But you know, we shouldn't judge."

Part of me is happy that Jesus' words have been so taken to heart. But another part of me doesn't like that line, "But you know, we shouldn't judge." I suspect that what some mean by that statement is this: "Well, yes, I think adultery is wrong, but that's just my opinion. Other people might look at it differently. So no one really knows what's right and wrong; it's just a matter of taste, a personal preference. And so we shouldn't judge." But that's not at all what Jesus meant in Matthew 7:1.

First, we need to look at the word "judge." Both the Greek verb for judge (*krinō*) and the English word have similar facets to them, like a coin with two sides.

On the negative side, we use the word "judge" to mean to condemn people, to pronounce them guilty, to pass sentence on them, to reject them, and even punish them. This is what the Pharisees were good at. But according to the Bible, this is not our work, but God's. Our knowledge of other people, their actions, intentions, and motives is too limited to pass verdict on their eternal destiny. Unlike God, we don't know the whole story. But God knows and God has the authority to reach a verdict on a person's life and give the appropriate response.

But there's a more positive side to judging as well. It can also mean to discern, assess, evaluate, weigh, consider, or sift through various options and actions. We might come to a negative conclusion, but we could also come to a positive conclusion. I evaluate options and judge which one is God's will. This is what we call using good judgment.

We don't often hear that phrase "good judgment" anymore. The two words "good" and "judgment" don't seem like they belong together, for our society tends to think all judgment is bad. But there is such a thing as good judgment, and the wisdom portion of Scripture encourages us to use good judgment and rebukes those who lack it:

> Teach me good judgment and knowledge, for I believe in your commandments. (Psalm 119:66, NRSV)
> My son, preserve sound judgment and discernment, do not let them out of your sight. (Proverbs 3:21, NIV)
> But a man who commits adultery lacks judgment; whoever does so destroys himself. (Proverbs 6:32, NIV)
> The lips of the righteous nourish many, but fools die for lack of judgment. (Proverbs 10:21, NIV)
> Whoever isolates himself seeks his own desire; he breaks out against all sound judgment. (Proverbs 18:1, ESV)
> I went past the field of the sluggard, past the vineyard of the man who lacks judgment. (Proverbs 24:30, NIV)

Good judgment is something wise people need.

So the word judgment has both a negative and a positive side, and what Jesus is forbidding in Matthew 7:1 is the negative kind of judgment. We could paraphrase it this way: "Do not condemn others, or you too will be condemned. For in the same way that you condemn others, you will be condemned." Jesus does not want us condemning others or turning our back on the lost because of their sins. He does not want us rejecting those who have moral problems, or criticizing those stuck in sin without offering help. Jesus did not judge in that kind of way.

But even though Jesus forbids a condemning judgment, he is not forbidding good judgment—making moral assessments of what God would have us do. We need good judgment just to survive.

For instance, when someone encourages you to join them in getting drunk and then driving home, you would be a fool to say, "I don't want to make any judgments about anything or anybody—like the Good Book says, judge not—so hey, whatever, let's do it."

If somebody tried to lure you into an adulterous affair, you would be a fool to say, "I don't want to make any judgments about what this might do to my marriage—judge not lest you be judged—so I guess I'll go with it."

When someone tells you how you can rip off the government, you would be a fool to say, "I really can't judge whether that that would be a bad thing to do—judge not, Jesus said—so tell me more how this works."

We continually need to exercise good judgment in the Christian life. We need good judgment to figure out what will help us draw near to the Lord and what won't, and which people will bring us up or down in our faith. We need good judgment to do that, and that activity is not forbidden by Jesus' words.

If Jesus wanted us to give up using good judgment, the whole Sermon on the Mount wouldn't make any sense. For example, Jesus said in that sermon, "Blessed are those who hunger and thirst for righteousness" (Matthew 5:6, NIV11). Without good judgment, we wouldn't know what this righteousness that we hunger for looked like. Jesus later said in the Sermon on the Mount to avoid not only murder, but also hatred, but if we didn't have good judgment, we wouldn't know the difference between love and hate.

And we not only need good judgment for our own sakes, but also for the sake of other people. If we have the right kind of relationship with another person (perhaps as their friend, elder, parent, etc.), we are called to use good judgment to help them. Right after Jesus told us not to judge, he told a mini-parable about a man who had a huge board in his own eye who hypocritically criticized a neighbor for a speck in his eye. The point of Jesus' little story was not for us to ignore the moral flaws of ourselves and others, but to help each other with them. That's why Jesus ended his story with these words, "You hypocrite, first take the log out of your own eye, and then you will see clearly to take the speck out of your brother's eye" (ESV).[1]

People with good judgment do not condemn others, but they do assess and work on their own moral problems so they can better help others. In fact, good judgment is needed to help anybody, because you can't help yourself or others until you assess what the problem is. That assessment is what good judgment is all about

Indeed, there is a bad kind of judging, and our world is very aware of that. So is Jesus. And we should be very aware of it in our own hearts. To all those who stick their nose in everyone else's business, who try to impose their opinions on others, who condemn and reject people stuck in sin, Jesus would say, "Judge not, lest you be judged." But when you or someone you know needs help in turning from sin and back to God, that's when the Lord says, "Use good judgment." In fact, in another verse not often quoted, Jesus said, "Do not judge by appearances, but judge with right judgment" (John

---

[1] For more on this, see the essay entitled "Specks and logs" on page 245.

7:24, NRSV). In that context, Jesus was especially calling people to judge him with right judgment, but this truth apples in other situations as well.

Moral and spiritual issues are not a matter of taste in which everyone does what is right in their own eyes. After all, what's right in our eyes are specks and logs that keep us from seeing God's reality. What's needed is good judgment so that we can help each other get rid of those obstructions to vision, and thus walk in the light of the Lord.

Justice [1]

For many progressives, the same-sex issue is not about sex, but justice. The main problem is not that the LGBT community is sinning, but that they are sinned against. They are treated unfairly by government policies, harassed by school bullies, denied housing and promotions, and demeaned by the church and individual Christians. Some are subjected to gossip; others are beaten up; and a few of them are even killed. The heterosexual world does not have a good track record in how they have treated the LGBT community.

Given this record of mistreatment, our first response should be repentance. When the subject of the LGBT community comes up, the gut reaction of conservatives is to think those people should repent, but we have plenty of repentance to do ourselves. Although Paul highlights same-sex behavior in Romans 1, it's not the only sin Paul condemns in that chapter. He also indicts those who are filled with greed, envy, strife, hatred, deceit, gossip, pride, and disobedience. In other words, everyone. And the larger context verifies this. In Romans 1 Paul condemns all those wicked people out there in the world. In Romans 2 Paul turns the tables on his readers and condemns all the religious sinners. And from this he concludes in Romans 3 that all have sinned. We must all repent and find hope in Christ alone.

Yes, same-sex sins are sins, but numerically speaking, opposite-sex sins far outweigh same-sex sins—adultery, prostitution, pornography, premarital sex, irresponsible fathering, rape, child abuse, and more. Heterosexuals have plenty to repent of, including how they have treated the LGBT community.

Jesus, the friend of sinners, calls us to stop the queer jokes and to repudiate violence and injustice. Jesus does not call us to merely tolerate the LGBT community, but to love them. They want and need the same thing we all want and need: love, respect, friendship, forgiveness, significance. We must be willing to pray with, eat with, and befriend those involved in same-sex behaviors. We conservatives eat with gluttons, shop with greedy people,

---

[1] Some of this essay came from an editorial entitled "Homo Sapiens and Homosexuality" which I wrote for *The Sunday School Guide,* Vol. 83, November 14, 2004, 17, 30-31. Used by permission.

compliment proud people, and relax with lazy people. Surely we can be-friend the LGBT community as well.

Does that mean, then, that we don't call same-sex behavior a sin? Of course not. When you love, you speak the truth. God loved us enough to tell us the truth about our sin. We do the LGBT community a disservice if we hide the truth. Yes, it would be much easier in our culture to say, "Oh go ahead." Easier to say, but not more loving. When it's appropriate to speak, we must speak the truth about the sinfulness of same-sex behavior. It is not hate speech to say that, because the same thing must be said about all the other sins, too.

Of course, we do not have to constantly remind them of this. If a grown child quits going to church, every parent knows it doesn't work to remind them each week that they should go. Maybe, when the moment is just right, the parent could say something once in a while, but usually parents should back off and let God do the convicting work. Their job is to keep loving and praying. It's the same with talking with someone about same-sex behavior. There may be God–appointed times to talk directly with an LGBT friend about sin, but if they already know where you stand, most of the time should be spent just expressing friendship and care, especially in times when they've been sinned against.

Others have written far more eloquently and knowledgably about injus-tices suffered by the LGBT community. So, for the purposes of this book, I'm going to focus instead on how the issue of injustice intersects with the issue of sinfulness. Sometimes when someone has experienced tremendous injus-tices in their lives, we feel sorry enough for them that we're reluctant to hold them accountable for *their* own wrongdoings. It would feel like we're kicking someone when they're down, and maybe even wrongly implying that their sin is what caused them to be treated unjustly in the first place. For example, if an adolescent had experienced abusive trauma when they were young, we might be reluctant to discipline in the way that we would discipline a child who had not been abused. Compared to the gravity of how they had been sinned against, it might seem mean-spirited to point out their misbehaviors.

You can see some of that same dynamic in how the United States treats Israel. The Jews experienced horrific injustices in the Holocaust and con-tinue to be victims of anti-Semitism. They were treated so badly that it seems mean-spirited and unsympathetic to point out how some of their own policies treat the Palestinians unjustly. And thus, many in the United States (wrongly) turn a blind eye to Israeli acts of injustice.

But we find in the Bible that even though God has a special heart for the poor and oppressed, they will still be held accountable for their own sins. Being treated unjustly does not give anyone a free pass to sin. You can see how that's so with the advice Paul gives the slaves in Colossae. He knows some of them have been treated unjustly (and he offers hints that slavery itself is unjust), and yet he warns slaves against their own forms of wrongdoing: "You are serving the Lord Christ. For the wrongdoer will be paid back for the wrong he has done, and there is no partiality" (Colossians 3:24-25, ESV). Slaves have been sinned against, but they are also still sinners themselves.

Paul does not specify what some of these wrongs might be, but slaves were not immune to the sins he listed earlier in this chapter: sexual immorality, covetousness, idolatry, anger, malice, obscene talk, and lying (Col 3:5-9). In his book *Roman Slave Law*, Alan Watson noted that "the individual slave is frequently in a good position to provide the master with a poor return on his investment, to cheat him, rob him, damage his property, or make him liable to others for property damage, to make disastrous contracts for him, to give damaging reports of him, to exploit him sexually, and even to assault or kill him."[2] Paul calls on Christian slaves, however, to turn from the wrong in order to avoid negative payback for any sins they commit.

Victims of injustice, then, do not thereby receive a free pass to sin. Even though it might seem mean-spirited to say so, sometimes those who have been wronged also need to hear where they have been wrong themselves. And that also applies to the LGBT community. We must grieve over how the LGBT community has been mistreated, and yet we cannot back down from the biblical truth that same-sex behavior is not God's design for human life.

---

[2] Alan Watson, *Roman Slave Law* (Baltimore: The John Hopkins University Press, 1987), 1.

LGBT

One night at the dinner table, my son made an announcement. Up until that time (this would be the early 90's when he was about ten years old), we had always called him either by his full first name (Benjamin) or the nickname my daughter had given him early on (Benj). But then in the middle of the meal—probably after we had asked Benjamin to pass some bowl—he declared, "I want to be called Ben." I guess from his perspective, Benjamin sounded too formal and Benj sounded too childish. He preferred Ben. His tone of voice was not one of anger or irritation, but it was firm enough that none of us questioned his call. After that, the rest of us always called him "Ben." It's a sign of respect to speak to a person with the name or label that they prefer.

Churches do that all the time when a new pastor begins his or her ministry among them. The members want to show respect toward the pastor and so they ask, "What would you like to be called?" In my case, did I want to be called Rev. Landegent, Rev. Dave, Pastor Landegent, Pastor Dave, Preacher Dave or just Dave or David? For better or worse, I went with Pastor Dave. It conveyed both respect and informality at the same time. Some of my son's friends, however, liked to call me P.D., which evolved into P. Diddy, the moniker of a better-known rap artist at the time. I didn't mind at all. Maybe they were poking fun of me, but I took it to mean that they thought I was at least a little cool.

So it's important for us to think about what names or labels we should use in the same-sex debate. The apostle Peter once said, "always being prepared to make a defense to anyone who asks you for a reason for the hope that is in you; yet do it with gentleness and respect" (1 Peter 3:15, ESV). So if we truly want to be respectful to those who do not identify themselves as heterosexual, then we must use the names and terms they prefer.

This means, of course, that we need to avoid terms that are regarded as derogatory, some of which were always used in a derogatory way, and some of which did not start out that way but took on negative connotations as time went by. I don't need to name the derogatory terms that have always been used in a nasty fashion, but it might be helpful to consider a term that has rapidly been losing favor, namely, "homosexual."

"Homosexual" is a versatile word in that it can function as both a noun (he is a homosexual) and an adjective (he has homosexual desires). The term comes from the Greek word for "same" (*homos*), not the Latin word for man (*homo*). I first ran into this as a young boy who was enamored with scientific things (my dad was a biology teacher). When I first learned that the scientific name for a human being is *homo sapiens* (man of wisdom), I thought it would be cool to refer to a person as a *homo sapiens.* So once day after church, while my dad was getting in the car, I said to my younger brothers about someone walking by, "Hey, there goes a *homo sapiens!*" My dad quickly said, "Uh...I don't think it's a good idea to call people that," and then tried to explain why not in a way that an elementary child might understand.

Although it's still used in many contexts, the term "homosexual" appears to be falling out of favor. For one thing, some people shortened the term to "homo" and used it as a slur against others. Secondly, at one time it was used as a diagnostic term to describe same-sex attraction as a mental illness.

Another problem with the term "homosexual" is that it causes a lot of unnecessary confusion in debates between progressives and conservatives. Whether they are consistent in how they use vocabulary or not, when conservatives talk about a homosexual, they are mostly talking about what someone *does*, namely, they engage (or want to engage) in same-sex behavior. But when progressives talk about a homosexual (which they don't do much anymore), they are thinking more about what a person *is* than what they do. This is their created identity, they say, which really cannot be changed, but instead should be celebrated.

So when a conservative says in a debate, "Homosexuals are sinners," what they really mean is, "Those who engage in same-sex behavior are sinning in that very action." But to the progressive—who thinks of homosexuality more in terms of identity than activity—it sounds as if the conservative is saying it's a sin for homosexuals to be who they were created to be, equivalent to saying it's a sin to be an African American or a Hispanic. About the only way a progressive could tolerate saying "homosexuals are sinners" is if we quickly add that all heterosexuals are sinners, too.

Because of this potential for confusion, then, it may be good that the term homosexual is used less than it once was, although it will be used in this book on occasion.

At this point in history, it appears that that preferred term is LGBT, an acronym formed from the first letters of Lesbian (same-sex attracted women), Gay (same-sex attracted men), Bisexual (men or women sexually attracted to both sexes), and Transgender (those who began life as biological males or females, but now identify themselves as the opposite sex, some of whom have undergone medical procedures or treatments to make that more of a physical reality).

LGBT mostly functions as an adjective. When referring to all those who identify as lesbian, gay, bisexual, or transgendered, people will speak of the LGBT community. When talking about an individual who is lesbian, gay, bisexual, or transgendered (but without wanting to specify which), they might speak of an LGBT person. When discussing issues relevant to or involving lesbians, gays, bisexuals, or transgendered individuals, they might refer to LGBT issues or LGBT matters.

Back in the 1970's people mostly spoke of the gay community, and then the gay and lesbian community. In the 80's bi-sexuals wanted to be included in the efforts toward civil rights, and so there was talk of the LGB community. In the 90's, however, transgendered people were added to this, even though many of their concerns were different from the others, and so LGBT became the preferred term.

In order to include those who do not feel they fit into any of these categories, sometimes other letters have been added. The most common additional letters would be Q for queer or questioning and A for asexual. And sometimes a plus sign is added to signify that this is not an exhaustive list. Thus you might also see LGBTQ+ OR LGBTQA+. Not everyone in the LGBT community agrees that it's a good idea to add more letters. It could look as if people are so keen on being different and avoiding categorization that they keep on multiplying letters. For the sake of simplicity, then, I have been using the acronym LGBT in this book, and hope that my readers will not take offense.

Of course, it's always possible that some do not like any kind of categorizing. They want to be treated as the unique human being they are, with a specific name and face. Recently I was in a denominational meeting that was discussing a situation involving a married gay man who felt called to be ordained. The man involved happened to be there as a delegate and he made it clear that he did not like being talked about as a subset in the category of married gay men; he had a name and he told us what it was. I can respect that. All of us are much more intriguingly complex than any label would ever suggest. We want to be treated as persons, not game pieces to move around in a competitive contest between progressives and conservatives.

Nonetheless, I could also understand why delegates had been using labels earlier when referring to him. For one thing, no one in the discussion had his prior permission to mention him by name, and to do so could just have easily been interpreted as a personal attack. But secondly, even if we want to treat people as persons and not categories, we still need a way to have "big picture" discussions of these matters. Naming everyone by name in a big picture discussion is impossible, and yet those discussions must happen whenever broader thinking is needed to inform broader policy.

And so the essays in this book refer to LGBT people more abstractly rather than by name. I will also use the term even though I have very little to say about transgender issues and know very little about their sexual desires.

I have always been curious about how the ordering of letters in LGBT was decided. The history suggests that B and T were added as additional groups who wanted to be included. But if the category began with the gay community, which then became the gay and lesbian community, then why didn't GLBT become the acronym (although I guess this variation does exist in some places)? Maybe it was done this way to avoid a patriarchalism in which men always come first. Or perhaps because a glancing look at the shape of the letters LGBT makes one think of positive words like LIGHT or LEGIT, while GLBT only calls to mind less-positive words like GLOB or GLIB.

I can understand why the LGBT community wants to be known as a community. Many of them have experienced isolation when growing up because they didn't feel like they fit in with their peers. The LGBT term, however, gives them a sense of belonging. I have noticed in the media that we often use the word "community" in conjunction with groups that have a keen sense of their minority status, especially those groups that have felt under attack by the majority. So, for instance, when a synagogue is torched, the media report on how the Jewish *community* is responding. Or when an unarmed African American teenager is gunned down by law enforcement, we are told how the African American *community* is reacting. The crimes are not regarded as merely attacks on an isolated building or individual, but as an attack upon a whole body of people who are together in their desire to move beyond such bigotry. In the face of such evil, they want to stand as a community. The LGBT community wants to stand together in that same way.

But we should not read too much into the term community with regards to LGTB people. While it's true that a number of LGBT people gravitate toward living in certain cities or neighborhoods, they don't actually all live near each other (nor do racial or religious communities). And while it's true that most of them are united in their goals to be treated justly and well by others, they don't all think exactly alike: some are Republicans, some Democrats; some are church-goers, some are not; most think LGBT sexual activity is perfectly acceptable, but a few still think it's a sin they must constantly resist. The LGBT community is not a monolithic group. Tensions rise between and within the groups who are under the LGBT umbrella.

While I aim to be respectful and use the terms LGBT and LGBT community, I do think it's important for both sides to ponder three ways that these terms do affect the debate, probably to the advantage of the LGBT cause.

First, this fairly innocuous-sounding term not only gives the discussion a more respectful tone (which is good), but it also makes same-sex activities themselves sound fairly innocent. But this is precisely the point of the debate. Conservatives do not think such activity is harmless, but rather poses spiritual, emotional, and physical dangers to those involved in it. But out of respect we are called to use nice language to talk about something that we do not think is nice at all. We can live with that (and my book will do just that), but I think it's important to point out how the LGBT term itself makes it more likely that we will overlook or downplay the seamier aspects of at least some same-sex behavior. LGBT behavior not only includes two people of the same sex being kind, tender and faithful to a partner, but it also encompasses orgies, prostitution, one-night stands, rape, sado-masochism, and other forms of deviance (and I should point out that heterosexual activity also includes similar seamier facets). Conservatives can be guilty of focusing on the worst of the worst to make their points, but that does not mean that progressives or the LGBT community should just turn a blind eye to all the evil things happening in their midst.

Secondly, while we want to use the terms that are regarded as respectful in the present day, we have to recognize that the ongoing shift from one favored term to another also affects the debate. About 40 years ago my denomination wrote some highly-regarded reports about LGBT matters, but some now dismiss those reports as insensitive. That's because they never used the term LGBT, but often used the now-less-favored terms homosexual and homosexuality. Maybe some of the content from those old reports actually was insensitive (even if ignorantly so), but good thinking should not be rejected simply because it does not use contemporary lingo. I can easily imagine the day coming in which LGBT will be regarded as an insensitive term, and then all the books written with that verbiage (like this one) will be consigned to the dustbin of outdated ideas.

Thirdly, use of the phrase "LGBT community" cannot help but call to mind similar-sounding phrases used for various ethnic groups, such as the African American community, Hispanic community, or Jewish community. This reinforces in the mind that being LGBT is just as genetically set as one's ethnic or racial identity. But this is precisely one of the points of contention for conservatives. I realize that there are other uses of the term "community" which do not carry this connotation (such as the evangelical community or the surfing community), but most commonly the term "community" is attached to ethnic and racial groups. Thus, every time we refer to the

LGBT community, I believe we are subtly reinforcing the belief that being LGBT is equivalent to being an African American in the sense of being born a certain way.

Perhaps at this point a progressive reader might be thinking, "I was glad and ready to listen when you said you wanted to respect people by using the terms they preferred. But now that you've spent so much time examining the term LGBT, and pointing out its potential pitfalls, it no longer feels respectful at all. It sounds more like you will only use the term 'LGBT' grudgingly." I will admit that at an earlier time, when I could tell the linguistic ground was changing under my feet, I probably did resent having to change my vocabulary. But I've gotten past that. Still I think it's important to bring to light how all this does factor into the discussion, because if it raises some issues for me, it certainly does for others as well. It will be very difficult to go forward if we can't just describe how language factors into our conversation.

Live and let live

One time I went to a community prayer meeting that included people from many denominations. The meeting was organized as a concert of prayer, which included prayers of thanks, confession, intercession, etc. At one point, however, they told us that they wanted everyone to pray in whatever way they chose. We could pray silently, we could pray aloud in tongues, we could sing a prayer, etc.

It probably sounded like a good idea when a committee met to plan this service, but it didn't work well in reality. Indeed, there was good participation, but not everyone actually got to pray in their preferred style. I intended to engage in silent prayer, for example, but with the guy in the pew behind me praying aloud in tongues, and the woman nearby offering up intense and loud intercessions, it was anything but silent. They got to pray in the way that they desired, but not I.

A lot of times in the same-sex debate, someone will say, "Why can't we all just live and let live? You deal with the issue in one way, and I deal with it differently, and we can each do as we see fit."

There's some sense to that. I have no need to control how everyone else minsters in Jesus' name, and I wouldn't like them controlling me in ministry. And that works best when we're not right next to each other. But if we're working side by side in a local church or denomination, things can get a little more difficult. We can say everyone should just do as they see fit, but as in my story of everyone praying as they saw fit, one way of doing ministry just might hinder someone else's way of doing ministry.

For example, if my church's ministry invites the LGBT community to experience new life through repentance and transformation, but another part of the denomination affirms the LGBT community and invites them to be ordained into gospel ministry, we're going to run into organizational difficulties. We'll each think the other is undermining our form of ministry.

In addition, from the theological perspective of conservatives, "live and let live" sounds more like the title of Paul McCartney's hit, "Live and Let Die." Since we believe that engaging in same-sex behavior jeopardizes one's eternal state before God (according to 1 Corinthians 6:9-10), then we would be endangering others if we raised no objections or warnings about this matter. We would be like the watchmen that the Lord spoke to in Ezekiel 33:6, "But if the watchman sees the sword coming and does not blow the trumpet, so that the people are not warned, and the sword comes and takes any one of them, that person is taken away in his iniquity, but his blood I will require at the watchman's hand" (ESV). Instead of living and letting live, we would be living and letting die.

Maybe this perspective places conservatives in danger of taking on the role of trying to run everyone else's life, so that others are just annoyed by our unsolicited advice and warnings. Well, we will try not to be obnoxious, but when we are in meetings where courses of action and policies are made about same-sex behavior, or when people genuinely want to know what the Bible teaches about it, we dare not just live and let die.

And I'm thinking that progressives should also be reluctant to "live and let live" with us conservatives. After all, if they really think that our approach genuinely harms members of the LGBT community and might cause them to turn their back on Jesus, why would they want to let us just carry on as usual, without warning us of the eternally harmful consequences of what we're doing?

"Live and let live"—it might be a good motto for people that really don't care about others, but it doesn't seem to fit well with Christian ministry.

Living in sin

You don't hear the phrase "living in sin" very much anymore. Not long ago, it was especially used in cases when a man and woman were living together (and having sexual relations) without being married. Other unmarried couples might also be having sex on a somewhat regular basis when they went on dates, but they still lived in different homes, so at this point it was not (quite) the regular feature of their lives that it would be if they were living together. They were sinning, but not yet living in sin. But if they were to move in together, the couple would be deciding that sexual sin was going to be (at least for the time being) an ongoing part of their life. They were living in sin—at least that was the line of thinking.

By extension, some also have applied this phrase to those who are living in a same-sex relationship—married or unmarried. Unlike a gay or lesbian person who sins through occasional sexual encounters, a same-sex couple who moves in together is deciding that sexual relations are going to be (at least for the time being) an ongoing part of their life. Again, conservatives would say that they were living in sin.

But the phrase "living in sin" is not heard as much anymore. In part, this is because the phrase was mostly applied to sexual sins, and that doesn't seem fair. Aren't there other sins that we persistently live in? Isn't the persistent gossip living in sin? Or the chronic liar? Or the one who gets drunk on a daily basis? Or the one who is constantly passing judgment on others?

But the other reason the phrase has fallen into disuse is that many no longer see any problem with two unmarried people "living together." I haven't seen any statistics, but it wouldn't surprise me if the majority of couples now getting married had first lived together. Most people today have someone in their extended family who is (or had been) living with a boyfriend of girlfriend. And many today are also adopting the same attitude toward those living in a same-sex relationship.

So where did this phrase "living in sin" come from? Probably from Paul—"What shall we say then? Are we to continue in sin that grace may abound? By no means! How can we who died to sin still live in it?" (Romans 6:1-2, ESV). According to Paul, then, the opposite of living in sin is not *occasionally* sinning, but *dying* to sin. So whether a person *occasionally* has premarital sex or has made it a *more ongoing* part of life by moving in with someone, in both cases the person is living in sin instead of dying to it. Likewise, occasional gossips and frequent gossips are both living in sin, too. Those who occasionally judge others and those who do it on an hourly basis are both living in sin. So the way to stop living in sin is not by doing a particular sin less often, but by dying to sin with Christ. Lower-frequency sin may bring fewer consequences, but it still is not God's will for us. The Christian is someone who has died to sin with Christ on the cross and is called to live into that death.

Paul was well aware that just because we have—in Christ—died to sin, that does not mean we no longer sin. That's why he not only announced that our sinful selves have died with Christ in Romans 6:6, but he also called us to live into that death in Romans 6:11-12: "So you also must consider yourselves dead to sin and alive to God in Christ Jesus. Let not sin therefore reign in your mortal body, to make you obey its passions" (ESV). We must die to sin, because that's who we are in Christ.

Paul does not regard sins by Christians as harmless little vices that have already been forgiven and will one day be overcome. He doesn't just shrug his shoulders when Christians sin and say, "Well, I guess until Jesus comes back, what else would you expect? That's just going to happen." No, he remains appalled by it. That's why he asks with some astonishment, "How can we who died to sin still live in it?" (Romans 6:2, ESV). Yes, Christians will sin—and they will sin a lot—but we should never remain comfortable with that.

This, in fact, is the main problem with living in sin. It's not the frequency of sin that's the main problem, but the fact that we have made a peace treaty with our sin. Rather than waging war against it—so that the sin that we're dead to in Christ will actually die—many of us make a peace treaty with sin and let it live comfortably in our hearts.

For me, this is the main problem with many engaged in same-sex relations. While it is always regrettable when sin is done, the main problem is not that people engage in same-sex behavior, or even that they do so frequently. Rather, the problem is that they have made a peace treaty with it. Instead of treating it as a sin in our hearts that they fight against—and perhaps often losing the battle—they treat it instead as something to celebrate and make their peace with.

Once at a regional cluster of churches in my denomination, we were having a lengthy discussion about the possibility of ordaining practicing gays and lesbians. When it was my turn to speak I said, "You know, the problem is not with ordaining a sinner: all pastors are sinners. The problem is not with ordaining someone who frequently falls into a particular sin: all pastors have particular sins that they fall into. The problem is with ordaining someone who has made peace with that sin, and even celebrates it; I would not favor ordaining people with that attitude."

Living in sin when we have died to sin in Christ is to live a contradiction. Whenever that contradiction happens in our hearts, we need to battle our way back to where Christ would have us live—in him, not in sin.

Love

The father sat in my office to talk. We had always been on good terms, but we had never had a conversation about his teenage son's journey concerning his sexual identity. More and more this son had been coming to church in women's attire, and his father wanted to talk with me about this. I thought maybe someone had made some rude remark to him, but that didn't seem to be the case. Everyone had been pretty accepting of his actions, even though there may have been some internal eye-rolling.

What the father was hoping for was that the church could take some kind of public stand in affirming his son on his journey. I told him as gently as I could that I didn't feel comfortable doing that. But I immediately began to talk about how much I loved his son. He was a gentle spirit and very talented, and he and I had always gotten along well.

The father seemed a bit relieved by my words and said something like, "Well, then, at least we can agree that it all comes down to love." Yes, it does. But I didn't think it would be helpful in the long run to just paper over our deep disagreement with generic ideas of love. So I said, "Yes, it is about love, but that doesn't necessarily resolve everything, because love has so many facets to it."

It's true that Christians have done a miserable job of loving those involved in same-sex relations. Disciples of Jesus must love all others no matter who they are or what they do. But even if we all agree that love is needed, that still does not resolve the debate, for we may not agree on how best to show love in any given situation or to any given person. As every spouse or parent knows, love is always a mixture of honoring, accepting, affirming, approving, overlooking, challenging, correcting, warning, and even rebuking. In loving my neighbor involved in same-sex relationships, there may be much I affirm and some things I overlook, but if I have earned the right to be heard by that neighbor, there may also be a time for warning. I would want others to do the same for me.

If a member of the LGBT community will only regard an *affirming* love as true love, then I feel sort of stuck. I will feel like no matter how highly I regard them, feel affection for them, help them, show generosity to them, and affirm their other qualities and actions, as long as I don't affirm their same-sex beliefs and actions, they will look on me as a hater (or at least not very loving). It's difficult to know how to proceed in convincing them of my love—without changing my convictions.

But Jesus did not say, "Greater love has no one than this, that he lay down his convictions for his friends." Nor did he say, "Greater love has no one than this that she lay down her faith for her friends." Rather, he said that laying down our lives for others was the way of love (John 15:13).

Somehow in some way—without dropping their convictions—Christians need to lay down their lives for their LGBT friends. Only then might the LGBT community believe Christians who profess love for them.

A few years back, a lesbian couple moved into the house immediately behind that of my parents. I asked my now-deceased father, who had conservative convictions on this, what he was going to do about his new neighbors. His response was immediate: "I'm going to be the best neighbor they ever had," which for my dad especially meant offering them produce and flowers from his large garden. That was vintage dad.

So even though love can include correction and warning, as I noted above, that is surely not the main response any of us should have toward the LGBT community. It's mostly a matter of being the best neighbor they've ever had.

There is a time to speak the truth in love, but there's also a time to be silent in love. One summer, between college and seminary, I lived in a Christian commune. My roommate was a Christian I knew from my home church (as well as from the "Jesus freak" coffeehouse I had been involved in during high school). Other people had told me that he was struggling with his sexual identity and that he believed he was gay. That summer we spent a lot of evenings just talking about all kinds of things of faith. But never once did "homosexuality" come up (as it was more commonly called then). I didn't feel compelled to talk about it, and he must not have either. He would have known where I stood, and he already knew what the Bible taught, so I didn't see any reason to belabor it. If he had wanted to know what I thought about homosexuality, I would readily have told him, but it didn't come up. After I left for seminary, he sent me a note, thanking me for never bringing up the issue of homosexuality, and instead just being his friend. When he was later dying from AIDS, I counted it a real honor for him to ask me to preach at his funeral.

As I said, there's a time to speak the truth in love, but there's also a time to be silent in love. "Love one another deeply from the heart" (1 Peter 1:22, NIV).

Making it personal [1]

I talked too much at the first national denominational meeting that I attended in the mid-80's. I was trying to limit myself from participating in the debate, but I kept finding myself at the microphone. One of the upcoming issues that year was about people having abortions for the sake of convenience. I knew the abortion issue had sometimes created controversy in the denomination, but I couldn't imagine how anyone could be in favor of aborting a child for convenience's sake. I thought this would be a non-controversial issue that would easily pass, so, I resolved ahead of time that I would keep my mouth shut for once.

After the issue was presented on the floor of synod, the first delegate to speak said that he was a pastor, that his wife had gotten an abortion, and that no one gets an abortion simply because it's convenient. Therefore, he said, we should not approve the recommendation. The meeting room got deathly still. To my amazement, no one stood up in support of the recommendation, the president called for a vote, and it was defeated.

I was stunned. What happened? I knew there were plenty of delegates there who opposed abortions for the purpose of convenience. I also knew that, even if that pastor didn't think so, there were people out there who had abortions for the sake of convenience (even though they might not admit this to themselves). And yet no one spoke.

In retrospect, I think that what happened was this: When the pastor spoke, then, wittingly or unwittingly, he changed the tone of the debate completely. No longer were we talking about abortion as a *theological* issue. Now it had suddenly become a *personal* issue. Anything said against abortions for convenience's sake could easily be construed as an attack on that particular delegate and his decisions. Even if we strenuously disagreed with what the delegate had said and done, none of us in that setting were quick-witted enough to know what to say without sounding harsh and mean-spirited. And so we said nothing. When the line between an incisive

---

[1] Based on an editorial entitled "Making It Personal," which I wrote for *The Sunday School Guide,* Vol. 82, November 30, 2003, 65, 78-79. Used by permission.

debate and a personal attack gets blurred, many Christians will back down and let questionable ideas go unchallenged. We don't want to be mean.

False teaching is easy to oppose in the abstract. Just set up a chart that contrasts a false doctrine with biblical doctrine. One side shows what the anonymous "they" believe, and the other side shows what "we" believe—all backed with appropriate biblical references. The chart shows that all the Bible verses are stacked in your favor. The teaching is wrong, case closed.

But when false ideas become personal, it's a whole different ball game. The ideas come in a flesh-and-blood human being who stands before you. They have a name, a family, a circle of friends, and a wonderful track record in ministry. They're charming, witty, even jovial. The fruit of the Spirit appears to grow in their life. But there's still this problem of them teaching doctrines contrary to Scripture. Now, in order to oppose their ideas, you have to oppose this very nice person.

Try as you might to speak the truth *in love,* you have to be intolerant of their teaching, even though it has the potential to make you appear to be a nasty person. You may even have to call for their ouster from ministry, although you know that will have a very negative effect on their family, their economic situation, and all the people ministered to by that person. It's no wonder many Christians don't have the stomach for opposing false teaching.

Even though the Apostle Paul told us to speak the truth in love (Ephesians 4:15), I think the devil likes to create situations in which it appears that we can only do one or the other. The devil will try to convince us that we can either speak the truth in a nasty way, or we can overlook the truth in the name of love. And if those are the only two options, then many of us will opt for the latter. But those are not the only two options. Truth and love always belong together in their opposition to false teaching.

False teaching is not only an assault on the truth, but it's also an assault on love. I see that happening with regards to same-sex debates. The teachings of those who approve of same-sex behaviors, for instance, pull us away from loving God, causing us to worship a false idea of God made in the image of our own thinking. False teaching with regards to same-sex relations also pulls us away from loving the church, for it causes us to mislead fellow believers and needlessly divide the church. And false teaching on this issue pulls us away from loving the world, for without the gospel of truth, we have no real help to offer a world in desperate need. False teaching is not only untruthful, but profoundly unloving.

So how can we lovingly speak the truth to those who are wrong?

(1) We can pray for them, get to know them, listen to their story, and show kindness to them. They may be enemies of the truth, but the Lord commands us to bless our enemies.

(2) We can acknowledge the parts of their teaching which may have the ring of truth. Not everything they say is false, and we should admit it. This helps builds bridges.

(3) We must avoid overstating our case. For example, it's possible to look in the Koran, ignore the context and find absolutely horrible quotations for making a case against Islam. But they could do the same against us by lifting quotations out of context from the Bible. We must be fair in assessing what someone is teaching, instead of putting them in the worse possible light. That also applies to LGBT concerns.

(4) We must speak respectfully to everyone in the debate. There is no place for name-calling (even though the Reformers were pretty adept at it). One of the ways we live out saving grace is by helping others save face in public. No one deserves to be mocked or put to shame in public. I've always had a hunch that most progressives did not start off rejecting biblical truth. Instead, they were believers who met just one too many conservatives who acted like jerks. In trying to get away from these nasty conservatives, they drifted into the progressive camp. This makes it important for all conservative Christians to avoid being the kinds of jerks that drive others away from the Bible.

(5) We must be willing to at least consider where we may be in error ourselves. Perhaps a false teacher is over-emphasizing a verse from the Bible because conservatives have de-emphasized it. For instance, those who approve of same-sex behavior often point out Ezekiel 16:49's teaching that Sodom's worst sin was economic oppression. We might want to ignore that verse, since it gets used against us, but instead we need to pay attention to it. The verse does not mean that the sin of Sodom is about injustice and not about same-sex behavior (as some contend); rather, Ezekiel 16:49 reminds us that economic sins and sexual sins usually go hand in hand. Greed and lust often get in bed together.

(6) As much as possible, we must keep the focus on the issue instead of the person. They might wrap themselves around the false teaching so much that it's hard to attack the teaching without also attacking them, but we must keep our eyes fixed on the issue. Paul had to deal with false teachers in many of his churches. But he almost never mentions any of them by name. Even though curious New Testament scholars would love to know more about these unorthodox teachers, Paul prefers not to drag their names in the mud. Instead, he usually refers to them in vague terms like "some people" (Galatians 1: 7), "those people" (Galatians 4:17), or "those 'super-apostles'" (2 Corinthians 11: 5). Paul wants to stick to the issues and not get involved in personal attacks.

(7) But having said that, we also have to remember that the things we are arguing about do affect real people. We are not just moving theological

chess pieces around in an effort to checkmate our opponent. Our words have the potential to affect (negatively and/or positively) the emotions, life situations, and faith of the LGBT community.

Maybe it's a good thing I didn't speak one more time at that denominational meeting I mentioned earlier, because I might have said the wrong thing in that moment. But if I were to speak today, I would've said, "I don't know my brother's situation very well or what led he and his wife to obtain an abortion. It's hard for me to comprehend. We may have to talk. But I do believe that there are some in our society who are using abortion as a convenient form of birth control, even if they do not admit that to themselves. Our denomination may not agree on everything about abortion, but surely we can tell the world that the convenience of those already born is not a good reason to throw away the life of those about to be born."

Marriage

Those of us who regard same-sex relations as not God's will for human life can find ourselves in an odd position when it comes same-sex marriage. Normally we would be in favor of people taking marriage vows and faithfully keeping their commitments. But if a same-sex couple asked me to perform their wedding so that they could take vows to be faithful to one another for life, I would not go along with it. But then they might say to me, "So you'd rather that we just live together without commitments? Would you rather that we be promiscuous?"

Of course not. I would not want them to follow those options either. What I would want—and what I believe God wants—is that they not be involved in same-sex relations at all. But if they're going to "do it" anyway, why would I not prefer that they at least have only one partner and remain faithful to that partner?

Perhaps we could compare it to being the parent of a teenage daughter. Despite your best efforts to train and discipline her, she intends to have sex with her boyfriend, but she wants birth control pills to avoid getting pregnant. You, as a parent, could say no, because what you really want her to do is not have sex at all until she's married. And you realize that if you obtain birth control pills for her, she will definitely feel even freer to have sex and to do it more often. But you believe in your heart that she's going to do that whether she has the pills or not, so the pills could at least possibly alleviate some unwanted consequences. When the daughter doesn't want the best, should you at least help her avoid the worst?

A similar dynamic might arguably be involved with regards to same-sex marriage. Even if I think same-sex relations are wrong, why wouldn't I marry the couple if it could help them avoid what's even worse, which would be a lifestyle of promiscuity and probably increased loneliness? Let me try to answer that question.

First, it's not my role to help people sin in less harmful ways. Maybe parents have to do that for their teenagers (I was thankfully never put in that situation), but that's not the role of the pastor. My role is to call people to repentance and faith, to turn from sin and turn to Jesus.

But this is not just about me keeping my conscience clean. I think I would be doing the same-sex couple a disservice if I were to marry them, for I would be saying, "It is good for you to make this ongoing sinful relationship permanent." But what needs to happen is for them to draw apart, not join closer together. When a same-sex couple is not married, there's a better chance for Jesus to speak into their situation and say to at least one of them, "Your life needs to change; you need to get out of this relationship and align your life with God's will." But that message will be harder (not impossible, but harder) to hear when the couple has made their relationship more permanent. It's not that I'd want to say, "Be promiscuous instead," but rather, "Don't make this relationship permanent; keep your ears and eyes open to the leading of Christ's Spirit who has a different will and way for your future."

Whatever sin we struggle with, to do that sin sporadically is always better than making peace with it and doing it on an ongoing basis. If sin is in our lives, it should only be there as an unwanted intruder, not a permanent resident, for Jesus said that if something causes us to sin—even if that something is as "permanent" as an eye or a hand—that thing needs to be lopped off.

Mission

It's a common complaint you hear on the floor of denominational meetings: "This issue is distracting us from our mission to bring the gospel to the world. When you look at all the great needs of the world and all the people in the world who have not really heard the gospel or seen it demonstrated, why are we spinning our wheels debating the morality of same-sex behavior?"

And naturally each side in this debate blames the other for perpetuating the debate, so that we get bogged down in a quagmire of controversy. If those progressives would stop ordaining gays and lesbians for ministry, say the conservatives, we could focus on mission. But the progressives think of the conservatives as one-issue people, whose only goal in life is to block the tide of history rolling in favor of the LGBT community.

Up until recently, I voiced the same complaint about how this debate was sapping our energy for missions. But I've been trying to look at it differently. Maybe this debate is a vital part of our mission.

The LGBT community appears to be much larger than many heterosexuals in the church would have guessed. Maybe some of this new perception is exaggerated by the fact that the media seems to be promoting LGBT causes. And whatever gets media attention seems to be larger than it actually is. Still, there is truth to the fact that there are more members of the LGBT community all around us...and many of them have not heard the gospel, or they have heard it and turned away. So there's a great mission field there.

And because of that mission field, the church needs to figure out what is the gospel call for such a time as this. That's what the early church had to do when they came to the realization that a huge mission field had just opened up to them, namely, all the non-Jewish people of the world.

The early church was wondering: With all these uncircumcised non-Jewish people around them, does the gospel call mean that they must be circumcised in order to come to Jesus, the Jewish Messiah? With all these idolatrous people around them, does the gospel call mean they must turn away from all idols, and even the things that are associated with idolatry (such as the meat in the marketplace that had first been dedicated to a god)? With all these sexually immoral people around them, does the gospel call mean they must change their sexual behavior in order to follow Jesus? These were mission questions, and the church had to answer these questions. The council in Jerusalem in Acts 15 especially dealt with the circumcision question, but questions about idolatry and sexual immorality were also in the mix.

Today we are dealing with similar missional questions. When we bring the gospel to the LGBT community, are we expecting them turn from same-sex behaviors in order to follow Jesus, or can the Lord sanctify those same-sex relationships so that they are lived out in a more Christ-like way? That's the issue we have been debating for many decades already. It's not necessarily a diversion from our mission to work on this. In fact, we should think of it as a vital part of our mission.

The problem is not that we are having this discussion, but that it's taking us so long to resolve it. The council of Jerusalem in Acts 15 made a decision in a relatively short amount of time. The controversy began when Peter brought the gospel to Cornelius the centurion's home, and it came to a head around the time Paul and Barnabas returned from their first missionary trip (probably a period of less than ten years). But once the church realized a decision needed to be made, the decision was made rather quickly. True, it did take a while for there to be general agreement with the decision, but the decision itself was made rapidly, and it stuck.

It would not have been helpful for the early church's mission to have a ten-year study about the inclusion of non-Jews in the church, followed by regional discussion groups, and then many years of prolonged debate at church-wide conferences. It would not have been helpful, because in the meantime proponents of both sides would have been operating with their own answers, with each side getting more and more entrenched in their beliefs. And the non-Jewish world would have been confused about whether they needed to be circumcised or not.

It's not that every missional decision in the past has been made as quickly as this one. The church took a long, long time to hammer out what it means for God to be spoken of as Father, Son, and Holy Spirit. So the Acts 15 story does not mean we should always make missional decisions quickly. But it does explain a bit why both sides in today's same-sex debates have been frustrated with the impact that our impasse has on missions.

It's not that we have not been doing any mission work since this controversy arose. No, we all have been carrying on in mission with our own answers to LGBT questions. And now both sides have become very entrenched in their way of doing missions to (and/or with) the LGBT community. This has divided the church in the same way it would have divided the church, if the Jerusalem Council had taken a long time to come to a decision about circumcision. It's hard to imagine what would have happened in the first century if half the congregations had been requiring circumcision for thirty years and the other half had not.

So it's probably time we get around to deciding the very missional question of what the gospel call means for the LGBT community. And if we cannot decide, then we probably need to go on separate mission trips. Time will tell. Maybe both mission trips will succeed—which will create its own sense of confusing division. Maybe one or the other will fail. But at least we will press forward in mission.

Moral logic

Why? It's the question all children have asked their parents when told to do something they didn't want to do. "Why do I have to clean my room? Why can't I drive the car yet? Why do we have to go to church?"

And then there are the "why" questions that we don't dare voice to our parents, lest they really come down hard on us: "Why can't I copy the homework answers from my friend? Why can't I try cocaine? Why can't I have sex with my prom date?"

Parents have answers for most of these questions, but not usually answers that will satisfy their uncooperative child.

"Why do I have to clean my room?"

"Because it's a mess."

"Why do you think it's so messy? My friends' rooms are a lot messier than mine."

"Because I'm not their parent, and I think it's messy and unsanitary?"

"I don't agree. But why do I have to do it now?"

"Because your grandparents are coming to visit."

"Why does that matter; they won't come in my room anyway."

And on and on it goes, with many parents finally saying, "Because I said so!" It's not really that they think there's no moral logic to what they are commanding other than their own will to power. It's just that they know there's no moral logic *that will satisfy the rebellious child.*

James Brownson's book, *Bible, Gender, Sexuality,* leans on the notion of moral logic in promoting the idea that at least some forms of same-sex behavior fit within the parameters of biblical morality.[1] The biblical commands about same-sex behavior must have a moral logic behind them, he argues, and if the moral logic of those biblical prohibitions only fits selfish same-sex relationships, but not monogamous and faithful same-sex relationships, then perhaps there is a place in the kingdom for some forms of same-sex behavior.

---

[1] James V. Brownson, *Bible, Gender, Sexuality* (Grand Rapids: Eerdmans, 2013), 3-15, 290. Brownson starts to build his case for the importance of moral logic in the introduction, and the index shows that references to moral logic are found throughout the book.

On the face of it, this makes sense to us. We assume God has reasons for his commands, and much of the time it's not that hard to figure out what some of his reasons might be. For example, we should not kill because, for one thing, human life is not ours to dispose of, and secondly, every person made in God's image belongs to God, and so it's not our call whether they live or die. And I'm sure we can think of other reasons why God commands us not to kill.

But the moral logic behind other commands is not nearly as clear to us. No reason is provided in Scripture for these commands, and so (especially if we agree with the command), we come up with our own plausible moral logic for them. For instance, no reason is given for the first command in the Bible, the one barring Adam and Eve from eating from the Tree of the Knowledge of Good and Evil. They were simply called to obey the command. Dietrich Bonhoeffer made the case that the fruit represented the temptation to form our own morality (to know and do the good) apart from God. I find his analysis very convincing, but I have seldom heard others follow Bonhoeffer's moral logic. Instead, they have proposed other reasons behind the command.

But what we might fail to notice is that the quest for moral logic is precisely the essence of the serpent's temptation. "Did God really say, 'You must not eat from any tree in the garden'?" (Genesis 3:1, NIV). The implication of the serpent's question is that there's no *good* reason for God to issue a command like this; so there must be a *bad* reason. And the serpent immediately proposes a bad reason: God doesn't want you to become like him (Genesis 3:4).

There are many commands in the Bible for which God does not provide reasons, or at least not reasons that make sense to us. God commands Abraham to sacrifice his only son through Sarah. God prohibits the Israelites from eating shellfish and having incestuous relations. God commands Joshua to annihilate the Canaanites—men, women, and children. We could probably come up with some moral logic behind these commands, but not to everyone's satisfaction.

The quest for the moral logic behind the commands of God is good, if it helps explain why the commands should be obeyed, but not if it helps us explain why they should be disobeyed—then we are acting like the serpent in the Garden of Eden.

Is there ever a time in which a command of God needs to be abrogated or changed? Yes, when God himself changes it (as happened in the New Testament with regards to the Old Testament food laws and circumcision laws). It appears that the coming of Jesus (in which the kingdom of God is expanded far beyond the kingdom of Israel) changed the status of various Old Testament laws. While Jesus clearly stated that he did not come to abolish any laws (Matthew 5:17-20), in the very next paragraphs he already begins to issue commands that alter the character of those Old Testament commands. By the end of the New Testament, we see clearly that Old Testament laws about unclean food, circumcision, and animal sacrifices have been changed by God. Might there be other changes to Old Testament laws that God could make even after the New Testament was completed? Possibly, but not those which were endorsed by the apostles, such as laws against same-sex behaviors.

Is there a moral logic behind the biblical prohibitions against same-sex behavior? Undoubtedly God knows there is, but I'm not sure we know completely. Probably all sides can agree on a moral logic about prohibitions against homosexual promiscuity, rape and pederasty, but the moral logic behind consensual same-sex behavior is not as obvious to one and all. My hunch is that it has something to do with how he created us to be male and female and the notion of biological fittingness. Others come up with more elaborate schemes of how men and women interact, some of which can lead to odd theories like Gagnon's idea that Adam was created as an androgynous being.[2] But one reason that conservatives come up with such weird theories is that they are trying to satisfy the progressives' demand for a satisfactory explanation. Most conservatives themselves, however, are satisfied with the far simpler "because God said so."

Would I like to know why God commanded certain things, including the prohibition of same-sex behavior? Indeed. But I know, as Abraham knew, even if one cannot satisfactorily figure out the moral logic of a command, the command must be obeyed nonetheless.

---

[2] See Brownson, 26-29, for a description and critique of Gagnon's ideas.

Normal

N ormal is an odd notion. A number of people say they just want to feel normal, to be thought of as normal, for life to be a little more normal for once. But another group of people can't stand the stifling feel of normality. When everything is so conventionally normal, life gets boring. And when others expect them to be normal, they might seethe with resentment. So is normal a desirable thing or not?

This issue is very much a real one for the LGBT community. They realize that many people regard them as abnormal. Some in the LGBT community might wear that badge proudly, because "who wants to fit into such a screwed-up society like ours anyway?" But others in the LGBT community long to be thought of as normal. But how do they reach that sense of normality? Two main ways: either they wish they themselves could change and have sexual desires like the majority of people in society, OR they wish society would change and regard same-sex behaviors as normal. The former way is losing favor in today's world. Instead, we are becoming a society in which same-sex attraction is increasingly believed to be as normal as opposite-sex attraction. The legalization of same-sex marriage went a long way toward making that happen.

But what is normal? We often use the word to describe the way things usually happen. It usually happens that dead people stay dead, that children are born with ten toes, that executive men wear suits to work, that people get married, and that men are sexually attracted to women. And we have different names for what to call it when what's normal doesn't happen. When the dead rise, it's a miracle. When a child is born with extra toes, we call it an abnormality. When an executive wears denim shorts to work, we call it unconventional. When a man doesn't get married, we call it odd (or if a woman doesn't get married, we might say it's unfortunate). And when men are attracted to men, we might call it a deviancy.

Why the differences in how we describe these departures from the norm? It depends on whether morality is in the mix. With regards to non-normal events in creation, we think of them as miracles if we like them and abnormalities if we don't. If we're talking about departures from social custom that are not really matters of morality, then we use words like unconventional or odd. But if we're speaking of moral behaviors, we turn to words like "deviant."

Most of the LGBT community doesn't appreciate being labeled as deviants (and who would?). So they use various approaches to the relationship between normality and same-sex behaviors. For instance, some might question if same-sex attraction is actually all that unusual. They might point to surveys which suggest that it's far more common than once believed. At one time, society regarded being left-handed as abnormal, but we now know it's actually quite common, and therefore, few people make it an issue anymore. Why not think of same-sex attraction in the same way?

Others say that same-sex behaviors are only a break from social convention. Just because societies at one time looked down on same-sex activities does not mean they must continue to do so. Social convention is always changing. Pastors at one time were expected to wear clerical robes, but then suits became the norm. Today about anything goes for how to dress in the pulpit. And what about all the different social conventions in all the different cultures across the planet and down through time? Surely we should be able to change our social conventions and regard same-sex attraction as now normal. At least that's what some think.

Still others just want to throw out the whole notion of normality altogether. Normal, they say, is not what usually happens, but is actually an attempt to impose the norms of some people on the rest of society. It's a word used to make a power play, so that the few can impose their own moral ideas on the many. It's no coincidence that the words "normal" and "norm" sound alike. They are related words, both rooted in the Latin term *norma*, the word for a carpenter's square, used as a pattern to form right angles. Normal are those things that fit the pattern set by the carpenter's square (*norma*), or those things that follow the moral patterns (*norms*) set by others. This notion of having to follow someone else's moral pattern, say some, is what needs to be eliminated.

These objectors are partly right. It's probably best not to use "normal" to mean "what usually happens," because what usually happens in a fallen world is sin. We are no longer surprised by mass murders anymore. We are not surprised when politicians lie, or pastors have affairs, or church members gossip. It's pretty typical for movies to be filled with gore and f-bombs. And so when we define what's normal as what usually happens, we end up saying that sin is normal. But when sin is normal, then the floodwaters of iniquity really overwhelm society.

That's why I'm inclined to go along with those who don't like to think of normal as "what usually happens." Rather, normal is what is established by a norm. But here is where I part company with the objectors to normality. They believe no one is qualified to establish norms for others. A character in

Jessica Park's ebook, *Flat-Out Celeste,* said it this way, "Who gets to say how we are supposed to be? Or who are we supposed to be? And how dare anyone make you feel inadequate for being who you are. It's not okay. It pisses me off." That character's attitude, however, sure sounds like they are now establishing their own norm for the rest of us—the norm being that no one gets to establish norms for others, except that person. But I'm not ready to give up on norms. I'm not, however, interested in norms set by society or a few influential people. What I *am* interested in are the norms set by God, as we find revealed in the Scriptures. Of course, by looking to God for our norms, we have not completely resolved our problems, because we still need to figure out which interpretations of the Scripture most accurately reflect God's norms. Nonetheless, the norms of God establish what is to be normal.

And at this point we must reach the astounding conclusion that in today's world, no one is normal, for no one lives up to the norms of God (Romans 3:23). We are all deviants in the sight of God. We might even say that we all are sexual deviants in his sight, at least to some degree. I say that because any degree of deviation is enough to throw off the life we are building, just as any degree of deviation for a bricklayer or carpenter from the *norma*, the carpenter's square, will throw off their work as well.

We won't fully experience God's normal in our own hearts or in our world until Jesus comes. And until that day, all of us—whether same-sex attracted or not—need to look to Jesus to forgive our deviancies and inch our lives more in alignment with his holy will.

Objects of desire

W hen someone says, "I covet your prayers," do you immediately assume they are breaking the tenth commandment, "Thou shalt not covet"? Of course not. Even though the word "covet" is used in both statements, only a very rigid understanding of language would rebuke someone who coveted prayers.

It makes a huge difference what it is that you are coveting. Are you coveting your neighbor's prayers or your neighbor's spouse? Are you coveting their intercessions or their house? The object of desire makes a difference here.

I bring this up because a case has been made that when Paul talks about shameful and degrading same-sex desires in Romans 1, he is only talking about *inordinate* same-sex desires, not moderate same-sex desires. In his book, *Bible, Gender, Sexuality*, James Brownson is particularly intrigued by the possibility that Romans 1 is not describing the sins of his readers, but mostly portraying the excessive lusts of the evil Roman emperor Caligula. What made same-sex behavior so evil in Paul's day, according to Brownson, is that it was so excessive. Not content with marital sex, people like Caligula added multiple partners of the opposite sex, and then moved beyond to their own sex.[1] Brownson concludes from this that Paul's words do not apply to gays and lesbians with more moderate desires of seeking a committed same-sex relationship. "Desire itself is not the problem; it is desire that is out of control."[2] In other words, it is not the object of one's desire that makes it sinful, but the degree of that desire. As long as one's desire is moderate, then it would be permissible for one to desire a committed relationship with one's own sex. In Brownson's words, "It would probably not be appropriate to speak of this kind of desire for long-term gay unions as 'lust,' since it lacks the intensity and excessive self-seeking and self-centered drive that lies at the heart of Paul's understanding of sinful lust."[3]

Brownson is driving a wedge between the moral quality of a given desire and the object of that desire. As long as the moral quality of a desire is

---

[1] James V. Brownson, *Bible, Gender, Sexuality* (Grand Rapids: Eerdmans, 2013), 156-60.
[2] Brownson, 164.
[3] Brownson, 168.

good, then it doesn't matter as much what the object of desire is. Brownson would not like that principle applied to other situations beyond same-sex relationships, but it's difficult to see how one can avoid it. A man and woman married to other people might believe that their sexual desires for each other are very moderate. A sexual threesome could regard their sexual desires as very moderate and not self-seeking. A father and his grown daughter could believe that their sexual desires are moderate, too. From the outside, we could easily see they are deceiving themselves.

It's because of this human tendency to rationalize one's own behavior that the Bible not only forbids desires that are poor in quality (that is so say, excessive and self-centered), but it also forbids certain objects or persons that we might desire. The husband who desires his neighbor's wife might think his desires are very moderate and understandable; after all, they're both miserable in their marriages, and they feel so alive when they're together during their little trysts. But no matter what he might be telling himself, his desires are wrong. How do we know this? Because the object of his desire is forbidden to him by God, and if he's willing to disobey God in the pursuit of a desire, that's reason enough to say his desire is excessive and out of control.

The same holds true for same-sex relationships. Two women might think their sexual desires for one another are moderate and good. But no matter what they might be telling themselves, their desires are excessive. And how do we know this? Because the object of their desire is forbidden to them by God, and if they're willing to disobey God in the pursuit of a desire, that's reason enough to say their desire is excessive and out of control. Even Brownson seems to admit as much himself when he earlier says that "excessive" is that "which directs itself toward what is not rightly ours, overcoming self-control *and obedience to God.*"[4]

Same-sex desire is not lust simply because it passes a certain level of intensity—all sexual desire is intense. It is lust because, in disobedience to God's command, we sexually desire what is not rightly ours, whether that be a pornographic image, a person of the opposite sex who is not our married partner, a person of the same sex, or someone from our biological family.

---

[4] Brownson, 164 (italics mine).

On being right

O ne of the delegates at our denomination's national convention was asked to lead in prayer before breaking for lunch, after a morning filled with lots of debate over LGBT issues. This woman quietly prayed that the Lord would free us from the need to be right.

A part of me understood exactly what she was talking about. There's an all-too-human (and sinful) desire to justify ourselves before others. We want others to see that we are right and they are wrong. So we hope that our snappy zingers will deliver the final blow to the opposition and all their defenses will crumble before the rightness of our cause. I have detected this desire to be right in plenty of words spoken by both sides of the LGBT debates—and even from my own mouth.

But there's another part of me that takes issue with the prayer (although it may be one more case of me wanting to be right). Shouldn't we want to line up with the righteous will of God? We shouldn't want to line up with this righteous will so that we can cram it down someone else's throat or haughtily display how we have chosen the right side. But surely—at least for ourselves, if not for those within our sphere of influence—we would want to be in the right, wouldn't we?

Because what's the alternative? I certainly would not want to pray to be on the *wrong* side of God's will. Maybe the person who prayed meant that there is no definitive right or wrong on some matters, and that we just need to live together in the tension of not coming to a conclusion. I could understand that. I have often said that I want to be as black and white on issues as the Bible, and also as grey on issues as the Bible. If the Bible provides no definitive right or wrong on a given issue, then I would be in the wrong to continue pressing for one side to be right and the other to be wrong. I would be needlessly dividing up the body of Christ. God must have had had some reason for not making things clearer. So rather than spending my time clarifying what God wants left unclear, I should ponder instead on what good reason God might have for doing so. Or perhaps I should learn to live with the unresolved tension (or mystery) of a particular issue. For instance, I could ask myself, "What do I need to appreciate about both sides of this issue?"

So, with regards to the prayer spoken at our denominational meeting, I do want to be freed from self-righteousness. I want to be freed from a bullying kind of righteousness. I want to be freed from a proud form of righteousness. But I don't want to be freed from the right and good ways of God. Instead, I want to attach myself more firmly than ever to that. If that means standing for what God has clearly shown to be right, or rejecting what God has clearly shown to be wrong, or appreciating both sides of what he has left unclear—then that's where I want to be. And that's where we all should be.

Pharisees

I am a Pharisee. A Christian Pharisee, of course, but a Pharisee nonetheless. I hesitate to say that because, in the minds of many believers, the label "Pharisee" conjures up images of crass hypocrites, pious and proud pretenders who worked hard to get Jesus killed. I don't want to be associated with images like that. Rather, what I mean by claiming to be a Pharisee is that my own disposition and position in society is very similar to that of the Pharisees in first century Palestine.

The Pharisees were middle class people who took Scripture and morality very seriously. They could see that immorality was hurting the nation, and, therefore, called the Jewish people back to the commands of God. They were pretty good people, which may not be much compared to the standards of perfection set by God, but compared to the wickedness common in their world, they were decent folks. Maybe most of them were not rich, but they took good care of their possessions and appreciated cleanliness. They thought having a good reputation was a good thing, and they tried to keep themselves and their families from being corrupted by the influences of the world. Doctrinal standards were important, because they were a people of the Book.

I look at a list like that, and I have to admit it's like looking in a mirror. I take God's Word seriously when it comes to doctrine and morality. I want to give God a good name by maintaining a good name myself. I like living in a clean house, in a clean neighborhood, and try to keep myself clean—even in my long-haired "hippie" days, I took a shower every day. I try to minimize the influence of the world on my spirit, keeping the intrusion of the media to a minimum.

So in many respects, I could think of myself as a Christian Pharisee. And my deep hunch is that many Christians in America could also be called Christian Pharisees. Churches are full of clean, hard-working, decent people, who believe the Bible, follow God's commands, avoid scandalous sins, and seek to avoid the influences of the world. The fact that Christian Pharisees can be found in today's churches should not surprise us. Some of the earliest followers of Jesus were Pharisees—Nicodemus, Joseph of Arimathea, and Paul, to name a few. According to Acts 15:5, some of the Christians in the Jerusalem church also belonged to the Pharisee party.

But even though the lifestyle of Christian Pharisees has much to commend it, we must also be aware of the temptations that are especially likely to trip up Pharisees who love Jesus.

First, there's the temptation towards legalism—the fussy concern over rule-making and rule-keeping, which threatens to overwhelm the gospel in terms of importance. The Pharisees of the Bible were so concerned about God's laws that they lost touch with God. When the Son of God himself arrived in their midst, they were unable to hear his words of truth. They were incapable of being awed by his miraculous power. They did not feel the heartbeat of God in his ministry. Instead, the only thing they could think of was that he broke their rules. Although we Christian Pharisees believe in Jesus—unlike many of the original Pharisees—it is very easy to allow our concern for morality to eclipse the role of Jesus. Sunday School lessons and sermons can focus on morality and miss the Christ. Like Eve, we are tempted to eat from the Tree of the Knowledge of Good and Evil, instead of from the Tree of Life called the cross. Paul reminds us that the righteousness we seek is not "a righteousness of my own that comes from the law, but that [righteousness] which is through faith in Christ" (Philippians 3:9, ESV).

Another temptation for Christian Pharisees is to play with the rules, stacking them in our favor. We may honor God's laws, but that doesn't stop us from fiddling with them. The original Pharisees, for instance, made elaborate loopholes, so that they could act unjustly, but still congratulate themselves for following the letter of the law. We also look for loopholes. For example, we may acknowledge that the Lord wants us to care for the needy, but we think we're exempt from this command if we have reason to believe the needy got themselves into their situation and probably wouldn't change if we helped them anyway. We also make loopholes with regards to sexual morality. We are outraged by those involved in same-sex activity, but we don't even blink an eye about the so-called "acceptable" sexuality exhibited on game shows and sporting events. Instead of looking for loopholes, Jesus calls us to a righteousness that far exceeds that of the Pharisees (Matthew 5:20).

Because we live pretty good lives, it's also common for Christian Pharisees to be tempted by pride. We freely acknowledge that our moral track record has some flaws in it, but we can't help but notice that others have even more blemishes on their record. Our thankfulness for God's sanctifying work in our lives easily slips into moral one-upmanship. It's only a few fatal steps from the oft-cited prayer, "There but for the grace of God go I" to the prayer Jesus condemned in Luke 18:11, "God, I thank you that I am not like all other men—robbers, evildoers, adulterers" (NIV11). Pretty good people need a pretty good dose of humility, for there's moral rottenness in even the best of us, and any good we do happens only through the grace of God (Philippians 2:13).

Another common temptation for Christian Pharisees is to forget the Great Commission. Jesus told us to go into all the world with the gospel, especially sharing it with the most immoral people around. Jesus explained his own inclination for reaching out to the prostitutes and extortionists by reminding us that it's the sick who need a doctor, not those who think they are well (Mark 2:17). This ministry focus drove the original Pharisees crazy. In their minds, it was not possible to reach out to obviously immoral people without being contaminated by their sin. Even in the book of Acts, when there was a big debate about opening the doors of the gospel to Gentiles, it was the Christians from the Pharisee party raising the most objections (Acts 15:5). Clean-living Christians are often exceedingly wary of coming in contact with notorious sinners. For example, if a congregation has a gym facility, it will make many Christians anxious when unchurched neighborhood children come in to mingle with their own children. And so it will be tempting for them to make rules about who can be in the building and when. The fear of spiritual contamination is often so big in the minds of Christian Pharisees that it seems safer to them to forget about the Great Commission on the local level. Let's evangelize people far away, they say, but not in our own community. Christian Pharisees must remind themselves continually that no fears should stop us from the mission we have been called to do.

And, of course, we cannot talk about Pharisees without mentioning the temptation toward hypocrisy. We might wonder what's so alluring about pretending to be better than we are. Doesn't everyone want to be real? But Pharisees (both Jewish and Christian varieties) have high stakes in maintaining a good reputation. When we live pretty good lives, we find that it's rewarding. We feel good about ourselves. We believe that we are making a positive difference in our communities of faith and serving as role models for our children and others. We like the compliments of others who appreciate our good qualities and good work. Then, when we come face to face with the stubborn sinfulness still in our hearts, we try to keep it under cover. We tell ourselves that the sin was just a little indiscretion, something out of character. If our hidden sin became known, we believe it would hurt our reputation—and our witness—and so it seems better for God's kingdom (according to our own egos) to hide that sin. If this goes on too long, we will find ourselves mired in the hypocrisy of a double life, white-washed tombs full of rotten bones. But the Lord calls us to come clean, to pray the tax-collector's prayer, "God, have mercy on me, a sinner" (Luke 18:13, NIV11).

So even though I'm thankful for Christian Pharisees, and glad to be one myself, I must acknowledge that this poses its own set of spiritual challenges and dangers, not least in the debates about same-sex behavior. If the LGBT community hears more from me about Sodom and the laws of Leviticus than they do about the forgiveness offered by Jesus, I'm falling into legalism. If I consider the LGBT community to be the worst of sinners, I'm falling into pride. If I'd rather talk about the evils of same-sex behavior than actually befriend someone in the LGBT community, I'm forgetting the Great Commission. If I'm exposing the brokenness of the LGBT community, but not facing up to my own brokenness—sexual or otherwise—I'm acting like a hypocrite.

Lord, fill an old Pharisee like me with love, humility, integrity, and joy over your good news. Fill me with Jesus.

Purity [1]

Purity—it's not a popular word in many circles. It gets lumped together with prim, proper, prude, prissy, and Puritan. Purity sounds like the kind of thing that only morally fussy people would care about, the kind who scrunch up their face, purse their lips, and utter a "tsk, tsk" about all the naughty things going on. These are the kind of folks who "hear no evil, see no evil, and speak no evil"—except that all their senses are keen to notice how other people are hearing, seeing, and speaking evil. "How could those people do such things?!" they cluck.

Even among many biblical scholars, it seems that purity is an antiquated notion, full of silly taboos. If some moral issue is raised, especially about sexual matters, they are quick to say, "Well, that's part of the purity concerns of the priests in the Old Testament and the Pharisees in the New Testament, but the coming of Jesus changed all that. We have learned not to call anything common or unclean because the Lord has declared it so" (see Mark 7:19; Acts 10:15).

But not so fast. I'd like to put in a good word for purity. Can the idea be misused? Undoubtedly, yes. Purity concerns did increase unnecessary fussiness about what to touch and eat. Purity concerns turned lepers into social outcasts and left all non-Jewish people on the outside of the kingdom. But the coming of Jesus did not eliminate the importance of purity.

There are two primary adjectives in the New Testament that can be translated as clean or pure: *katharos* and *hagnos* (along with their related verbs and nouns). *Katharos*-purity is often, but not always, translated with words about clean and cleansing, so readers might miss the purity angle.

Some New Testament verses simply tell us that purity is a good thing. Jesus pronounced a blessing on the *"pure* in heart" in Matthew 5:8. Paul says we are to call on the Lord from a *pure* heart (2 Timothy 2:2), that our love should issue from that same *pure* heart (1 Timothy 1:5), and we should

---

[1] The middle part of this article which discusses forms of pure sex was based on an editorial entitled "Purity" which I wrote for *The Sunday School Guide,* Vol. 96, June 19, 2019, 57, 69. Used by permission.

hold the mystery of faith with a *pure* conscience (1 Timothy 3:9). James observed that heavenly wisdom is first of all *pure* (James 3:17).

Because Protestants—always wary of salvation by works—often focus more on what God does for us than on what we ourselves do, there is a tendency on the part of some to assume that purity comes as a gift from God that doesn't necessarily need to come to expression in our own lives. The (usually unspoken) thought seems to be: "Since purity is God's work, and that work won't be completed until Jesus returns, then let's just rest in the purity we have in Christ and not get too fussy about actually living in a pure way." But that's not the attitude we find in the New Testament. Some verses do indeed speak of the purifying work of Christ. According to John 15:3 and Ephesians 5:26, Jesus purifies us with his word. The book of Hebrews says that Jesus was "making purification for sins" on the cross (Hebrews 1:3, ESV), for Jesus offered himself to "purify our conscience from dead works to serve the living God" (Hebrews 9:13, ESV; see also 9:28). John adds that the blood of Jesus *purifies* us from every sin (1 John 1:7), and as we confess those sins he will continue to forgive and purify us (1 John 1:9).

But this purifying work of Jesus was expected to not just give us a "pure" standing before God, but was also working to transform us even now. Note in Titus 2:14 that Jesus gave himself for us "to purify for himself a people for his own possession *who are zealous for good works* (Titus 2:14, ESV; italics mine). And when Peter notes that if we do not add a number of good qualities to our faith, then we have forgotten the whole purpose of being purified: "Whoever lacks these qualities...[has] forgotten that he was cleansed [*katherismos*] from his former sins" (2 Peter 1:9, ESV).

More surprising yet are the verses in which we are called to purify *ourselves*, and not just have Jesus do it for us. When Paul was rebuking those who still dabbled with idolatry, he cited a number of Old Testament texts about God dwelling in our midst as our Father, and therefore we should "touch no unclean thing" (1 Corinthians 6:17, ESV, which is his loose paraphrase of Isaiah 52:11). His very next words are these: "Therefore, since we have these promises, dear friends, *let us purify ourselves* from everything that contaminates body and spirit, perfecting holiness out of reverence for God" (2 Corinthians 7:1, NIV11, italics mine). James called on his readers to "come near to God and he will come near to you. Wash [*katharizō*] your hands, you sinners, and purify [*hagnizō*] your hearts, you double-minded" (James 4:8, NIV11). Earlier he noted that religion that is pure before God means helping those in need and keeping oneself unstained by the world. Paul urged Timothy to keep himself pure (1 Timothy 4:12; 5:22), and he had the same advice for younger women (1 Timothy 5:2) and wives (Titus 2:5; and so did Peter in 1 Peter 3:2). 1 John 3:2 notes that when Jesus appears someday we will become like him, but this good hope does not mean we run on idle until then, for then John says, "And everyone who thus hopes in him *purifies himself* as he is pure" (1 John 3:3, ESV, italics mine). Additional verses that imply human participation in the divine work of purifying would be 2 Corinthians 11:2 (in which Paul expressed his desire to present the Corinthian church like a *pure* virgin bride to Christ the groom) and the call of Philippians 4:8 to think on whatever is pure.

Sometimes Christians unfortunately assume that purity is only about sexual matters. Actually, that's only one of many facets of purity. We need purity of speech and motives, with no trace of deceit mixed in. We need purity of love, instead of an artificial niceness. We need purity in our faith as well, with no double-mindedness added to it. Yet, sexual purity is also part of the equation, which is hinted at in references to the purity of Christ's bride and the need for young men (like Timothy) and young women to be pure.

When I was a kid, Ivory soap advertised itself as "99 and 44 one-hundredths pure soap." I always wondered, what else was in there? What's the other 56 one-hundredths in Ivory Soap made of? Did they throw in cow bones? or candle wax? How about some saw dust or charcoal? Although 99 and 44 one-hundredths is pretty good, you still cannot say Ivory soap is pure soap. There's some other foreign element in there too, which keeps it from being pure soap.

When the writer of Hebrews 13:4 said that the marriage bed should remain pure, he was not talking about soap that's pure, but sex that's pure. It's sex that doesn't have some foreign element mixed in: "Marriage should be honored by all, and the marriage bed kept pure," 100% pure.

So what are the things that make sex impure? What are the bad ingredients people mix in with sex that keep it from being what God intended it to be?

We're not asking this question so we can shame some people and think of them as worse sinners than ourselves. When it comes to sexual matters, none of us is pure. Everyone from teenagers on up has something in their past or present life that's sexually impure. So our purpose is not to shame a few really bad people. We're all guilty in this respect.

But we also don't want to go the way of the world here. The world says, "Yeah, we've all got stuff in our lives, so let's just all agree to overlook it. I won't point out your sins if you don't point out mine." No, it's important for us to see God's standard. And that's because God loves us and wants the best for us, including the best in terms of sexuality. He wants us to thrive in the fullness of being human, and he shows us the best way to make that happen.

So what are some of the ways we make sex impure?

First, some mix sex with same-sex behavior—men having sex with men and women with women. Even though the media wants to celebrate this, that's not the way God planned it. Romans 1:25-27 indicates that same-sex behavior is not God's will for us. To say that doesn't mean we turn our backs on the LGBT community. We have a built-in sympathy for them. Each of us knows what it's like to struggle with a sin and never feel like we get victory over it. Maybe it's anger, gossip, envy, or bitterness, and we're tempted to excuse it with, "That's just the way I am." All sinners would like to make that claim—we were born that way—but God has a better plan. Same-sex behaviors are not pure sex, but sex with disobedience mixed in.

Others mix sex in with promiscuity. They move from one person to another without any commitment. In the world of promiscuity, people don't talk about husbands and wives, but about sex partners. Whether we're talking about prostitutes, one night stands, or date rape—promiscuous behavior treats the bodies of others as tools for personal gratification, with no further obligations.

Although the words "promiscuous" and "promise" sound alike, they are opposites. A promiscuous person seldom makes promises and certainly has no intention of keeping promises. They want sex without commitment. But promiscuous sex is impure sex. It's mixing sex with selfishness and irresponsibility. It's going through the motions of love without any love. Pure sex, however, is not about selfish pleasure, but about pleasure that cares, pleasure that's completely committed to the other person, pleasure that keeps its promises. If you're not committed completely to someone, you have no right to use their body for sexual pleasure.

Third, some mix sex with a less-than-full commitment. To their credit, they're not promiscuous. They're in an ongoing dating relationship, and the relationship is growing closer. Maybe they're even talking about getting married or have already gotten engaged. But since they have this "kind of" commitment, they think it's okay to go ahead and have sex. "Well, we love each other, so why not?" they ask. Because it's backwards, that's why. There's no way to have pure sex unless you have complete commitment first, which happens in marriage. Saying "I love you" is not complete commitment. Planning to get married is not complete commitment. Moving in together is not complete commitment. All those are just "I hope to" or "I plan to" commitments. But that's not what pure sex is about.

A full commitment will declare that commitment to one's partner and to the world. In our culture, we declare it to the world with a ceremony and legal papers. Other cultures do it differently. But in some way, marriage means committing all the way. The purest sex comes after marriage, not before. You wouldn't think of getting a drink by first pouring the water, and then getting a glass. That's just a mess. You get the glass first, and then you pour the water. This same dynamic is true of sex and marriage. Just as you need a glass before you pour the water, so you need to have marriage before you have sex.

Fourth, some ruin sex by mixing in a third person. Sex is only supposed to be between two people with a husband and wife committed to each other. Sex is ruined when one spouse breaks the commitment by getting sexually involved with another person. According to some studies, about 60% of husbands and 35% of wives have done this. The problem here is not an iffy commitment, but the breaking of the commitment already made. It's what we call adultery

When something is pure we say it's unadulterated. When something's impure, it's adulterated. Adultery is adulterated sex, impure sex. This is the fastest way imaginable to destroy a marriage. When couples wed, the two become one flesh. So when one spouse cheats, it's like ripping up that flesh. Some marriages survive this pain; most don't. For how can you love when you don't trust?

Those who commit adultery often think marriage is all about the feeling of being in love, and when they don't have the feeling, they think it's alright to look outside the marriage. But pure marriage is not just about feelings. It takes commitment, hard work, and being a person of your word. This can only come from Jesus. He is faithful so we can be faithful. Only then can there be pure, unadulterated sex.

Fifth, pure sex can be ruined by mixing in lust. It's not just what you do with your body, but also your mind. This may, in fact, be the biggest problem of all. When it comes to sex, Americans seem to be watching it and thinking about it more and more, but doing it less and less. And this is most evidenced by the huge porn industry. Yet Jesus told us plainly, lust and adultery come from the same dirty bed: "You have heard that it was said, 'Do not commit adultery.' But I tell you that anyone who looks at a woman lustfully has already committed adultery with her in his heart" (Matthew 5: 27-28, NIV).

Today's propaganda for lust tries to say that lust is natural, healthy, normal, and honest. But surrendering to lust leads to jealousy, lies, concealment, broken homes, misery, addiction, disease, death, and hell. Sexual sin never happens suddenly. It always traces back to previous lustful decisions. As someone once said, "Sow a thought, reap an action. Sow an action, reap a habit. Sow a habit, reap a character. Sow a character, reap a destiny." If you weaken a dam, it collapses. If you weaken your soul with lust, it will collapse too.

So yes, there are many things people are mixing in with sex so it's not the pure, unadulterated pleasure God intended. The only way to find pure sex is through the married, committed love of a husband and wife. All other sex—pleasurable as it may seem at the time—is not God's best. Pure sex is what we are to honor above all else.

But some have tried to muddy the water on pure sex, even some Christians. They have taken some texts about purity and tried to use them to create space for same-sex practices. They look at the New Testament teaching on purity and note that sometimes a distinction is made between inward and outward purity. So they turn this distinction into a wedge, which allows them to say, "Outwardly what some people are doing may look impure to you, such as same-sex behavior, but if what they think and feel internally is pure, you can't really object." Let's look at a few of these texts:

(1) **Matthew 23:25-26.** This text comes from a series of rebukes that Jesus spoke against the Pharisees toward the end of his earthly life: "Woe to you, scribes and Pharisees, hypocrites! For you clean [*katharizō*] the outside of the cup and the plate, but inside they are full of greed and self-indulgence. You blind Pharisee! First clean [*katharizō*] the inside of the cup and the plate, that the outside also may be clean" (Matthew 23:25-26, ESV).

Since Jesus mentioned greed here, let's first think of how this might apply to *greed*, both internally and externally. Jesus is declaring that ritual purity on the outside is worthless if our greedy attitudes have made us impure on the inside. What's needed is that we first purify ourselves of internal greed in order that we might become externally pure as well. But we would be in error if we also concluded that internal purity alone is good enough, or that internal purity makes any and all external actions pure as well. We would not agree with a man who said, "Well, I don't have any greed in my heart [internal], so it doesn't matter if I underpay my workers [external]." Nor would we accept the excuse of a man who said, "The fact that I have cleansed my heart of greed means that the external thing of underpaying my workers can also be considered pure."

The same dynamic holds true for same-sex behavior (or any other sexual sin). A man might argue that as long as his heart is pure in his same-sex activity, that's all that matters, or that somehow his pure lust-less motives sanctify his same-sex activities. That doesn't seem to be Jesus' point. Rather, he would be saying that the place to start is by purifying what's in the in heart with regards to sexuality, and then this will lead to pure *external* sexual actions as well.

(2) **Luke 11:39-41.** Luke remembers a different time Jesus issued a stinging rebuke to the Pharisees. It happened earlier in his ministry when a Pharisee invited Jesus over for a meal and was surprised that Jesus did not wash before the meal. Jesus said in response: "Now you Pharisees cleanse [*katharizō*] the outside of the cup and of the dish, but inside you are full of

greed and wickedness. You fools! Did not he who made the outside make the inside also? But give as alms those things that are within, and behold, everything is clean [*katharos*] for you" (Luke 11:39-41, ESV). Because the Pharisees erred in forgetting about what's inside, Jesus reminded them that God made both the inside and the outside. And then more enigmatically Jesus calls the Pharisees to give as alms those things that are within. In other words, what's inside the heart must come out, and when it comes out—assuming it's something pure—give it to the needy. If you internally purify your heart, then you will externally help those in need. And then Jesus adds one of those statements that always managed to take people by surprise: if your internally pure stuff comes out in the form of externally helping the needy, then all things will be clean for you.

It's possible to interpret this to mean that as long as you give alms from a pure heart, then anything that used to be thought of as evil or impure has been transformed into something pure. That could range all the way from unclean foods and unclean hands to murder, incest, not paying your workers fairly, gossip, or same-sex relations. I doubt that many people think that's what Jesus is trying to say here. Sin is still sin, and cannot be transformed into something pure just because you purified your heart enough to give alms. Jesus is not undermining all forms of morality, but is focusing instead on undermining the Pharisees' fussiness about ritual purity.

(3) **Mark 7:15-23**. In the gospel of Mark, Jesus responded to a similar incident. This time the Pharisees questioned Jesus about why his disciples did not follow the time-honored tradition of only eating with washed hands, but instead ate with "common" (*koinos*), unclean hands. Jesus rebuked them for paying more attention to tradition than to the Word of God, and then said to a nearby crowd, "Nothing outside a man can make him 'unclean' [*koinoō*] by going into him. Rather, it is what comes out of a man that makes him 'unclean'" [*koinoō*] (Mark 7:15, NIV). A few verses later Jesus explained this further to his disciples: "'Don't you see that nothing that enters a man from the outside can make him 'unclean'? For it doesn't go into his heart but into his stomach, and then out of his body.' (In saying this, Jesus declared all foods 'clean.') He went on: 'What comes out of a man is what makes him "unclean." For from within, out of men's hearts, come evil thoughts, sexual immorality, theft, murder, adultery, greed, malice, deceit, lewdness, envy, slander, arrogance and folly. All these evils come from inside and make a man "unclean."'" (Mark 7:18-23, NIV).

Jesus wants to make us aware that internal impurities are much more damaging to us and our world than external impurities. Some Christians then extend this idea to the sphere of sexuality. After all, they might argue, the two main spheres in which something outside the body comes into the body are food and sexual activity. When they apply Jesus' teaching to same-sex behavior, their reasoning goes like this: as long as a same-sex attracted man has good things in his heart, then he is not made impure by same-sex behavior, that is, he is not made impure by semen coming into his mouth or anus." (I have not heard it expressed this bluntly, but that's what's going on, at least in gay sex.) But we wouldn't think of applying this principle to heterosexual acts: that as along as a man has good things in his heart, he would not be made impure if the vaginal liquid of a prostitute was entering his mouth, or if pornographic images were entering his eyes.

There is definitely a distinction between internal and external impurity, but we should not turn this distinction into a wedge, as if they operated in separate spheres. When Jesus lists impurities in Mark 7:21-22, we might think he is going to list only internal attitudes, such as pride, lust, and evil thoughts. But his list mixes together both what is *internal* (evil thoughts, greed, malice envy, arrogance, and folly), and also what is *external* (sexual immorality, theft, murder, adultery, deceit, lewdness, and slander). That's because the internal and external work together. Jesus is not advocating that external purity become a non-issue (except for what involves food), but instead he expands our ideas of purity to also include what's within. Every impurity that may seem external came from an internal source, and every internal impurity bears external fruit. Adultery comes from lust, lust leads to adultery. We would be in error to say that external adultery is okay as long as the person avoided internal lusts. Likewise, it would be wrong to say that external same-sex behaviors are okay as long as one avoids internal lusts.

The Bible speaks of both internal and external impurity because of our great tendency toward self-deception. On the one hand, if we think we're good because our observable *outer* behavior appears to measure up to God's standards, then Jesus calls us to a purity on the *inside*. On the other hand, if we think we're good because of our own assessment of our *inner purity*, then Jesus tells us about our need for *outwardly* pure actions. We've all heard of abusive spouses who thought they had nothing but pure love for their partner. They were wrong. Internal and external purity must work in tandem.

(4) **Titus 1:15.** When writing Titus, Paul warns him of all the false teachers at work in his area. They are insubordinate and arrogant, and many of them belong to the "circumcision party," thus indicating that they are either Jews or non-Jews who have become enamored with the Old Testament—reading it with an orientation toward the law and not the gospel (Titus 1:10). This perception of the problem is further reinforced by their dedication to Jewish myths and their man-made commands (Titus 1:14; see also Titus 3:9).

They likely had an interest in Old Testament commands about purity issues (such as washing and diet), for Paul next says, "To the pure, all things are pure, but to the defiled and unbelieving, nothing is pure; but both their minds and their consciences are defiled" (Titus 1:15, ESV—the three references to "pure" in this verse are all the Greek adjective *katharos*). In other words, those who are truly "pure" in the Lord don't worry about such things as washing and diet, while the false teachers who focus on that kind of purity are actually impure in all that they do.

Again, some read these verses and conclude that as long as one is internally pure in the Lord, then all their outward actions are pure as well. All those Old Testament taboos, such as those against same-sex behaviors, no longer apply. But if you look at the rest of Titus you realize this is not what Paul is saying. If you are internally pure in the Lord, then you will live in a godly way (Titus 1:1). You will not be open to the charge of debauchery or insubordination (Titus 1:6), nor will you be arrogant, quick-tempered, a drunkard, violent, or greedy (Titus 1:7-8). God's grace does not mean that we can be inwardly pure and do as we please. Instead, his grace is "training us to renounce ungodliness and worldly passions" (Titus 2:12, ESV). Jesus' goal is "to redeem us from all lawlessness and to purify [katharizō] for himself a people for his own possession who are zealous for good works" (Titus 2:14, ESV). Those who are pure in the Lord should be "careful to devote themselves to good works" (Titus 3:8, ESV). To say that "to the pure all things are pure" does not mean all formerly sinful actions—including same-sex actions—are now okay, but only that the Old Testament laws about diet and man-made traditions about washing no longer hold. I suppose someone could argue that Old Testament same-sex prohibitions belong in the same category as the no-longer-in-effect purity laws about diet, since they are both found in Leviticus. But then we would have to also say that prohibitions against incest (as well as lying and stealing) are no longer in effect either since they are in that same section of Leviticus. For that matter, the command to "love your neighbor as yourself" is found in this same chapter (Leviticus 19:18). [2]

(5) **Acts 10:15; 11:9.** Shortly before the conversion of the first uncircumcised non-Jew (Cornelius), Peter had a vision or dream in which a sheet of unclean animals was lowered from heaven, along with a voice commanding him to kill and eat. Peter protested that he had never eaten anything unclean before, but the heavenly voice then said, "What God has made clean [katharizō], you must not call profane" (Acts 10:15, NRSV). And then this same sequence of events in the vision happens twice more. Peter learns from this not only that formerly unclean foods are now acceptable to God,

---

[2] For more on this, see the essay "Seven texts" on page 211.

but so are the non-Jews whom he had previously regarded as unclean. And we know this is what Peter learns, for when he goes to Cornelius' home, he says, "You yourselves know that it is unlawful for a Jew to associate with or to visit a Gentile, but God has shown me that I should not call *anyone* profane or unclean" (Acts 10:28, NRSV, italics mine). When asked to explain his going to the home of a non-Jew in the next chapter, Peter recounts his vision and repeats the exact same words from the heavenly voice about not calling common what God has made clean.

Obviously, God has the prerogative to purify whatever and whomever he wishes—even things and people that he had previously declared to be unclean. If God so chose, he could also purify various actions that he formerly regarded as evil. If God so chose, God could purify killing (which he did in the holy wars of the Old Testament). If God so chose, God could purify lying and theft. If God so chose, God could purify slavery, pedophilia, incest and same-sex behavior. But the key issue is: has God so chosen? Because God's choices line up with his character, it would seem that he has not made those choices, nor will he. In Acts 10 we have a dramatic case of God making a choice to purify unclean animals and the unclean nations (as long as they are washed in the blood of Jesus), but we have no similar record or indication that God has chosen to purify actions that he has revealed in the New Testament to be sinful. We might have our favorite sins that we wish God would purify so that we could continue in them, but that's just wishful thinking, not biblical thinking.

(6) 1 Corinthians 6:12. Amid all the issues Paul had to deal with in 1 Corinthians, one of them was that some of the newly-converted men thought it was still okay for them to visit brothels. Paul argued strenuously against such behavior, reminding them that the body is not meant for sexual sin, for our bodies belong to the Lord, who bought us at a price. So if we are uniting our bodies with a prostitute, we are dragging the Lord Jesus into our sin. What's needed is for us to flee sexual sin and instead glorify God with our bodies (1 Corinthians 6:12-20). But in the beginning of this section he makes a surprising statement, "'All things are lawful for me,' but not all things are helpful. 'All things are lawful for me,' but I will not be dominated by anything" (1 Corinthians 6:12, ESV).

When Paul says that "all things are lawful for me," most translations and commentators assume Paul is quoting a popular slogan in the Corinthian church. Perhaps the words came from some false teachers, or it's a sloganized version of something Paul himself said, but it had been taken out of context to justify actions like visiting prostitutes. Paul's intent is to correct the slogan. Yes, there is a sense in which all things are lawful for Christians—they don't have to be fussy about dietary matters from the Old Testament. They can, in the later words of Augustine, love God and do as they please, because when they love God what pleases them are the things that please God. But this does not apply to sins, because sins are not helpful in our walk with the Lord or in the life of the church; and sins will dominate us. Even if these sins were "lawful," why would you do them? They can only hurt you and enslave you.

So even if someone were to argue, "Because Christ has come and transformed Old Testament purity laws, it is lawful for me to engage in same-sex behaviors and relationships," they would find no support from this text (or any other one). But even if it were true—that such behaviors were now lawful—it would still be the case that such behaviors were harmful and enslaving. Christians are called to flee these actions and instead glorify God with their bodies. And we know this applies to same-sex behaviors (as well as heterosexual sins) because of the context. The verses immediately before 1 Corinthians 6:12 list same-sex behaviors (and some other sins) as actions that could prevent a person from inheriting the kingdom of God. These actions also formerly characterized some of the Corinthians, but not anymore. Now they have been transformed—washed, sanctified and justified in the name of Jesus and by the power of the Holy Spirit (1 Corinthians 6:9-11).[3]

I hope you can see by now that purity, including sexual purity, is not a bygone concern of prissy priests and prudish Pharisees, but is an important element of what the Lord has done and is doing in the lives of his people.

---

[3] For more on this text, see the essay "Seven Texts" found on page 211, especially pages 220-223.

Red letters

O ver the years I have gone through hundreds of yellow hi-lite markers. They are an essential reading tool for me. I will highlight ideas
I've never thought of before. I will highlight sentences that nicely
state what I've thought myself for a long time. I will highlight the flow of the
argument. Then years later, when I pick up that book again, rather than
taking the time to reread the whole book, I can quickly skim through the
highlighted sentences.

When I first became a Christian I also did this with my hot-off-the press
Living Bible paraphrase. When I finished reading it, my Bible had a large
number of favorite promises and important commands in bright yellow.
And then when I got other translations I would start marking all over again.
Even my groovy *Letters to Street Christians*, which was a hippie-fied para-
phrase of Paul's letters, got the same treatment.

But I quickly realized that whenever I looked in my Bible, my eyes
immediately went to the yellow-marked verses. It would be easy to get
stuck on what struck me the first time around in reading the Bible and
overlook important truths found in the unmarked verses. So in addition to
my marked-up Bibles I also would read Bibles that I left unmarked. In this
way, my eyes would be more open to seeing things I had never seen before.

But I'm not the only one with a marked-up Bible. Some publishers are
willing to mark it up for you. I once envied a friend who owned a Bible with
a seven-fold color scheme designed to help dispensationalist readers know
which verses applied to which dispensation. They definitely divided up the
word of truth, but I'm skeptical whether they were "rightly dividing" it, as
their interpretation of 2 Timothy 2:15 (KJV only) claimed.

Much more common are those Bibles that print the words of Jesus in
red letters. When I first professed my faith in Jesus at my home church, they
gave me one of these red-letter Bibles (Revised Standard Version) which I
used until the pages got all wrinkled when I was doused with water outside
my college dorm. I'm sure the purpose of the red letters was for showing respect toward what the Lord said while he walked on earth. One of the ef-
fects of this practice, however, is that some Christians will place more
weight on the red letters than the black letters—as if they were somehow

more inspired or at least more important. At times this can be a needed corrective. In 2012, for instance, Shane Claiborne and Tony Campolo wrote the book, *Red Letter Revolution*, for the purpose of calling people back to the Jesus' words of radical discipleship—words too easily ignored by the middle class American church.

In this same vein, some involved in today's LGBT debates will point out that the red letters in our Bibles never speak about same-sex relationships. Jesus was silent on the issue. For them, his silence speaks volumes, for it indicates that in spite of all the sound and fury of our debates, it does not appear to be a major issue for Jesus.

Silence, of course, is multi-interpretable. It could mean Jesus had no opinion about this matter. But it could also mean that it was not a "hot topic" in his day, or that it was not a prominent practice among first-century Jews (although it was among the non-Jewish nations) and thus did not need to be addressed. Possibly Jesus' silence meant that he believed the Old Testament already addressed this issue well, and he had nothing to add to it (unlike some other Old Testament moral issues). Or maybe he believed that his general words about other sexual matters provided enough guidance for this issue.

Although we don't know exactly why Jesus did not speak of same-sex issues, we do know that "all Scripture [not just the red lettered portion] is breathed out by God and profitable for teaching, for reproof, for correction, and for training in righteousness" (2 Timothy 3:16, ESV). If we get ourselves pitting Jesus' silence against other biblical commands, we will quickly lose our way.

There are many issues about which Jesus was silent, and yet we do not therefore assume that such things are permissible. For instance, we have no specific word from Jesus about stockpiling nuclear weapons, polluting the earth, racism, drug abuse, capital punishment, abortion, slavery, child abuse, idolatrous images, warfare, etc. There are also some heterosexual practices about which Jesus said nothing, and yet we do not assume these are permissible either—such as incest, bestiality, group sex, and rape. Silence does not mean we have nothing to say about such matters, but that we must rely on other words of Jesus and other portions of Scripture for guidance.

But in spite of what I've just said about not confining our thoughts about same-sex matters to the red letters, at this point I would like to focus on some words of Jesus that might indeed say something to the issue at hand, even if none of them specifically address it. And I want to do this in light of another essay in this book entitled, "Why Do You Want to Know?" Let's consider a variety of people who have different agendas for coming to Jesus with their questions about LGBT matters and then imagine how the actual words of Jesus recorded in the Gospels might address these people. First, I'll describe a person who comes to Jesus with a question or comment about the morality of same-sex behavior, followed by a "red letter verse" from the mouth of Jesus, which I will put in bold print, not in red. (By the way, if I add any clarifying words to show the connection, I'll put them in brackets.)

A man doesn't like LGBT people and wants nothing to do with them, because they're just not normal. He's hoping Jesus will tell him that they are so "other" that he doesn't have to love them.

Jesus replied, "A man was going down from Jerusalem to Jericho, and he fell among robbers, who stripped him and beat him and departed, leaving him half dead. Now by chance a priest was going down that road, and when he saw him he passed by on the other side. So likewise a Levite, when he came to the place and saw him, passed by on the other side. But a [gay man], as he journeyed, came to where he was, and when he saw him, he had compassion. He went to him and bound up his wounds, pouring on oil and wine. Then he set him on his own animal and brought him to an inn and took care of him. And the next day he took out two denarii and gave them to the innkeeper, saying, 'Take care of him, and whatever more you spend, I will repay you when I come back.' Which of these three, do you think, proved to be a neighbor to the man who fell among the robbers?" He said, "The one who showed him mercy." And Jesus said to him, "You go, and do likewise." (Luke 10:30-37, ESV)

A woman has had some bad experiences in dating men and so she has been finding solace in lesbian pornography. She hopes Jesus will tell her that he understands why she's doing what she's doing.

You have heard that it was said, "You shall not commit adultery." But I say to you that everyone who looks at a woman with lustful intent has already committed adultery with her in his heart. If your right eye causes you to sin, tear it out and throw it away. For it is better that you lose one of your members than that your whole body be thrown into hell. (Matthew 5:27-29, ESV)

A man doesn't like the gay agenda that seems to be taking over city hall. He believes there should be laws *against* the LGBT community, not laws protecting them. There are some sodomy laws on the books that have never been repealed, so he brings his Bible to the city council to prove his point and call on the council to enforce the laws.

"Let him who is without sin among you be the first to throw a stone. (John 8:7, ESV)

A young man had been struggling for a long-time with his sexual identity and had some same-sex encounters. When he finally came out to his church-going parents, they were at first puzzled and dismayed, but then began to rail against him every chance they could. He was struggling under a burden of shame.

Neither do I condemn you; go, and from now on sin no more. (John 8:11, ESV)

A man has been having an affair, but he thinks he's justified in it because his wife has not been very nice to him, and besides what he's doing is not as sick as what those LGBT people do—right, Lord?

Why do you see the speck that is in your brother's eye, but do not notice the log that is in your own eye? Or how can you say to your brother, "Let me take the speck out of your eye," when there is the log in your own eye? You hypocrite, first take the log out of your own eye, and then you will see clearly to take the speck out of your brother's eye. (Luke 7:3-5, ESV)

A couple is struggling with what to do now that a lesbian couple has moved into their neighborhood with their backyards adjoining. They can see the couple sitting outside in the evening holding hands, and it bothers them. They even think about moving out.

You shall love your neighbor as yourself. (Matthew 22:39, ESV)

It has come to light that one of the church members has left his wife to move in with a gay lover. The board of elders is meeting to figure out how they should respond.

If your brother sins against you, go and tell him his fault, between you and him alone. If he listens to you, you have gained your brother. But if he does not listen, take one or two others along with you, that every charge may be established by the evidence of two or three witnesses. If he refuses to listen to them, tell it to the church. And if he refuses to listen even to the church, let him be to you as a Gentile and a tax collector. Truly, I say to you, whatever you bind on earth shall be bound in heaven, and whatever you loose on earth shall be loosed in heaven. (Matthew 18:15-18, ESV)

A woman wrote a letter to her church board, expressing her disgust that the church would be spending valuable time, money, and energy in a ministry to gay men who were in the hospital because of sexually-transmitted diseases. Certainly there were better causes than helping these people who had hardened their hearts to the Lord.

> **Those who are well have no need of a physician, but those who are sick. I have not come to call the righteous but sinners to repentance. (Luke 5:31-32, ESV)**

A gay college senior thinks the freshmen should be exposed to the fact that gay sex is a good option in life. So in the dorm he actively encourages young men to give same-sex experiences a try. Who knows, they may discover they're actually gay and experience a whole new world of pleasure.

> **Whoever causes one of these little ones who believe in me to sin, it would be better for him to have a great millstone fastened around his neck and to be drowned in the depth of the sea. Woe to the world for temptations to sin! For it is necessary that temptations come, but woe to the one by whom the temptation comes! (Matthew 18:6-7, ESV)**

A racist was feeling pretty smug that his church had established a policy against allowing same-sex marriages in their sanctuary, unlike that church down the street that spent so much time on social issues that he doubted they ever preached the gospel.

> **Woe to you, scribes and Pharisees, hypocrites! For you tithe mint and dill and cumin, and have neglected the weightier matters of the law: justice and mercy and faithfulness. These you ought to have done, without neglecting the others. You blind guides, straining out a gnat and swallowing a camel! (Matthew 23:23-24, ESV)**

A gay man who had been raised in a Bible-believing home realized one lonely night that he had been doing horrible things to and with other men. He was overwhelmed with a sense of guilt and thought the Lord would never take him back. And another man in that city also came to the realization that he had been treating people in the LGBT community as less than human. He had even beaten a gay man badly outside of a bar. He didn't think he could ever be forgiven of such hatred. Both fell despondently to their knees and prayed.

> **Man, your sins are forgiven you. (Luke 5:20, ESV)**

When a son told his parents he was gay, they told him to keep it quiet and they didn't want to hear any more about it. No sense telling anyone else. What would other people in their church and neighborhood think of them, if they knew their son was "one of them"? They had a reputation to maintain.

Woe to you, when all people speak well of you, for so their fathers did to the false prophets. (Luke 6:26, ESV)

A lesbian was spitting angry about the way others talked about LGBT people. She was about ready to blow her stack and call them all a bunch of stupid bigots. She had already participated in some marches where she could let off some steam and chant hateful things toward these morons.

But I say to you who hear, Love your enemies, do good to those who hate you, bless those who curse you, pray for those who abuse you…If you love those who love you, what benefit is that to you? For even sinners love those who love them. (Luke 6:27-28, 32, ESV)

A father was so angry when he found out his son was going to marry another man that he refused to talk to his son, meet his partner, or go to the wedding. He vowed in his head that he'd never speak to that son again.

Be merciful, even as your Father is merciful. (Luke 6:36, ESV)

When the pastor found out that a nearby pastor performed a gay wedding, he said to himself, "And I thought he was a Christian. Too bad he'll be rotting in hell."

Judge not, and you will not be judged; condemn not, and you will not be condemned; forgive, and you will be forgiven. (Luke 6:37, ESV)

A gay man used to be ashamed of his same-sex desires, but the events of the past decade had changed him profoundly. Now he was a gay activist, and his life was defined by this cause. He was living out his true identity.

If anyone would come after me, let him deny himself and take up his cross daily and follow me. For whoever would save his life will lose it, but whoever loses his life for my sake will save it. For what does it profit a man if he gains the whole world and loses or forfeits himself? (Luke 9:23-25, ESV)

An older man can remember a time when America was truly great, and there was none of this nonsense about homosexuality. Men were men and women were women. We need to bring America back to the good old days. And our churches, too.

No one who puts his hand to the plow and looks back is fit for the kingdom of God. (Luke 9:62, ESV)

People on both sides of this issue come to Jesus, wanting him to confirm that they are in the right.

Therefore be careful lest the light in you be darkness. (Luke 11:35, ESV)

There are a number of people on both sides of this issue who know how to talk nicely when they are with people they disagree with. But once they gather with their allies, they mock the other side and make sarcastic remarks about them.

Nothing is covered up that will not be revealed, or hidden that will not be known. Therefore whatever you have said in the dark shall be heard in the light, and what you have whispered in private rooms shall be proclaimed on the housetops. (Luke 12:2-3, ESV)

Some people on both sides of this issue are afraid of what will happen if the other side wins this debate. If the conservatives win, will they try to purge every LGBT person from the church? If the progressives win, will they destroy Western civilization and the institution of marriage?

But I will show you whom you should fear: Fear him who, after the killing of the body, has power to throw you into hell. Yes, I tell you, fear him. (Luke 12:5, NIV)

A church leader who has been very involved in ecumenical matters does not believe the church should ever divide over any issue, much less the LGBT issue. We have to stay together no matter what.

Do you think that I have come to give peace on earth? No, I tell you, but rather division. For from now on in one house there will be five divided, three against two and two against three. They will be divided, father against son and son against father, mother against daughter and daughter against mother, mother-in-law against her daughter-in-law and daughter-in-law against mother-in-law. (Luke 12:51-53, ESV)

A man thinks that AIDS was especially sent by God to punish those involved in same-sex relations. And they deserve their misery.

Do you think that these [gay people] were worse sinners than all the other [people], because they suffered in this way? No, I tell you; but unless you repent, you will all likewise perish. (Luke 13:2-3, ESV)

Both sides in the denomination's battle over LGBT matters were getting weary of the impasse. They both wanted to either leave or have the other group leave—and this was the year to make it happen.

A man had a fig tree planted in his vineyard, and he came seeking fruit on it and found none. And he said to the vinedresser, "Look, for three years now I have come seeking fruit on this fig tree, and I find none. Cut it down. Why should it use up the ground?" And he answered him, "Sir, let it alone this year also, until I dig around it and put on manure. Then if it should bear fruit next year, well and good; but if not, you can cut it down." (Luke 13:6-9, ESV)

A man knew he was not perfect, but he did know he was far more advanced spiritually than that gay neighbor down the street who sometimes attended his church.

Two men went up into the [church] to pray, one a [pillar of the church] and the other a [gay man]. The [first one], standing by himself, prayed thus: "God, I thank you that I am not like other men, extortioners, unjust, adulterers, or even like [that gay man over there]. I fast twice a week; I give tithes of all that I get." But [the man who was gay], standing far off, would not even lift up his eyes to heaven, but beat his breast, saying, "God, be merciful to me, a sinner!" I tell you, this man went down to his house justified, rather than the other. For everyone who exalts himself will be humbled, but the one who humbles himself will be exalted" (Luke 18:10-14).

A man who was gay was becoming increasingly obsessed with sexual encounters. This was what life was about. The rest of the time he spent was just for making enough money so that sexual experiences could happen.

Truly, truly, I say to you, everyone who practices sin is a slave to sin...So if the Son sets you free, you will be free indeed. (John 8:34, 36, ESV)

There was a lot of animosity on the floor of the denominational meet-ing, with each side trying to prove its point about how God views LGBT issues.

By this all people will know that you are my disciples, if you have love for one another. (John 13:35, ESV)

Some in the denomination were contending that the church must be one, even if there is disagreement about LGBT matters. Others were saying, however, that unity must not come at the expense of truth.

Sanctify them in the truth; your word is truth...I do not ask for these only, but also for those who will believe in me through their word, that they may all be one, just as you, Father, are in me, and I in you, that they also may be in us, so that the world may believe that you have sent me. (John 17:17, 20-21, ESV)

An LGBT activist insisted that all this talk of purity and commandments was just Old Testament legalism, and that we now needed to focus on salvation by grace.

For I tell you, unless your righteousness exceeds that of the scribes and Pharisees, you will never enter the kingdom of heaven. (Matthew 5:20, ESV)

Some in this debate are judging others without ever getting to know or empathize with any of them. Others are saying that any attempt to make a moral call about LGBT behavior, other than giving it the OK, is to wrongly judge others.

Judge not, that you be not judged. (Matthew 7:1, ESV)
Do not judge by appearances, but judge with right judgment. (John 7:24, ESV)

A man who was gay believed that what a person does with his body doesn't matter as long as his heart is in the right place.

What comes out of a person is what defiles him. For from within, out of the heart of man, come evil thoughts, sexual im-morality, theft, murder, adultery, coveting, wickedness, deceit, sensuality, envy, slander, pride, foolishness. All these evil things come from within, and they defile a person. (Mark 7:20-23, ESV)

As you can tell, the verses I matched to various scenarios are shaped by my prior beliefs about LGBT behavior. But if some of them struck you as wrong, you are invited to match up your own verses and scenarios. What I've done is not a definitive thing, but a thought-experiment. I hope you can see that even if Jesus never explicitly addressed the issue of same-sex behavior, his words can still speak into various related situations.

Yet, as we saw at the beginning of this essay, if we believe the entire Bible is inspired by God, we still need to learn from the biblical texts that are not printed in red.

Repentance

L ately I've been hearing conservatives use the word "repentance" more frequently in debates about same-sex issues. I think it's because we're hearing more members of the LGBT community tell us they believe in Jesus, and yet they continue living a same-sex lifestyle. That just doesn't compute for conservatives. It makes us wonder if we're saying too little when we say, "Everyone who calls on the name of the Lord will be saved" (Romans 10:13, ESV), or, "Believe in the Lord Jesus, and you will be saved" (Acts 16:31, ESV). Maybe the idea of repentance can help us spell out what it really means to call on or believe in the Lord.

After all, Jesus began his ministry by combining faith and repentance in his initial message: "The time is fulfilled, and the kingdom of God is at hand; repent and believe in the gospel" (Mark 1:15, ESV). While we might associate the message of repentance with John the Baptist, the gospel writers only mention that once (Matthew 3:2). The primary voice of repentance in the Bible is Jesus himself. He called people to repent (Matthew 4:17) and warned them that if they did not repent, they would perish just like those who had died suddenly in a recent accident or had been put to death at the hands of the Romans (Luke 13:3, 5). In fact, Jesus said that if the people did not repent in response to his message, their fate will be worse on Judgment Day than it will be for the Old Testament cities that were notorious for the wickedness: Nineveh, Tyre, Sidon, and Sodom (Matthew 11:20-24; 12:41; Luke 10:12-13; 11:32). But whenever a sinner does repent, the angels in heaven will throw a big party (Luke 15:7, 10).

And Jesus doesn't quit delivering a message of repentance after he atones for sin on the cross. In the book of Revelation, he speaks to seven churches in Asia Minor and calls five of them to repent or face harsh eternal consequences (Revelation 2:5, 16, 21; 3:3, 19). And as for the unbelieving world, they too face fiery eternal consequences when they refuse to repent (Revelation 9:20-21; 16:9, 11; see Jeremiah 5:3).

So Jesus issued the call to repent, and his disciples followed suit, not only before the cross (Mark 6:12), but also afterward. Peter's first sermon after the outpouring of the Spirit on Pentecost was a call to repent and be baptized (Acts 2:38). He repeated this call in Acts 3:19. Paul also summoned both Jews and non-Jews to repent (Acts 17:30; 26:20). With regards to some Corinthian believers who persisted in their sexual sin, he wrote, "I may have to mourn over many of those who sinned earlier and have not repented of the impurity, sexual immorality, and sensuality that they have practiced" (2 Corinthians 12:21 ESV).

To believe in Jesus, then, definitely involves the need for repentance. But what is repentance? The usual Old Testament verb for repent is the Hebrew word *shuv*, which simply means to turn or turn back. You may have been going in one direction (perhaps away from God and toward sin), but in response to the call to repent, you turn back to God. In the New Testament, the usual Greek verb for repent is *metanoeō*, which means to change one's thinking (*noeō* means "to understand"), and the noun for repentance is *metanoia*.

There are a number of components to repentance. For one thing, when you repent, it changes your *thinking* (this is especially seen in the Greek word for repentance). Some of the very activities, objects, and relationships you once thought so valuable and life-enhancing, you now see as worthless and dangerous; they will be the death of you. And some of the things of God that you despised at one time, you now regard as of infinite worth. This may be what Paul was talking about when he said, "But whatever gain I had, I counted as loss for the sake of Christ. Indeed, I count everything as loss because of the surpassing worth of knowing Christ Jesus my Lord" (Philippians 3:7-8a, ESV).

The *emotional* component of repentance happens when you realize with horror just how much you have been hurting others and offending God. Without using the word "repent," this is what James 4:8-9 is talking about: "Draw near to God, and he will draw near to you. Cleanse your hands, you sinners, and purify your hearts, you double-minded. Be wretched and mourn and weep. Let your laughter be turned to mourning and your joy to gloom" (ESV). Paul also referred to this when he spoke of an incident that happened in the Corinthian church: "I see that that letter grieved you, though only for a while. As it is, I rejoice, not because you were grieved, but because you were grieved into repenting. For you felt a godly grief, so that you suffered no loss through us. For godly grief produces a repentance that leads to salvation without regret, whereas worldly grief produces death" (2 Corinthians 7:8b-10, ESV). This aspect of repentance might seem over-the-top to some, especially those of northern European descent like myself who tend to squelch our emotions. But it's an important component of repentance.

But even though becoming aware of your sin and feeling badly about it are good things, those two things alone don't constitute repentance. Repentance includes an *action* component (and this is especially seen in the

Hebrew word for repentance, which involves turning). You move in a new direction and live out new behaviors. A recent *Christianity Today* gave the moving testimony of a woman who heard the voice of God telling her that her lesbian relationship would be the death of her, and she knew that voice was right. So even though she still dearly loved her partner, she knew she had to move out.[1]

There is no need to set up a sequence of repentance that moves from new thoughts to transformed emotions and then to new actions. Any one of these three elements could happen first (for as is commonly said, you can think your way into new actions, and you can act your way into new thinking). There's no need to set up a flow chart. But all three elements should happen to some degree.

If you're reading this book, you already know that I believe those involved in same-sex behaviors need to repent—to change their thinking about same-sex behaviors, their emotions about it, and their actions. But I would also remind myself—and my conservative allies—that we need to repent as well. Most of the calls to repentance in the Bible, with some notable exceptions, were issued to the people of God, many of whom would probably be regarded as conservatives—the Jews in the Old Testament, the Pharisees in the Gospels, and the church (as especially seen in 2 Corinthians and Revelation). We have abandoned our first love and the works we did at first (Revelation 2:4-5). We have tolerated false teaching about idols and sexual immorality (Revelation 2:14-16, 20-21). We have fallen asleep at the wheel (Revelation 3:2-3). We have been lukewarm and resisted the Lord's discipline (Revelation 3:15-20). And of course, we have not been loving toward those among us, including the LGBT community.

The best way to repent is to fix our eyes on Jesus (Hebrews 12:2). If we look to Jesus, our thoughts will be taken captive to obey him (2 Corinthians 10:5). Our hearts will be drawn to him. And our steps will follow behind him, running the good race.

I know that this essay assumes that same-sex behavior is sinful, and if you do not make that assumption, you will likely resist what I've said. All I can ask is that—no matter where you stand on this issue—you keep your heart open to the new possibilities and open doors that repentance brings into our lives.

---

[1] Jackie Hill Perry, "The Boring Night That Made Me a Christian," *Christianity Today*, 62 (September 2018), 71-72.

Room for all

L ike a number of denominations, mine has two sub-factions that advocate on one side or the other of the divide over same-sex behavior. The progressive group has adopted a name that has a very positive feel to it: Room for All. It makes me think of the old gospel hymn, "There's Room At the Cross for You" and the open arms of Jesus, ready and willing to receive all who call on his name. It's a good name.

And because of the situation, what that group especially has in mind is that there is room in the church for the LGBT community. Their desire for the denomination is that the LGBT community not only be welcomed, but also affirmed and empowered to serve, including in an ordained capacity.

The larger, conservative wing of the church does not want to go in this direction. Some of this wing has aligned itself with a group called The Gospel Alliance, partly because they want to focus on more than the same-sex issue, but also because it's hard to think of a catchy name for a group that doesn't want same-sex behaviors affirmed. It just doesn't sound right to have a group called Room for Many, Room for Some, Room for the Chosen Few, Room for Heterosexuals, or Room for Repentant Sinners. They just don't express as well the wideness of God's mercy.

But even though the name Room for All is rhetorically effective in an age of sound bites, we are still left with the question of what it actually means and if that meaning is true.

For one thing, I'm not really sure the group would actually want to follow the full implications of their name. They use it to imply there's not only room for all of the LGBT community to show up, but also that they will be affirmed in their lifestyle, so that they can continue to engage in same-sex behaviors. But would they feel the same way about white supremacists who show up at church? Would they really want white supremacists to be affirmed in their beliefs and encouraged in what they post on line? Would they advocate for white supremacists to seek ordination as elders, deacons, and ministers of Word and sacrament? Is there room for them, especially to remain as they are?

I'm pretty sure the answer would be, "No" (and I'm glad). But perhaps I've chosen the wrong comparison because a white supremacist is dedi-

cated to *not* having room for all. For them, there's only room for white people. So it would be an unbearable contradiction for Room for All to welcome
and affirm those who only wanted room for some.

But this gives me a clue already as to the inevitable logic Room for All
will have toward conservatives like me. If Room for All were to prevail in
my denomination, would there be room for people like me? After all, according to their way of looking at my position, they should view me as a
heterosexual supremacist (I don't see myself that way, and they might not
call me that, but their positions should tag me with that label). So if they
follow their own logic, Room for All would not want to welcome and affirm
those who only want room for some, such as white and heterosexual supremacists.

Currently, they won't say this because they are in the minority. But if
the day were to come in which they were in the majority (at least in terms
of power and influence), it would not surprise me at all if moves were
slowly made to ensure there was no room for the conservative position on
this issue in the denomination.

Many decades ago our denomination was wrestling with allowing
women to be ordained as ministers of Word and sacrament. When the step
was finally made to allow it, a "conscience clause" was added to the constitution, which created room for those who were against the ordination of
women. No one could any longer block a woman from being ordained, but
neither would anyone be required to endorse it. I personally did not need
this conscience clause because I was favorable toward the ordination of
women, but I knew others believed that Scripture taught otherwise, and the
biblical texts themselves were ambiguous enough to make room for all on
this issue. But years later, when the ordination of women had become more
widespread, complaints were made about the conscience clause as de-
meaning toward women, and it was removed from our constitution. That
seemed to be a pretty good indication of what could happen with regards to
same-sex issues. If Room for All actually prevailed, eventually the conservative position would be officially disallowed.

And if this were to happen, then in a strange twist of history, Room for
All would actually function as a Room for Some group, or even a Room for
Sinners Who Repent of Their Supremacist Ways group. No group can truly
have room for all if they want to stand for anything. There may be a big tent,
but even big tents have outsides to them.

It's possible that Jesus' Parable of the Wedding Banquet is one source
behind the moniker Room for All. In the parable as told in Matthew 22, a
king had invited the usual expected guests to his son's wedding banquet.
But all the invitees gave lame excuses for not being able to come. So the
king opened his doors wide and had his servants go to the highways and

byways to invite all the people who are usually left out of those gala events: the blind, the crippled, the riff-raff. As Robert Capon put it, it didn't matter if they smelled worse than pigs or if they didn't know what hors d'oeuvres are, or if they ate with their fingers and didn't use napkins; the King invited them to the wedding banquet.[1] Rich, poor, old, young, men, women, respected, disreputable, good, bad—there's room for all.

Jesus is a living illustration of that open invitation. He opened his life to all kinds of people. Religious leaders avoided women; Jesus befriended them. Disciples chased away kids; Jesus hugged them. Pharisees shunned crooks and hookers; Jesus ate with them. Jews wouldn't touch the unclean, but Jesus did, and he healed them. Jesus is an open invitation into the presence of God. He invites us all—*good & bad*—to come to him. It's like the old hymn says, "Just as I am, without one plea... O Lamb of God I come; Just as I am poor, wretched blind...Just as I am though tossed about with many a conflict, many a doubt, fightings and fears within, without." God has invited everyone to his "come as you are" party.

But then the parable ends with a twist that is often overlooked (especially since it's not included in Luke's version—Luke 14:16-24). At the banquet, the King meets a man who came as he was (in his grubbies) and who stayed that way. We might feel sorry for him. We figure he had nothing else to wear. But we don't realize that a king would typically issue appropriate garb at the door. The King doesn't blame the man for coming in dirty clothes. But he does blame the man for staying in them. Wedding clothes were issued at the door, but this man must have refused to put them on. So the king asks, "Friend, how did you get in here without a wedding garment?" (Matthew 22:12, ESV). And then the king abruptly has the man bound and cast into the darkness. Jesus ends his parable by saying, "For many are called, but few are chosen" (Matthew 22:14, ESV).

The Lord issues the invitation, "Come as you are," but the full invitation would read, "Come as you are and be changed." There is room for all to enter, and there is room for all to be transformed, but there is no room for the one who refuses transformation. Again, it's like that old hymn, "Just as I Am": "Just as I am Thou wilt receive, wilt welcome, pardon, cleanse, relieve." When we come to Christ as we are, we'll never be the same again. And the transformation is not only one of finding the psychological peace we experience in being welcomed, but also the reality of ongoing moral and spiritual renewal in our hearts and lives.

So even though the conservatives may not be operating under the Room for All name, they still want to issue the gospel invitation to one and all, "come as you are to Jesus Christ and be changed."

---

[1] Robert Capon, *The Parables of Judgment* (Grand Rapids: Eerdmans, 1989), 124-125.

Of course, sometimes such hospitality gets a little awkward. Many years ago, my wife and I had some visitors in our home, and one asked matter-of-factly, "Do you mind if I smoke?" We can't stand the smell of cigarette smoke and we also know it's bad for our lungs. But before we could even respond, they had lit up. At the moment, I suppose we could have raised a fuss about it, but we tried to do the hospitable thing, and found some dish that could serve as an ashtray. It was awkward. I still don't know how I'd do it any differently without being confrontational.

A similar kind of awkwardness can happen when an LGBT person comes to a conservative church that wants to be welcoming to one and all. Things may start off well, but if the LGBT person asks on their first visit, "Do you accept gays and lesbians?" or "Would you perform our same-sex marriage?" or "Can a gay or lesbian be baptized here?"—right away things get tense. Before we even have a chance to build a relationship, we have to declare ourselves. They likely won't come back and probably think that we were not very welcoming or loving. Maybe that saves us all from wasting time, but it's hard to come across as hospitable—with room for all—when the guests demand that we be a certain way before they'll accept hospitality.

Yet that awkward scenario doesn't always happen. The Lord calls all of us Christians to be more diligent and loving in showing hospitality, so there's room for all to come to Jesus and be changed.

Seven texts

There are seven texts in the Bible that specifically address same-sex behaviors. This may not sound like very many to some people, but to me these seven texts sufficiently address the issue. Yet some people today question how relevant these verses are in today's situation. So we need to consider them here.

1. Genesis 18:16-19:29 (especially 19:5)

The story of Sodom from the time of Abraham is the most vivid of the texts about same-sex behaviors. Abraham was chosen by God so that his family would be a blessing to the world by keeping to the way of the Lord in righteousness and justice (Genesis 18:18-19). Sodom did not have that reputation. The Lord tells Abraham, "Because the outcry against Sodom and Gomorrah is great and their sin is very grave, I will go down to see whether they have done altogether according to the outcry that has come to me. And if not, I will know" (Genesis 18:20-21, ESV). Two angelic messengers are sent to investigate, but Abraham knows before the investigation even begins that Sodom will live "down" to its reputation and deserve destruction. But in fulfilling his calling to be a blessing and not a curse to the nations, Abraham attempts to dissuade the Lord from this course of action. As if he were haggling down a price, Abraham pleads with the Lord to be merciful because there may be a few righteous people who live there...50, 45, 40, 30, 20, 10. And the Lord agrees to spare the city if only ten righteous ones are found.

But the angels only find four righteous people (Lot, his wife and two daughters)—and even their righteousness was pretty dubious. Lot was reluctant to flee (Genesis 19:16). Lot's wife looked back (ruefully?) at the destruction of Sodom and dies because of it (Genesis 19:26). Lot's daughters seduced their father by getting him drunk so that they could bear children (Genesis 19:30-38). The righteous ones are still deeply flawed.

But even worse are the citizens of Sodom, especially the men. None of them but Lot offered the angelic visitors hospitality, which was normally an expectation of that day. Instead, the men of Sodom came together after dark, surrounded Lot's home, and demanded that they be given a chance to "know" the two strangers (Genesis 19:4-5). This is not an innocent request for a "meet and greet" time. What they have in mind is a gang homosexual rape of the two strangers. Lot knows this, for he pleads with them not to act so wickedly (Genesis 19:7). And then he makes a horrendous offer: to have his daughters raped instead of his guests, which demonstrates not only how far hosts were expected to go in protecting their guests, but also how little valued women were in that day. The men of Sodom had no interest in Lot's offer and were angry to have Lot talk to them in such a moralistic, judgmental fashion (Genesis 19:9). The angry crowd of men would have gotten their way had it had not been for the quick action of the angels in rescuing Lot and blinding the men of the city.

What can we learn from this narrative?

First, we vividly see here that the wages of sin is death. Much as we don't like to think about this, God stands in opposition to sin. Indeed, the Lord describes himself as "merciful and gracious, slow to anger, and abounding in steadfast love and faithfulness, keeping steadfast love for thousands, forgiving iniquity and transgression and sin" (Exodus 34:6-7a, ESV). But we also need to read the rest of that text, where God reveals himself as one "who will by no means clear the guilty, visiting the iniquity of the fathers on the children and the children's children to the third and fourth generation" (Exodus 34:7b, ESV). The coming of Jesus, of course, adds another layer of grace and mercy, but if a person insists on rejecting the sacrifice of Jesus, the wages of their sin is not canceled.

Second, we learn from this story that it is the calling of God's people to pray for the Lord to show mercy to the wicked. Abraham prayed for the unrighteous people of Sodom, and it is our calling to pray fervently for God to be merciful to those who are evil. The basis for Abraham's prayer was that God would be merciful to Sodom for the sake of the righteous who live there; and the basis for *our* prayer is that God would be merciful to all sinners (including ourselves) for the sake of the one Righteous One who bore their sin on the cross.

Third, we see here the sins for which Sodom was especially condemned. The most horrific of the sins is the attempt to commit a homosexual gang rape. Another facet of this action is the violation of hospitality (which stands in stark contrast to Lot's hospitality and even more in contrast to the hospitality that Abraham showed to God and the two messengers in Genesis 18:10-15). And then beyond this is a more generalized sense that the city did not practice righteousness and justice (as Abraham's descendants are called to do in Genesis 18:19). All of these sins produced victims—one gets the impression that this is not the first time that strangers to the city were treated thus—and it is the outcry of these victims that had risen against the city (Genesis 19:13).

There have been a number of attempts to downplay the role of same-sex sin in this story. Some prefer to focus on the more generalized pattern of injustice in the city. Quite commonly, they will use the elaborate parable of Ezekiel 16 to make their point. In that chapter, the Lord wants Jerusalem to understand how abominable her actions are. She had always regarded herself as pretty good, especially when compared to other sinful nations like the northern kingdom centered in Samaria. To counteract her self-assessment, Ezekiel tells a parable of how God had rescued an abandoned girl (Jerusalem), provided for her, and married her when she grew up. But rather than being grateful, this young woman cheated on her husband, promiscuously throwing herself at every man (nation) that would come by. She was even worse than a prostitute because she paid her customers instead of the other way around. To expose the horror of her sins even further, God declared that she was not only like her sisters—Samaria to the north and Sodom to the south—but even worse. "You not only followed their ways, and acted according to their abominations; within a very little time you were more corrupt than they in all your ways" (Ezekiel 16:47, NRSV). Then the Lord describes what the sin of Sodom was: "This was the guilt of your sister Sodom: she and her daughters had pride, excess of food, and prosperous ease, but did not aid the poor and needy. They were haughty, and did abominable things before me; therefore I removed them when I saw it" (Ezekiel 16:49-50, NRSV).

It's at this point an old dividing line between progressives and conservatives kicks in, with conservatives focusing on sexual sins and progressives focusing on economic sins. Some progressives will read Ezekiel 16 and conclude, "See, we told you that the Sodom story was not really about sex, but about the unjust treatment of the poor." But why should we treat this as an either/or issue? It appears to me that sexual sins and economic sins are often intertwined together. In Colossians 3:5 Paul lists five sins that he believes Christians should put to death in their lives, the first four of which are usually linked to sexual sin: sexual immorality, impurity, passion, and evil desire. And then he ends the list with greed (other sins, chiefly revolving around anger, are added in verse 8). Some may see greed as not quite fitting in the list, but Paul knows that lust and greed have a lot in common. It should surprise no one, then, that the person or culture that gives in to its materialistic desires will also give in to its sexual desires, and vice versa. As Walsh and Keesmaat said, "If the empire is all about economic growth driven by a lifestyle of consumption, then *all* of life becomes a matter of consumption—including our sexual life."[1] Sodom appears to be one of the places where sexual and materialistic consumption fed off each other.

Even Ezekiel would likely agree, for his description of Sodom's sin does not end with verse 49 (concerning pride, prosperity, and oppression of the poor), but also adds verse 50, which includes a reference to the abominable things of Sodom. Sometimes those who wish to downplay the sexual aspect of Sodom's sin only quote verse 49, but the abominable sins mentioned in verse 50 were also a part of Sodom's terrible legacy. Perhaps Ezekiel is trying to say economic oppression is an abomination, but given the biblical story of Sodom, sexual sins are just as likely a part of the deadly mix in the city.

At the end of the day, however, it must be acknowledged that the particular sexual sin described in Sodom is homosexual rape, not consensual same-sex activities between partners who have pledged themselves to be faithful to each other. So if we only had this story to discern the morality of same-sex relations, it would be of limited value in many of our contemporary discussions. I'm assuming that everyone on all sides of the LGBT debate would readily acknowledge that what happened in Sodom is sin.

Still, I think what made Sodom such a symbol of sin and judgment is how its sinfulness was layered with the worst of the worst. Yes, there was evil economic oppression, and then on top of that a horrible failure of hospitality was added. Then the story adds another layer involving rape—violent, non-consensual sex. And then finally, to indicate a further layer of depravity, it depicts the move toward *same-sex* rape. All sin is an abomination to God, but for the Jews, the same-sex activity of this story is highlighted to fill one with a sense of horror.

2. Leviticus 18:22

Of the verses that mention same-sex behavior, very few of them do so in the form of a command. The words about Sodom are in the form of a narrative, for instance. And Paul's words about the matter are part of a description of what happens when people suppress the truth about God.

In Leviticus 18:22, however, we run into a direct command against same-sex activity: "You shall not lie with a male as with a woman; it is an abomination" (NRSV). The command is addressed to men, not women, for it was a patriarchal society. The thought is expressed euphemistically, for laying with a man as with a woman is not about how you sleep in a bed, but the sexual activity you would do in that bed.

---

[1] Brian J. Walsh and Sylva Keesmaat, *Colossians Remixed: Subverting the Empire* (Downers Grove, IL: InterVarsity Press, 2004), 161-162.

The command is found in what is called an apodictic form, that is, in a "do not do *x*" form. There are no particular nuances here about what kind of relationship is forbidden. If God had wanted to include nuances, he could easily have said, "Do not rape another man," or, "Do not molest young boys or slaves," or even, "Do not form long-term commitments of regularly lying with the same man as you would a woman." Rather, the form of the command suggests that all same-sex activities—no matter what the intentions of those involved or who is involved—are forbidden. Why? Nothing is said. We simply take it as God's word that such activities are not fitting for those who belong to God—and not only not fitting, but detestable, or abominable.[2] We are in dangerous territory when we insist that God must answer to us concerning the rightness of his commands, and that if God does not justify his commands in a way that we see fit, we reserve the right to ignore his words.

The command here is so straight-forward that many wonder why this verse alone doesn't settle the debate. Well, as in real estate, it's all about location. If this command were found in the Gospels on the lips of Jesus, or in a letter from Paul or John, there would be little to debate. But this verse is found in what is called the Holiness Code—that part of Leviticus which describes what it means for Israel to be holy as God is holy—and it is contested how this section of Scripture applies to people of the new covenant in Christ.

The first part of Leviticus contains many directions for the nation (and especially the priests) for the proper way to offer sacrifices to God—many of which restore a holy status to defiled individuals, priests, or the nation. Then in chapters 18-20 we find a number of directives for how God's people ought to live. A common refrain is that God's people need to be holy as God is holy: "Be holy, because I, the Lord your God, am holy" (Leviticus 19:2, NIV11; see also 11:45; 20:7, 26; 21:8). But holiness is not self-generated, for it is God who claims to be the one who makes us holy (Leviticus 20:8; see also Leviticus 21:8, 15, 23; 22:9, 32 for how God does the same with regards to the priests).

To get a sense of what we're talking about here, it will be helpful to summarize various commands found in the relevant part of the Holiness Code (Leviticus 18-20):

18:1-5	general summons to obey God and not follow the practices of the nations
18:6-18	commands against incest
18:19	command against sex during menstruation

---

[2] For more on this, see the essay "Abomination" on page 3.

18:20	command against adultery
18:21	command against idolatrous child sacrifice
18:22	command against same-sex behavior
18:23	commands against bestiality
18:24-30	general reminder to obey God and not follow the practices of the nations
19:1-2	a call to be holy as God is holy
19:3	commands to honor parents and the sabbath
19:4	command against idolatry
19:5-8	time limit concerning how long you have to eat a sacrifice
19:9-10	command to help the poor by leaving produce behind during the harvest
19:11	commands against stealing and lying
19:12	command against swearing falsely by God's name
19:13	commands against defrauding or robbing others and not paying wages owed to a worker
19:14	commands against mistreating the disabled
19:15	commands against perverting justice through favoritism
19:16	commands against slander and endangering others
19:17	commands against hating others and for rebuking a sinner
19:18	commands against revenge and for loving others as one's self
19:19	general call to obey commands and the commands about not mixing things together: animal breeding, seed planting, making clothes
19:20-22	punishment for having sex with a slave girl betrothed to another
19:23-25	commands about how to long to wait before harvesting from a fruit tree
19:26	commands against eating meat with blood in it and practicing divination
19:27-28	commands forbidding certain haircuts, cutting skin, and tattoos
19:29	command against hiring one's daughter out as a prostitute
19:30	commands to honor the sabbath and the tabernacle
19:31	command against consulting mediums and spiritists
19:32	command to show respect to the elderly
19:33-34	command to love the alien and stranger as yourself
19:35-36	commands to use true weights and not false ones
19:37	general command to obey God
20:1-5	punishment for those who burn their children as sacrifices
20:6	punishment for those who consult mediums and spiritists

20:7-8	general call to obey God
20:9	punishment for those who curse their parents
20:10	punishment for those who commit adultery
20:11-12, 14, 17, 19-21	punishment for those who commit incest
20:13	punishment for those engaging in same-sex behaviors
20:15-16	punishment for those who commit bestiality
20:18	punishment for those who have sex during menstruation
20:22-24	general call to obey God and not follow the nations
20:25-26	commands to not eat unclean animals
20:27	punishment for those who are mediums and spiritists

Although all the different types of sins forbidden in these verses are intertwined, it might be helpful to categorize them thus (ranking them in order of the most verses for each type of command):

Commands about sexuality (33 verses)
18:6-20 • 18:22-23 • 19:20-22• 19:29 • 20:10-21

General commands to obey God (20 verses)
18:1-5 • 18:24-30 • 19:1-2 • 19:37 • 20:7-8 • 20:22-24

Commands about idolatry and idolatrous practices (13 verses)
18:21 • 19:4 • 19:26b • 19:27-28 (?) • 19:31 • 20:1-6 • 20:27

Commands about eating (10 verses)
19:5-8 • 19:23-26a • 20:25-26

Commands about the weak, poor, and disabled (6 verses)
19:9-10 • 19:14-15 • 19:33-34

Commands about economic sins (4 verses)
19:11a • 19:13 • 19:35-36

Commands about honoring parents and the elderly (3 verses)
19:3a • 19:32 • 20:9

Commands about the tongue (3 verses)
19:11b-12 • 19:16

Commands about sacred times and places (2 verses)
19:3b • 19:30

Commands about violence, revenge, hatred, and love (2 verses)
19:17-18

Commands about mixing things that are not to be mixed (1 verse)
19:19

I'm fully aware that these are my categories and that other categorizations could also work (and even that categorizing itself may be wrong-headed, for it makes us compartmentalize life). Some of the commands could possibly belong to more than one category. For instance, commands about parents might also be designed to protect them in the weakness of their old age. Commands about the poor could also be grouped with commands about economic sins. And many of the categories (such as sexual behavior, mixing items, and eating) may be related to the commands about idolatry. An over-arching theme seems to be that the sins listed were practiced by the nations and that God's people need to live differently.

There is a great temptation on the part of Christians to try to make distinctions between moral and ritual commands, with the former still in force for Christians and the latter not so. Maybe a better way forward would be to look at which laws were definitely transformed and/or somehow abrogated by the coming of Jesus, and which ones seemed to still be in force in the teachings of Jesus and the apostles.

The commands that seem to still be in force after the coming of Jesus would be: general commands about obeying God, turning from idols, honoring parents, caring for the weak, avoiding economic sins, taming the tongue, loving others, and not seeking revenge. Other commands, however, seemed to have been abrogated in some way (dietary commands) or unmentioned (such as tattoos, mixing clothes, cross-breeding cattle, sabbath observance, etc.). And one command, about eating meat with blood in it, was regarded as still valid by the early church (see Acts 15:29), but this was never mentioned again in the New Testament.

Actually, in looking through these verses, I had been expecting to find a lot of no-longer-valid commands in the Holiness Code, but I was surprised to see how the bulk of the code is still regarded as valid today. So to those who dismiss the commands about same-sex relations simply because they came from Leviticus' Holiness Code, some new thinking needs to happen. It's just not that easy to toss out the Holiness Code, unless you are prepared to toss out verses that are seen as foundational commands for Christians (like loving your neighbor as yourself).

What is contested, of course, are the laws about sexuality. Of the thirty-three verses with commands about sexuality, twenty are about incest, two about adultery, three about bestiality, four about unusual situations (having sex with a betrothed slave girl and hiring out your daughter to others as a prostitute), two about sex during menstruation, and two about same-sex relations. Except for the last two, we hear no groundswell in the church about overturning any commands about incest, adultery, or bestiality. The command about refraining from sex during menstruation is a source of much speculation. Some see it as yet another example of bigotry against women, while others believe it's somehow wrapped up in ideas about blood and its ability to cleanse as well as make unclean. Although the issue is never raised in the New Testament, it could easily be that the coming of Jesus and his bloody death on the cross forever canceled out all ideas of blood making one unclean.

And so we are left with the commands about same-sex relations being the ones that are the most contested. By themselves, the two Levitical texts may not resolve the issue, but their flat statement of "this is the way it should be," coupled with some New Testament texts, indicate that same-sex relations are not the will of God. We should not want to gut the power of these commands any more than we would want to gut the commands in Leviticus about justice and love.

3. Leviticus 20:13

I won't say much more about this verse since it is also found in the Holiness Code of Leviticus. But we should take note that it is a command framed in a different form. While Leviticus 18:22 is in the apodictic form (do not do *x*), Leviticus 20:13 is in the casuistic form, which follows a general pattern of "If someone does the forbidden act of *x*, then..." Much of Leviticus 20 is couched in this casuistic form (verses 9-18, 20-21)—with the consequence being death in eight of the cases (including same-sex behavior), being cut off from God's people in two cases (20:17-18), and being childless in two cases (20:20-21).

There are some people in the LGBT discussion who worry that if we were to regard the Levitical laws as being valid for God's people today, then we would have to go all the way and also impose the death penalty on those engaging in same-sex relations. I can understand their fears, especially in light of LGBT persecution through the years. That might be true if we were still living in the theocratic kingdom of Israel, but the coming of Jesus has completely transformed the meting out of consequences. Yes, there are some cases in the New Testament of Christians who are so hardened in their sin that they need to be treated like an outsider (see Matthew 18:17; 1 Corinthians 5:5, 13; 2 John 10-11). And we do have a few instances in the

New Testament of God himself imposing a death penalty on a person hardened in their sin (Acts 5:1-11; 1 Corinthians 11:29-30). But our model in how to deal with those who have broken the laws of the Holiness Code is Jesus. When a woman was brought to him caught in the act of adultery, Leviticus 20:10 said both partners must be put to death (unfortunately, as is so often the case, it was the woman who was threatened with the consequences and not the man). But even though Jesus agreed with the Holiness Code that such actions are wrong (Leviticus 18:20), he refused to follow the Holiness Code's way of delivering consequences. Instead he said, "Neither do I condemn you; go, and from now on, sin no more" (John 8:11, ESV). Mercy is the way forward.

4. 1 Corinthians 6:9-20 (especially verses 9-10)

There's no command in these verses about same-sex behavior, but there is a list of the kinds of sinners who will not inherit the kingdom of God.

Paul believed it was necessary to spell this out because some of the new converts in Corinth were not understanding what it meant to follow Jesus. Some were dividing up the body of Christ based on their favorite teachers (1 Corinthians 1), while others were celebrating what they regarded as a freedom to commit incest. Still others were filing lawsuits against fellow believers, participating in idolatrous feasts, overlooking the poor in celebrating the Lord's Supper, boasting about speaking in tongues, and denying the resurrection. It was a mess. And yet, God was at work. So Paul wrote this letter to deal with various errors in theology and practice.

In chapters 5-6 Paul is especially dealing with the problem of sexual immorality in the church: a case of incest in chapter 5 and what appears to be a problem of Christians visiting prostitutes in chapter 6. Paul is not writing about morality in order to fix the world, but in order to keep the church on the right track with the Lord. There's no way they can avoid running into various chronic sinners in their neighborhoods and workplaces (1 Corinthians 5:9-10), but they should not let chronic sin fester in the church: "I am writing to you not to associate with anyone who bears the name of brother if he is guilty of sexual immorality or greed, or is an idolater, reviler, drunkard, or swindler—not even to eat with such a one...Purge the evil person among you." (1 Corinthians 5:11, 13, ESV). This is not intended to be an exhaustive list, but to provide some examples of the kinds of chronic sinners who need to be kept from corrupting the body of Christ.

After a brief aside about the wrongness of suing one another in the early part of chapter 6, Paul returns to matters of sexual immorality and other chronic sins in the remainder of the chapter. The unrighteous will not inherit God's kingdom, he says, and then lists examples of the kinds of people he means, including the sexually immoral, idolaters, adulterers, thieves, greedy people, drunkards, revilers, and robbers (see 1 Corinthians 6:9-10). This list is very similar to the list in chapter 5, but then chapter 6 adds adulterers, thieves, and two words associated with same-sex behaviors. It's these last two terms we will focus on.

The first one is the plural form of the adjective *malakos*, which normally means "soft." It's about the soft ones. Most likely this is a reference to men who are soft, dainty, fancy, and effeminate. The only other uses of this term in the New Testament are the parallel verses of Matthew 11:8 and Luke 7:25, in which Jesus contrasts the desert-hardened John the Baptist with princely types who lounge in soft clothing. The Greek translation of the Old Testament (the Septuagint) only uses *malakos* twice: Proverbs 25:14 speaks of the power of a soft tongue and Proverbs 26:22 says that the words of a knave are soft but harmful. So none of the other uses of this word are evenly remotely related to same-sex behavior. There is general agreement, however, that it refers to the more effeminate male in a same-sex encounter or relationship.

The second term is *arsenokoitēs*. This word is not found in the Old Testament, and the only other usage in the New Testament is 1 Timothy 1:10 (which we'll look at shortly). It's a compound noun formed from *arsēn* (male) and *koitē* (bed). The more common Greek word for man is *anthropos,* which can be also be used to describe humans in general. But when writers want to specify that they are speaking of males in particular, they will use *arsēn*. So, for example, the Greek translation of Gen 1:27 says that God created man (*anthropos*) as both male (*arsēn*) and female. When Jesus quotes this verse in Matthew 19:4 and Mark 10:6, he also uses *arsēn*. *Koitē* often means just bed, but it also can function as a euphemism for sexual relations that happen in the bed. Thus, the compound term literally means, "male-bedder," that is a male who goes to bed with another male for sexual relations. This definition is further reinforced by the fact that when Leviticus 18:22 and 20:13 (the previously considered verses) speak about males having sex with other males, the ancient Greek translation of the Old Testament uses both *arsēn* and *koitē* to say this: "And you shall not sleep with a male (*arsēn*) as in a bed (*koitē*) of a woman" (NETS).

Translators, however, have not always agreed what to do with these two words. The King James version went with "effeminate" and "abusers of themselves with mankind" (which seems like an elaborate euphemism). The NRSV spoke of "male prostitutes" and "sodomites." The original NIV translated them as "male prostitutes" and "homosexual offenders," and the latter term was changed to "practicing homosexuals" in the TNIV revision. The ESV decided to just join the two terms into one phrase, "men who practice homosexuality," and the 2011 NIV revision followed a similar course with "men who have sex with men."

One cannot help but wonder how the current debates over LGBT matters affect these renderings. Translations backed by more conservative causes (such as the NIV and ESV), for instance, are more eager to use terms that would apply to all forms of same-sex behaviors. The downside is that they sacrifice accuracy by mashing the two separate terms together. Also, by choosing the "rapidly-losing-favor" terms "homosexual" and "homosexuality," they risk sounding bigoted. If they were translating today, they might choose "men who engage in same-sex behaviors."

But it's not just the translations backed by conservatives that appear to be skewing their renderings. Translations that have more backing from progressives (like the NRSV) seem to prefer words that could be construed as only applying to specific kinds of same-sex behaviors, such as male prostitutes. Even the word "sodomy" used in the NRSV seems an odd choice for a few reasons. For one, it's on its way toward becoming an archaic term, so that the reader might think it only applies to ancient forms of same-sex behavior and thus has little do to with more contemporary forms. Second, by using this term the translation moves the reader toward thinking about Sodom, and thus they might interpret this verse to mean that only homosexual rapists are condemned here. Third, when the word sodomy is used today, it sometimes denotes anal and oral sex of either heterosexual or homosexual varieties. So for readers who see nothing wrong with anal or oral sex between a man and a woman, they are more likely to see this text as hopelessly outdated.

So even though what Paul meant by "soft" is less-than-clear to us, his second term (men-bedders) is clearly about those who engage in same-sex behaviors. If they persist in this behavior, and harden their hearts in it, says Paul, they cannot enter the kingdom of God. This is issued both as a warning to those who practice such things and as a reminder that the church must be vigilant in not letting this kind of behavior be tolerated and affirmed in the church.

But there are a few more things to glean from this text. First, it is not just same-sex behaviors which create problems for the church and individuals in it. There are other sins here that we so quickly overlook because many regard them as more "normal" (such as adultery) or "socially acceptable" (such as being greedy or slanderous). Another factor is that it's hard for others to tell if some of these sins are being committed or not. We might suspect that another person is greedy or idolatrous, but there's no clear line they have crossed (except perhaps worshiping a statue). Sexual sins, on the other hand, get called out more often because it's easier to tell when a line has been crossed.

But Paul's concern is not that people are barred from God's kingdom because they slandered someone a few times or felt greedy on occasion. I don't think he's even writing off those who occasionally fall into a sexual sin—heterosexual or otherwise. What he's talking about are Christians who persist in a sin, even celebrating that they have the freedom to do so, almost daring others to object (as was happening with the man involved in incest in 1 Corinthians 5).

As for non-Christians doing these things, Paul expresses no interest in getting them to shape up morally. What he wants for them is to come as they are to Jesus, and it is Jesus who will wash, sanctify, and justify them by the power of his Spirit (1 Corinthians 6:11). And this has indeed happened in Corinth, for the church seems to have many people who at one time were indeed sexually immoral, idolaters, adulterers, thieves, greedy people, drunkards, slanderers, and people engaging in same-sex behavior. But they have experienced transformation from the Lord, and Paul is warning them not to return to what they once were.

And this leads to a second gleaning from this text, namely, that Paul does not regard same-sex behaviors as something that express a person's built-in identity. Even if at one time they bore an identity like men-bedder, (or in our day, gay or lesbian), the label does not need to define them for life. It's not who they really are. They can be transformed by the life-giving Spirit of God. I know there are plenty of skeptics about this, but I have seen with my own eyes God doing this transforming work in someone I know well. Many want to say, "The people in the LGBT community just are who they are, and rather than trying to shame them into a failed attempt to change, let's celebrate who God made them to be." But such a statement denies the transforming power of Jesus Christ.

Is change always easy and instantaneous? Hardly ever, but it's real. There will be setbacks and difficulties, but the Lord is there to keep on working in us, as long as we don't give up.

Finally, we should recall that Paul is writing to a permissive culture and a permissive church by reminding them that even if some of the forbidden behaviors were allowed and/or legal, they still would not benefit us, but instead have the great potential of enslaving us (1 Corinthians 6:12). These are wise words for a permissive age.

5.   1 Timothy 1:8-11

As he did in 1 Corinthians 6:9-10 (and also in some of his other letters), Paul here makes another list of the people who are on the wrong track morally. The purpose of the list, however, is slightly different. In 1 Corinthians 6 Paul is addressing the church, especially those who wrongly think their freedom in Christ allows for deviant sexual behavior. Paul warns them that those who do such things cannot enter God's kingdom.

Here Paul is addressing his co-worker, Timothy, but not because Timothy is in danger of slipping into deviant behavior. Rather, he is warning Timothy of an increasingly-popular false teaching. Although we don't know the full nature of this teaching, it involves some kind of speculation about Old Testament genealogies and laws (see 1 Timothy 1:3-7). Later in the letter, Paul reveals that these speculations led to the imposition of laws on the church about avoiding marriage and various foods (see 1 Timothy 4:1-10). Paul would have none of this.

Paul will admit that the law is good, but it has limited value, for it cannot save anyone or make them righteous. That's why the law is not that helpful to those who have been justified by Christ. But its best purpose is that of warning sinners that they are on the wrong track (with the implied hope that they will turn to Jesus for forgiveness and transformation). In 1 Timothy 1:9-11, Paul lists who these people on the wrong track might be. He begins with general evil: the lawless and disobedient, the ungodly and sinful, the unholy and profane. Then he lists some more specific sins, including those who kill or strike their parents, enslavers, liars, perjurers, the sexually immoral and, of particular concern to us, *arsenokoitēs*—the "male-bedders" that were mentioned in 1 Corinthians 6:9.

Again, the translations vary from "sodomites" (NRSV) to the more generic "perverts" of the original NIV to those who practice homosexuality (ESV, NIV 2011 revision).

Because Paul mentions a good aspect of the law here, he implies that the Old Testament laws against men-bedding to still be in force. It is an expression of rebellion against the will of God, and people need to know this.

But Paul is not interested in just railing against bad people, for he will quickly remind us that the good news of Jesus is exactly what "bad people" need. And he knows this from his own personal experience. As he points out in the immediately following verses, Paul himself had been a blasphemer, a persecutor, a violent man, but Jesus still showed him mercy and grace (1 Timothy 1:13-14). And if he, the worst of all sinners, could be forgiven and transformed by Christ, so can everyone else, for "Christ Jesus came into the world to save sinners" (1 Timothy 1:15, ESV).

This is something that conservatives on this issue sometimes forget. Our aim is not to make sure "bad people" are put in their place and that the rest of society agrees with us. Our aim is to offer the good news that Jesus came to save sinners, including those involved in same-sex relations.

6. Jude 7

Like Paul in 1 Timothy, Jude is also vexed by the problem of false teachers misleading the churches. But while Paul was opposing false teachers who tried to impose extra rules and regulations on the believers, Jude is dealing with false teachers who have a message of permissive grace, which allows people to do as they please instead of what pleases the Lord. Jude warns the churches that "certain men whose condemnation was written about long ago have secretly slipped in among you. They are godless men, who change the grace of our God into a license for immorality and deny Jesus Christ our only Sovereign and Lord" (Jude 4, NIV).

In the next paragraph (verses 5-7) Jude provides three examples from the Old Testament of God's judgment on those who rebel. First, he notes that some of the Israelites that God rescued from Egypt did not truly believe and thus were destroyed. Jude's point is that the false teachers of his day similarly appear to have been rescued by God at an earlier time (like the Israelites), but have subsequently proven that they did not really believe, and will thus be judged.

His second example (of those who had been "in" God's kingdom, but are now "out") is provided by the angels who rebelled during the time of Noah. Jude is following a popular understanding of Genesis 6:1-4, which notes that the "sons of God" had sexual relations with the daughters of men. These "sons of God" were widely understood in Jude's day as a reference to angels who had sexual relationships with women and were punished by God with everlasting bondage (see the apocryphal book 1 Enoch 69 for more on this). Jude sees here another example of God punishing those who at one time had been on his side, but had rebelled—in this case through sexual deviancy—and the false teachers seemed to be on that same path.

Picking up on the sexual deviancy aspect of the previous example, Jude ends his trio of examples by pointing out how Sodom and Gomorrah were destroyed for their sexual immorality and perversion. This particular example does not correspond to the false teachers as well as his earlier examples. I say that because unlike the unbelieving Israelites or the angels, the people of Sodom and Gomorrah never even pretended to be on God's side. But there is a correspondence in that both false teachers and the cities of

Sodom and Gomorrah will be punished with eternal fire, and probably both were involved in sexual sin.

The doomed cities were condemned for committing-sexual-sin (all one word in Greek, *ekporneuō*) and going (*aperchomai*) after (*opisō*) other (*heteros*) flesh (*sarx*).

The verb *ekporneuō* is made from the common verb for committing sexual sin (*porneuō*) with the preposition *ek-* (out of or from) as a prefix. The addition of the prefix puts a slight emphasis on going out after sexual sins. *Ekporneuō* is only used here in the New Testament, but it is used 44 times in the Greek translation of the Old Testament for the Hebrew verb *zanah,* meaning to "whore after" either a sexual partner[3] or an idol.[4] Some instances of the verb point to both sexual immorality and idolatry because they often went hand in hand (perhaps with pagan rituals including sexual acts or pagan women leading Israelite men into idolatry).[5] The NRSV and ESV translate this verb as "indulged in sexual immorality" in Jude 7, while the NIV and its revisions go with "gave themselves up to sexual immorality." In any case, the men of Sodom were not merely seduced into sexual immorality, taken in a moment of weakness; they were "out" looking for it.

I have translated the other phrase used to describe the sins of the doomed cities as "going after other flesh," which is the most literal translation. The various English translations render this phase as "pursued unnatural lust" (NRSV), "pursued unnatural desire" (ESV), and "perversion" (NIV and revisions). I suppose these translations were designed to clarify things, but given how the English words "perversion" and "unnatural" have sometimes been flash points in the LGBT debate, they don't seem that helpful (although, to their credit, the footnotes of the NRSV and ESV do provide a more literal translation).

The word "going" (*aperchomai*) is a common word for going or departing (used 117 times in the New Testament), and the word for "after" (*opisō*) is also a fairly common word, often in the sense of following after Jesus. Only occasionally is it used about following after something evil—false prophets (Luke 21:8, Acts 20:30), desires of the flesh (2 Peter 2:10), and Satan (1 Timothy 5:15), also known as the Dragon (Revelation 13:3). The only other time *aperchomai* and *opisō* are used together, as in Jude 7, is Mark 1:20 where the sons of Zebedee follow after Jesus.

The phrase "other flesh" is from two common words, *heteros* and *sarx*. But apart from the context, it would be unclear what Jude meant by it. No

---

[3] See Genesis 38:24; Leviticus 17:7; 21:9; Numbers 25:1; Deuteronomy 22:21; Hosea 1:2
[4] See Exodus 34:15-16; Leviticus 19:29; 20:5-6; Deuteronomy 31:16; Judges 2:17; 8:27, 33; 2 Chronicles 21:11, 13; Hosea 2:5; 4:18; 5:3; Ezekiel 6:9; 16:16-17, 20, 26, 28, 30; 20:30; 23:3, 5, 30, 43.
[5] See Numbers 15:39; Hosea 4:12-13; Jeremiah 3:1

biblical text uses that or an equivalent phrase to describe deviant sex. In fact, in the Greek translation of the Old Testament, *sarx* is used for talking about human frailty, but not human sinfulness (unlike the way that Paul often uses the word).

A possible candidate for the meaning of "other flesh" would be that the men of Sodom were sexually desiring the flesh of angels (whatever the flesh of angels might be). Perhaps Jude is providing a counter-balance to the example in verse 6. While the angels wanted to have sex with women in the time of Noah, the men of Sodom wanted to have sex with angels. But there is no indication from the Genesis stories that the men of Sodom knew that Lot's guests were angels—and in any case, the men of Gomorrah, who were not visited by the angels, would not have been guilty of that desire.

More likely is that the men of Sodom were sexually desiring flesh that was "other" than what they were supposed to desire, namely, being one flesh with their wives. The main weakness here is that we have no other evidence of any such phrases used in the Bible or elsewhere to refer to a man going after the flesh of his wife (or even someone other than his wife). Yet we'd be hard-pressed to find any other meaning here that has something to do with the Sodom story.[6]

Because of the lack of clarity here, this text is not the strongest one for deciding the morality of LGBT behavior, but it does say something. There is a clear sense that it is the *sexual* activities happening in Sodom and Gomorrah that were wrong, and not merely economic injustices or the lack of hospitality. While homosexual gang rape is the specific sin condemned in Genesis 19, it's doubtful that Jude would make use of the story if that's the only form of homosexual sin that he believed was wrong. Rather, Jude believes that the false teachers in his day were preaching a message that gave people a license to commit a variety of sexual sins, for they "defile the flesh" (Jude 8, ESV), "following their own sinful desires" (Jude 16, ESV), and "their own ungodly passions" (Jude 18, ESV), as well as a number of other non-sexual sins, like grumbling, boasting, showing favoritism, and causing divisions.

Because Sodom-like sins here and in 1 Timothy 1 are associated with false teachers, it should not be surprising that conservatives are suspicious of progressives who promote their new perspectives on LGBT behaviors. Conservatives wonder, "Are these progressives like the false teachers who "secretly slipped in...[the] godless men, who change the grace of our God

---

[6] Some have found irony in how the Greek word for "other," *heteros*, is used differently in this text and in today's terminology. Conservatives use *hetero*-sexual to mean God's design for people to have sex with the "other" gender, not the same (*homos*) gender. But Jude condemns the men of Sodom for sexually desiring "other" (*heteros*) flesh, that is, flesh that is other than what they were supposed to desire.

into a license for immorality" (NIV)? We conservatives don't want to think of progressives in this way, but it's difficult to think otherwise.

7. Romans 1:18-3:18 (especially Romans 1:24-27)

Paul writes this letter to properly introduce himself to the church in Rome and to point out that his message is one needed in a church that has experienced some division between Jewish and non-Jewish believers. In Romans 1:1-6 he gives a quick summary of the gospel message and his role in proclaiming it, followed by his standard procedure of greeting and blessing the church, thanking God for them and expressing his desire to visit them (verses 7-15). This is followed by an even shorter summary of the gospel which is offered to the Jews first and then also to the non-Jews.

Then at verse 18 Paul begins the body of his letter, the goal of which is to show how the gospel meets the needs of both Jews and non-Jews. But before he gets to the good news of how Jesus brings this salvation to both parties, he wants them both to realize the predicament they had been in before Jesus came. He begins with the predicament of the non-Jewish world (Romans 1:18-32), followed by the predicament of the Jews (Romans 2:1-3:8), followed by a summary of how both groups and the individuals in them are lost in sin (Romans 3:9-20).

We will focus our attention on the sin-problem of the non-Jewish world in Romans 1:18-32, but always with an awareness that even religious people, chosen by God, face the same sin problem.

According to Romans 1:18, even though God loves a lost and sinful world, he also stands in wrath against that world. Some might think it's unjust for God to respond in this way, for these people did not know about God or his will for their lives. Unlike the Jews, who had received revelation from God, these people were wandering in darkness. How were they to know? But they *did* know, says Paul. They may not have known all the details of what God was like or doing, but they have no excuse because God has revealed enough of himself through creation. God had made the truth of his presence and power plain to anyone who looks at the created world, but in our sinfulness, we suppress that truth (see verses 18-20). We know it, and then, because we don't want to know it, we hide it from ourselves. Knowledge, of course, involves intellectual ability, but the will is also involved. If we don't want to know something—perhaps because it would interfere with the way we want to live—we can figure out ways to not know it. That's what suppressing the truth is all about.[7]

---

[7] For more on the suppression of truth, see R. C. Sproul, *The Psychology of Atheism* (Minneapolis: Bethany Fellowship, Inc., 1974), 56-80.

Because they suppressed the truth about God, refusing to worship or thank him, the most immediate consequence was foolish thinking about God and creation. In their god-less wisdom, they got the two mixed up and began to worship the creation instead of the Creator (see Romans 1:21-23).

So God revealed his wrath against this we-want-to-make-our-own-god world. We might imagine that God would show his wrath by sending natural disasters or plagues or maybe just a general sense of unease in life. Those can, of course, be forms of God's wrath, but here Paul emphasizes a form of wrath we might not expect. He punishes sin by "giving us over" to it. We want to rebel and go our own way? "Fine," says the Lord, "have at it." As C. S. Lewis put it, if we won't say, "Thy will be done" to the Lord, then the Lord says to us, "Thy will be done."[8] We will get the freedom-from-God that we wanted…and we won't like it at all. This is the wrath of God at work. It's often been said how fearful it will be to fall *into* the hands of an angry God, but perhaps what's worse is to fall *out of* the hands of an angry God. The worst punishment for sin is for God to hand us over to even more sin.

Three times in this section we hear the awful refrain, "so God gave them over." And what did he give them over to? First, he gave them over to "the sinful desires of their hearts to sexual impurity for the degrading of their bodies with one another," which is somehow wrapped up in their worship of the creation instead of the Creator (verses 24-25, NIV11).

Secondly, and relatedly, "God gave them over to shameful lusts," which Paul specifies as same-sex behaviors: females exchanging natural relations for unnatural ones, and males burning with lust for other males and committing indecent acts with them. These actions have even further negative paybacks in the future (verses 26-27, NIV11).

And then thirdly, God gave them over to a depraved mind to do lots of other things that should not be done. And here Paul lists a wide variety of sins, ranging from greed and depravity to gossip and boasting, from murder and deceit to disobedience to parents and more (verses 28-31). And even though the wages of these sins is death (Romans 6:23), the people living under God's wrath will continue to do them and approve of others doing them (verse 32). The fact that God gives sinners over to *all* these sins helpfully reminds us that this section of Romans is not just about same-sex behaviors. All sins—even the ones some of us might think are a little more respectable or "normal"—are a consequence of that basic sin of repressing the truth about God.

What can we glean from this text about same-sex relations?

First, this negative assessment of same-sex behaviors does not come to us in the form of a command, such as "thou shalt not engage in same-sex relations." Only the Leviticus texts give us straight-forward commands. But

---

[8] C. S. Lewis, *The Great Divorce* (New York: The Macmillan Company, 1946), 72.

that does not mean the assessment is any less negative, for same-sex sins are highlighted here as a particularly potent example of what happens when God gives us over to sin. The first example of God doing this speaks more generally of God giving us over to sinful desires for sexual impurity in which we degrade our bodies with another. This could easily be about same-sex behaviors, but also other forms of sexual impurity. The last example of God giving us over specifies a multitude of sins. It's the middle example that combines the general and specific, for here God gives idolatrous humanity over to the particular sexual sin of same-sex behavior.

Why would Paul choose to highlight this sin? Paul does not say, but it seems to fit the context of a darkened understanding of Creator and creation. If we foolishly refuse to know the Creator, God gives us over to foolish thinking about the creation as well. One example of this would be the worship of images of people, birds, animals and reptiles (verses 23, 25). Another example of getting things mixed up about creation is that people try to have sexual relations with others of their same sex. But from the very beginning, God created men and women, and he formed them biologically in such a way that they would be able to be fruitful and multiply only with the opposite sex (see Genesis 1:27-28). Does this mean that sex and sexual play is *only* for procreation, and any non-reproductive sexual relations are sinful? No, male and female couples can have sex simply for experiencing intimacy and pleasure, and nothing in Scripture forbids them from engaging in non-reproductive forms of sexual play, such as oral sex. But the key is that God designed our bodies for sexual activity between gender opposites: male with female. To refuse to acknowledge this basic biological reality is to misunderstand creation as well as the God who made it. It's likely, then, that Paul highlights same-sex behavior because it especially points out the kind of foolish thinking about creation that happens when we reject the Creator.

Is it the only sin that expresses this? No. In a sense, all sin shows foolish thinking, not only about God, but also creation. Greed forgets that created beings cannot "have it all." Murder shows that we have forgotten that other people are also created in the image of God. Boasting overlooks the fact that we are totally dependent creatures, not self-made men and women. Those who disobey parents have foolishly rejected the very humans who brought them into this world. Those who abort, abuse the environment, threaten others with nuclear weapons, torture others, live selfishly—these all represent profound misunderstandings of God's creation. And same-sex behaviors do the same.

Another thing to notice here is that this is the only place in Scripture that not only gives a negative assessment of male-to-male sexual relations, but says the same about female-to-female sexual relations. Why is nothing said elsewhere? We don't know. Possibly it is because the Bible is generally written from the perspective of Jewish males, and so the writers were less aware of lesbianism. But Paul's increasing contacts in the non-Jewish world might have made him more aware that this practice was prevalent enough to need mentioning here.

Paul's wording also suggests he's not attempting to make fine distinctions here, nor should we. I say this because a prominent argument for those who view same-sex behaviors more positively is that Paul is only talking about certain kinds of same-sex behaviors, that is, those which are impure, lustful, and indecent—the kinds of sexual behavior done by those who are insatiable, promiscuous predators, often taking advantage of those who are younger or weaker. But Paul says nothing—so goes the argument—about those involved in same-sex behaviors who are pure, chaste, and properly desirous. These would be the kinds of people who are faithful to one partner, and for whom sexual relations are only one aspect of their life together. This line of thinking is often based on the thought that the "nasty" kind of same-sex behaviors were the only kind in the ancient world, while the "faithful" kind of same-sex relationship is a new phenomenon in history. Therefore, whatever Paul says about this only applies to the kind of "nasty" stuff happening in his day. Some writers who hold this position almost make it sound as if the only people Paul is condemning are wealthy, powerful men (like the various Caesars) who misused their position to indulge in all kinds of promiscuous perversions with both men and women.

Others use a different tack and say that the primary form of same-sex behavior in the ancient world were a kind of pederasty in which older men sexually abused boys and young men, more often through persuasion than coercion. Some of these relationships were long-standing, but still they were characterized by a great difference of power and social status between the same-sex partners, with the older and more powerful ones sexually using the weaker ones. For their part, the younger and/or less-powerful ones may have had their own motives for participating in the relationship; it was a way to curry favor with the more powerful partner and thus gain both status and wealth. Again, the idea being proposed is that Paul is only condemning this kind of same-sex behavior, and not what we see today.

There is yet another method that some use to consign Paul's condemnation to a smaller subset of same-sex behavior. This tactic emphasizes the use of "natural" in verses 26-27. The idea is that we should follow our "nature" when it comes to sexuality. So if, by nature, we are heterosexual in orientation, then we should only engage in heterosexual sexual behavior. But if we are gay or lesbian by "nature," then we should follow our nature and only engage in same-sex behaviors (and those who are bi-sexual by nature should be allowed to follow their "nature" too). According to this perspective, then, what Paul is condemning are only heterosexuals who go against their own nature and engage in same-sex behaviors. Conservatives see two main problems with this approach: (1) It assumes that one's sexual orientation is completely given from birth, which is precisely the assumption that most conservatives do not accept; and (2) It assumes that Paul understood that he was making a distinction between those who are same-sex in orientation by nature and those heterosexuals who indulge in same-sex behavior by perverted choice. Ultimately, if we follow this line of thinking, it forbids nothing because a heterosexual by "nature" involved in same-sex behaviors is really no different from someone who is bi-sexual by "nature."

All of these approaches which aim to limit Paul's words to only a few same-sex behaviors feel very much like special pleading. Maybe my historical imagination is impaired, but it is difficult for me to imagine Paul saying at this point, "Of course, I'm not talking about ordinary people whom God created to be gay or lesbian, and who just want to find a steady, faithful same-sex partner. May they celebrate who God has made them to be." In the end, you either have to decide whether Paul is wrong or right in his assessment. Most progressive Christians would not prefer to say straight-out that Paul was wrong. Much more commonly they would prefer to say that Paul meant well, but his words here do not have the final say because his understanding was limited by his own culture and era. And what about Scripture being inspired by God and our only rule of faith? Well, they might not say so plainly, but progressives seem to think God made sure Paul used words that were ambiguous enough to create space for them to insert their own preferred message.

I frankly fail to see the ambiguity or the space between the words that allow for God's approval of any same-sex behaviors. It's not in his plan for human life. Rather, this sin clearly demonstrates what happens when people want to define reality for themselves instead of submitting to the realty of God and God's creation.

The seven texts, then, show the heart of God concerning same-sex behaviors. He loves the people caught up in these behaviors, but he wants to call them to their true place in his creation and family.

Sides

Whe I'm in a discussion about LGBT issues and attempting to describe what is happening in our denomination, I will often use the word "sides," as in "my 'side' looks at it this way." And I invariably find myself using my fingers to make little quotation marks when I say the word "side."

I do that because I have come to realize that some people totally dislike the use of that term in this discussion. Once, when I was serving on a task force about our ecumenical relationships with denominations that allow for same-sex weddings and pastors, every time I used the word "side," another person on that task force would rebuke me. This person didn't want me to use that word, even though there were obviously two sides (if not more) represented in our small group. I never had an opportunity to explore why this person disliked the word, but I think I can hazard some guesses:

First, to use the term "sides" seems to reinforce our differences. It's not just "you think this and I think that," but "we're both here to represent separate constituencies of people who think like we do. It will be impossible to come to any agreement with you because my loyalty to my side must prevail."

Secondly, and relatedly, the term "sides" makes us forget that ultimately we are on the same side. Generically speaking, we are both humans and we're on this planet together. But more importantly for Christians, we both belong to Jesus Christ. We're not here to work against each other, but with each other for the sake of the Lord's work in this world.

Thirdly, the terms "sides" can easily push us toward hostility and violence. Warfare is usually a matter of one side versus another, a fight to the finish. Even if we try to focus on a less violent versions of "sides," such as found in athletics, we know too well that even athletics can devolve into acts of violence on the football field, the basketball court, or the hockey rink. Even the fans can turn to violence in support of their "side." In a world already full of hostility, do we really need to talk about sides in our theological discussions?

And then fourthly, there's the problem of how the term "sides" tempts us to oversimplify issues, especially in thinking there are only two sides to an issue. We see this constantly happening in American politics, which unlike many European nations with their multitude of political parties, has never gotten beyond a two-party system. Many in the United States, for instance, associate the Republican party today with being pro-life and the Democratic party with advocating for social justice. But what if you want to be both pro-life *and* advocate for social justice, where do you go then? Most people feel forced to choose one side or the other, even though the two concerns are tied together in many ways. The same holds true in the LGBT discussions. If there are only two sides, then it often appears as if you have to back either everything or nothing in the LGBT cause. But what about the person who believes same-sex behavior is not God's will for humanity and yet wants to work against bigotry and injustices shown to the LGBT community? What side is that person on?

So these are some of the problems in looking at the LGBT issue in terms of sides. Yet I think the term "sides" is still needed in order to discuss matters. We cannot make profound differences between us disappear by simply refusing to use the word "sides." Vocabulary alone cannot dissipate the reality of our deep disagreements.

It might be helpful to consider some biblical texts that refer in some way to "sides." The problem is that the Hebrew and Greek words that could be translated as "sides" do not really refer to opposing groups of people (either militarily or otherwise). Sides in the Bible are mostly about the physical sides of: a body (Eve was made from Adam's side), a structure (like the tabernacle) or an item (like the ark of the covenant). Although the body, structure, or item may have opposite sides, these sides are not in opposition to one another, but part of the same thing. A house with only one side on it is no house at all. Perhaps this is an important reminder to us that even while Christians talk about being on different sides of an issue, we are still part of God's temple, the body of Christ—unless we believe that the views of these others mark them off not merely as another side, but as outsiders. But that's a much more serious charge.

The whole notion of "outsiders" can be a dangerous one for believers. Focusing on the distinction between insiders and outsiders leads to unholy forms of exclusivism, which take a sick delight in ostracizing, condemning, rejecting, mocking, or even persecuting those—even other Christians—who are not like us. Yet as much as the outsider/insider mentality can be dangerous, there is no avoiding the fact that such language can be biblical.

Let's consider Colossians 4:5 as an example: "Walk in wisdom toward outsiders" (ESV). Who is Paul regarding as an "outsider"? Obviously for Paul, no one should be regarded as an outsider because of their ethnicity or social class (see Colossians 3:11). The more immediate context suggests that an outsider is anyone on the other side of the door that Paul is praying to be opened, that is, someone who has not yet heard or believed the gospel of Jesus (see Colossians 4:3).

Ultimately, Christ is the dividing line between insider and outsider. People are either in Christ or not. Insiders are holy ones and brothers and sisters in Christ (Colossians 1:2), while outsiders do not belong to the Lord or his family. Insiders have been relocated to the kingdom of God's Son, while outsiders are still enslaved under the authority of darkness (Colossians 1:13). Insiders are reconciled through Christ and remain in the faith, while outsiders remain alienated from Christ (Colossians 1:21). Insiders know the mystery of "Christ in you, the hope of glory" (Colossians 1:26-27), while outsiders do not have Christ within them, nor the hope that he grants. Insiders walk in Christ, rooted, built up, and established in him, while outsiders are captivated by human traditions and elemental-orders (Colossians 2:6-8). Insiders are in Christ to such an extent that they have died with him to sin and have been raised with him to new life, but outsiders are still dead in their sins (Colossians 2:11-14; 3:5-17). Insiders are fully alive, joined to Christ as a body to the head, while outsiders are disconnected from Christ, perhaps living in a flimsy shelter of religiosity (Colossians 2:16-23). Whenever the insider/outsider dynamic is found in this letter, Christ is the dividing line.

Some might conclude from this "outsider" talk that Christianity is just another exclusive religion fostering hatred and bigotry. But they may be overlooking the most important element of the insider/outsider dynamic, namely, that being an "outsider" is not meant to be a permanent condition. Even if many people are outside of Christ, we are not to be smugly content with that situation. Rather, we are called to invite outsiders to enter in.

Every outsider is a potential insider, a "future fellow-believer," as Karl Barth put it,[1] and we eagerly join the Lord in working to see that happen. Some unbelievers might still be offended by this perspective because they don't think of themselves as outsiders who need to be drawn inside; that cannot be helped. Yet this perspective is far better than the insider mentality that wants to keep others out.

In the Old Testament we see that Abraham was chosen to be God's "insider," not so he could hoard God's blessings, but so all the outsider nations of the world could be blessed through him (Genesis 12:2-3). Many Old Testament stories, for example, celebrate the "outsider" who becomes part of God's family and kingdom, including the Canaanite Rahab (Joshua 2), the Moabitess Ruth, the Syrian general Naaman (2 Kings 5), and others.[2] The psalms joyfully anticipate the day when all the "outsider" nations become

---

[1] Karl Barth, *Church Dogmatics* IV.3.2. (Edinburgh: T. & T. Clark, 1962), 495.
[2] For more on this, see F. A. Spina, *The Faith of the Outsider: Exclusion and Inclusion in the Biblical Story* (Grand Rapids: Eerdmans, 2005).

"insiders" (Psalm 86:9). The prophets have the same hope: "I will make you as a light for the nations, that my salvation may reach to the end of the earth" (Isaiah 49:6b, ESV).

When Jesus came, he was especially concerned for outsiders within the nation of Israel: the prostitutes, the tax collectors, the lepers, the prodigals, the lost sheep, the disabled, the women, the children. If people were on the outside, Jesus wanted to invite them in, even if that meant excluding those who had been on the inside before (Luke 13:28-29). And Jesus wanted this invitation extended to the whole world, which is why he charged his disciples to bring all nations into the circle of insiders (Matthew 28:19-20).

Paul, of course, took this commission seriously. He affirmed in 1 Corinthians 9:19-23 that he must do whatever it takes to win all outsiders to Christ. He joined Jesus in preaching "peace to you who were far away and peace to those who were near" (Ephesians 2:17, NIV), for his aim was to present every person complete in Christ (Colossians 1:28).

An undercurrent in our LGBT discussions, which we often do not like to admit to the other side, and probably not even to ourselves, is that both sides are trying to discern whether or not people on the other side of the issue are actually outsiders. Is that gay man who wants to be ordained really a Christian? Is that hot-headed conservative really a believer? We know we're not supposed to judge others in the sense of thinking we have the last word on their eternal destiny, but still we wonder if they're truly a part of the body of Christ, or intruders who have secretly slipped in to the church. On the one hand, intruders posing as conservative Christians might be like the "false believers" of Galatians 2:4 "who slipped in to spy on the freedom we have in Christ Jesus, so that they might enslave us" (Galatians 2:4, ESV). On the other hand, those posing as progressive Christians might be like the sneaky intruders of Jude 4 who "pervert the grace of our God into licentiousness and deny our only Master and Lord, Jesus Christ" (NRSV).

It's easy to suspect that there are imposters in the other side (on the LGBT issue as well as other ones), but both sides should also admit that there may be imposters on their own side as well. But what do we do about the presence of outsiders posing as insiders on "our side" or "their side." Perhaps in very obvious cases of such, we need to expose them (as did Paul and Jude). But often things are not as clear. The church must be watchful for this, but not paranoid. If the suspicion of others becomes our predominant mode of life together, then the church becomes like the body of Christ with an overactive immune system, so vigilant that the body ends up attacking itself. There may be times to root out what is evil in our midst, but mostly we need to follow the wisdom of Jesus' parable of the wheat and the weeds (Matthew 13:24-30, 36-43). While it's true that the devil plants false believers like weeds in a wheat field, sometimes the weeds (false believers) look so much like the wheat that uprooting the weeds is not the solution. As the owner of the field explained to his servants who asked if they should uproot the weeds, "No, lest in gathering the weeds you root up the wheat along with them. Let them both grow together until the harvest," when they would be separated (Matthew 13:29-30, ESV).

Still, if you can't help but wonder whether someone on the other side (or even your own side) is actually an outsider, what should you do (besides trying to suppress your judgmentalism)? Love them, of course. Even in a "worst case" scenario, in which they actually *are* false believers, it would be good to follow Colossians 4:2-3 by walking in wisdom toward outsiders, with speech salted with lots of grace. And we do this because, after all, our hope for outsiders is not that they be shunned or rejected, but that they become insiders.

Of course, our first instinct should not be to think of others in this discussion as outsiders, but as fellow believers in Jesus. There is a great difference between thinking of someone as a false Christian and thinking of them as a Christian who believes false things. Because in reality, all of us are Christians who believe some false things (unless you have happened to reach the point of doctrinal perfection). So if *you* want others to regard you as a Christian, even though you have some wrong beliefs, you should return the favor and regard other professing Christians in the same way (unless they've given you very obvious reasons to think otherwise).

But we are not done looking at other biblical texts that may have something to say about "sides." Some texts refer to sides (at least in English) which have more of a militant feel to them. For instance, the story of David and Goliath refers to literal "sides" as the armies of Israel and Philistia stand on the sides of opposing hills with a valley between them.

In 2 Kings we read of Elisha indirectly anointing General Jehu to purge the northern kingdom of the idolatrous dynasty of Omri and Ahab. In carrying out his mission (with perhaps too much zeal; see Hosea 1), Jehu asks some eunuchs who are in a tower with queen Jezebel if they are on his side. If they are, they should throw the queen out of the tower window; and they do (2 Kings 9:32). In the next chapter Jehu tells some government officials in Samaria that if they are on his side, they should behead seventy sons of Ahab; they also comply (2 Kings 10:6). It's stories like these that make us wary of taking sides in LGBT discussions. We wonder if the winners in the theological battles will show no mercy toward those who are defeated.

Of course, when we are in distress and even under attack, we are glad to know that God is on our side: "The LORD is on my side; I will not fear. What can man do to me? The LORD is on my side as my helper; I shall look in triumph on those who hate me" (Psalm 118:6-7, ESV; the Hebrew does not use a word for side here, but says more simply, "The Lord is with me," as reflected in the NIV). But this good news of God being with us and on our side can quickly turn into thinking that God backs us in all that we do and say, and he stands in opposition to those on the other side.

When we get to thinking like that, we need to remember what happened to Joshua before the battle of Jericho. As he was surveying the sight of the future battle, he saw a man with a drawn sword; so Joshua asked him, "Are you for us, or for our adversaries?" (Joshua 5:13, ESV), in other words, "Who's side are you on?" The man could have answered Joshua in a reassuring way: "Can't you see that it's me, God? Of course, I'm on your side. I'm the God who made all those promises of being your God and loving you with an everlasting love. I will never leave you or forsake you." God could have responded in that way, and often he does (as seen in the promise of Romans 8:28-29 that nothing will separate us from his love).

But God does not give the same reassurance to Joshua. Instead, when asked which side he is on, God answers through his angel representative, "No; but I am the commander of the army of the LORD. Now I have come" (Joshua 5:14, ESV). It's an odd answer because Joshua has not asked a yes or no question. Rather he gave God two options. It's like dishing up ice cream and asking a friend, "Chocolate or vanilla?" only to have them respond, "No." That means they don't want either option you gave them; maybe they wanted strawberry ice cream, or a different dessert entirely. By saying "No" God is rejecting Joshua's question as irrelevant. Joshua had been assuming there were only two sides (the Israelite side and the Canaanite side) and that this Stranger needs to pick one. But God is saying that the real question is not whether God is on our side, but whether we are on God's side. And Joshua understands this immediately, for even though he's a mighty commander, he quickly falls to the ground in worship.

This is important for us to remember in any theological discussion. While each side is tempted to think God is on their side, the real issue is whether or not we are on God's side. God has a will and a way, and we need to line up with that—not only in what we think, but also in how we act. Being doctrinally correct is important, but if your correctness lacks the fruit of the Spirit, you are not being on the Lord's side at all.

But there is one more difficult Old Testament story about being on the Lord's side which seems to undercut what I just said. When Moses was on Mount Sinai, the Lord said he was about to destroy the Israelites because the nation had begun to worship a golden calf at the foot of the sacred mountain. Moses pleaded for God to show mercy. But when Moses himself descended the mountain and saw the idolatry with his own eyes, he said, "'Who is on the LORD's side? Come to me' [again, the Hebrew does not have a word for "side" here, but more literally says, "who is for the Lord?"]. And all the sons of Levi gathered around him. And he said to them, 'Thus says the LORD God of Israel, "Put your sword on your side each of you, and go to and fro from gate to gate throughout the camp, and each of you kill his brother and his companion and his neighbor."' And the sons of Levi did according to the word of Moses" (Exodus 32:26-28, ESV). Notice that Moses is calling people to come to the *Lord's* side, not *his* side. And yet the results of some being on the Lord's side is the death of many on the other side.

I imagine some conservatives out there could read these verses as a justification for acting violently toward LGBT people, whom they would regard as not on the Lord's side. But such a reading fails to see how the coming of Jesus changes things. If there was anyone who was on the Lord's side in terms of thinking and acting, it was Jesus, the Son of God. And yet Jesus did not take up the sword to smite all those who were not on the Lord's side. Instead, Jesus traded places with them on the cross. He was willing to be on the wrong side and bear their punishment, so that they could be relocated to the Lord's side and live in his righteousness. "God made him who had no sin to be sin for us, so that in him we might become the righteousness of God" (2 Corinthians 5:21, NIV11). So even if it's actually true that we are on the Lord's side on a certain issue, that doesn't mean we are called to punish, ostracize, or kill those on the wrong side. Jesus already bore that punishment for them on the cross. Does there remain a future punishment for those who refuse to accept the sacrifice of Jesus on their behalf? I believe the biblical warnings of hell say there will be, but that's a judgment we leave entirely to God. For the present, even those we think are on the wrong side are to be loved.

Now at last I come to what I thought would be the main point of this essay, but it has turned into more of an addendum. That's the issue of what are the main two sides in the LGBT discussion in the church and what do we call those two sides? While there are many sub-issues here that even people on the same side will disagree over, the main issue is this: does God regard *all* same-sex behavior as sin, or are there at least *some* forms of same-sex behavior that God would approve?

I know many people like to simplify the division between those who think same-sex behavior is sinful or those who do not think it's sinful. But that would be an over-simplification because even those Christians who would be very supportive of LGBT concerns would acknowledge that at least some forms of same-sex behavior are sinful (such as orgies, rape, adultery, promiscuity, and same-sex acts with minors). There may be a few grey areas for those who are supportive of LGBT concerns (some may think same-sex behavior is only allowable within same-sex marriage, and others may permit it if the same-sex couple are faithful to each other). But still, every Christian in this discussion would agree that some forms of same-sex behavior would be sinful. So the division is not really over whether same-sex behavior is sinful or not, but whether *all forms* of same-sex behavior are sinful or not.

And what do we call the two sides of this discussion. I wish I had better labels, but I will acquiesce to current lingo which uses the term *progressive* for those who believe some forms of same-sex behavior is God-approved, and *conservative* for those who believe all same-sex behavior is not God's will for human life (another way of saying sinful).

I use these terms under protest. Let me elaborate, but only a little, on the term "progressive," lest I come across as too disrespectful for those who embrace that label. The assumption of that label is that the LGBT cause is one of progress (and in the minds of many, progress is always inevitable). There may be some elements of progress that have already happened. For instance, it's a good thing that we are all learning to be more respectful and kind toward the LGBT community and that important civil rights have been recognized for them. But overall, a society that celebrates same-sex behavior appears to me to be one that is *regressing* instead of *progressing*. While Christian progressives will currently acknowledge that some forms of same-sex behavior are sinful, we have likely opened the door in general society to thinking that no forms of sexual behavior—homosexual or heterosexual—will be regarded as sinful. That's not progress, but a return to something more akin to pagan morality.

But what about the term "conservative," which I use to describe my side in this debate. I really dislike this term. Its intended meaning is that rather than letting moral values get corrupted and rot away, a conservative will be one that conserves those values. Just as the conservation movement of an earlier time tried to help farmers do the kinds of things to make agriculture sustainable into the future, so the conservative tries to help society live out the values that will preserve the good life. While some sectors of society like that word, there is a sizable portion of today's world for whom "conservative" connotes old codgers who think righteousness means stopping people from having fun. I may be very conservative on sexual issues and pro-life issues, but I can't say I'm conservative about many issues of social justice, race, the environment, warfare, or the size of government.

The other common term to describe my "side" is "traditional," but I like that term even less. In the Gospels Jesus always speaks negatively of tradition. He asks the Pharisees, "And why do you break the commandment of God for the sake of your tradition?" (Matthew 15:3, NRSV). A few verses later he declares, "for the sake of your tradition you make void the word of God" (Matthew 15:6, NRSV).

Paul—the only other NT writer to speak of traditions—refers to both good and bad traditions. Good traditions are the relatively new teachings and practices passed down from Jesus through the apostles to the church:

"Maintain the traditions even as I delivered them to you" (1 Corinthians 11:2, ESV); "Stand firm and hold fast to the traditions that you were taught by us" (2 Thessalonians 2:15, NRSV). He even commands the Thessalonians to "keep away from any brother who is walking in idleness and not in accord with the tradition that you received from us," (2 Thessalonians 3:6, ESV). On the negative side, Paul confesses that he had wrongly persecuted Christians because he had been "extremely zealous for the traditions of my fathers" (Galatians 1:14, NIV). This is the kind of zeal which Paul said he now regarded as rubbish in order to know Christ better (Philippians 3:4-8).

Tradition in itself is not the problem, for there is nothing wrong with handing over good teachings and practices to other nations, generations, peoples, and institutions. What is objectionable are those traditions which are merely "human" traditions—devised by people, but treated and enforced as if they came from God.

Colossians 2:8 warns against the "tradition of men," which is nearly the same phrase used by Jesus when he said, "You leave the commandment of God and hold to the tradition of men" (Mk 7:8, ESV). Paul similarly warns of those who promote circumcision, Jewish myths, and human commands (Titus 1:14), and those who preach a man-made gospel (Gal 1:11). What we need is not man-made tradition, but God-given revelation.

That's why if I had to come up with an adjective to describe my "side," it would be "biblical." I don't want to be conservative, traditional, or progressive in my approach to LGBT matters. I want to be biblical. But I'm fully aware that I can't co-opt that term for my side because the other side would regard that as an insult to their position. If you're a progressive and reading this, I hope you'll forgive my bold statement. But I also hope that you have been tempted to want to call your position biblical as well, because isn't that what we truly want—to be biblical in how we live out our faith?

So I follow common practice and refer to my side as the "conservatives" and the other side as the "progressives." But even as we take sides, let's keep looking to Scripture, so that we can learn to be more and more on the Lord's side.

Sinner-friendly churches [1]

Nearly every day my wife and I work on our newspaper's crossword puzzle. Puzzles like these get easier as time goes by, because it doesn't take long to notice that the same clues (and answers) appear again and again. Puzzle-makers keep using these "crossword" words because they have the letters that can be fit easily into a puzzle.

One clue that we see quite often is something like "church subject" or "sermon topic." Before I started doing crosswords, I would have guessed the answer would be grace, Jesus, or Bible. But instead the answer is "sin." In the mind of the crossword puzzle maker, church is a place that focuses primarily on the subject of sin.

It's quite likely that most unchurched people have that same perception of the church. Church is either the place where you go to be spiritually mugged (beaten and robbed of your self-esteem by a speaker who points out all your sins) or else it's a place where you go to join the other hypocrites in talking about how sinful the rest of the world is. In either case, it's all about sin—yours or theirs.

Where does the world get this impression of the church? My own experience indicates that churches today really don't talk about sin very much (with the notable exception of a few media preachers who have their judgmental sound bites trumpeted on television). In the past churches may have been known for moralistic preaching that catalogued all the evil sins of the world, the church, and the soul. But today many preachers carefully tiptoe around any text that might be construed as guilt-producing, and many churches purposely avoid including a confession of sin in the order of worship.

Since the world doesn't want to hear about sin, and the churches are no longer talking about it, you would think that the people of the world would start flocking to church. But it's not working out that way. And that's because not facing up to the truth never works. Both the world and the church seem to be avoiding the plain reality that we are sinners. Even if we don't

---

[1] Based on an editorial entitled "A Sinner-Friendly Church" that I wrote for *The Sunday School Guide,* Vol. 83, May 8, 2005, 17, 30-31. Used by permission.

talk about it, or name it, sin is still the basic human problem. So while it's true that the world doesn't want to hear about sin, the solution is not to avoid the subject, but to talk about it in a new way.

Maybe instead of trying to become welcoming churches, affirming churches, inclusive churches, or seeker-friendly churches, we should instead make it our goal to become sinner-friendly churches. We need to keep the terminology and consciousness of sin in the church, but not so that we can reject sinners, or tolerate sinners. Instead, we talk about sin because we are called to befriend sinners. We want to be sinner-friendly churches, where sinners are befriended by Jesus and his people.

After all, Jesus himself is the model for this kind of ministry. When we read of Jesus' earthly ministry in the Gospels, many people come away with two impressions: First, Jesus laid it on the line when talking about sin and righteousness. He pulled no punches about grudges, lust, divorce, violence, pride, worry, greed, hypocrisy, or doubt. Those who believe the myth of a sin-tolerant Jesus have not read the Gospels recently. But the other strong impression in the Gospels is that this hard-hitting Jesus drew sinners to himself by the crowdfuls. He had a reputation for being a friend of sinners—the very sinners he rebuked in his sermons and conversations. Jesus was able to speak the truth in love, to ruthlessly expose sin in a spirit of gracious forgiveness. Jesus is a sinner-friendly Savior.

We Christians should understand this need to be sinner-friendly, for we ourselves have been on the receiving end of Jesus' sinner-friendly ministry. When we talk about being sinner-friendly, we're not only talking about how we believers need to befriend those sinners out there, for we believers are also sinners. We may be saved by grace, but we are *sinners* saved by grace.

Once when I was candidating at a church looking for a pastor, the opening part of the service was handled by someone else. The order of service indicated that my very first verbal contact with the congregation was to happen right before the confession of sin. So when it was my turn to speak, instead of first giving a brief biography of myself, I said, "Hi, I'm Pastor Dave Landegent, and in order for you to know me, it's important that you know I'm a sinner, a sinner forgiven by Jesus Christ. Let's go to the Lord in confessing our sin together." We can be sinner-friendly congregations because our churches are already filled with sinners who have been befriended by Jesus.

So how does a sinner-friendly church operate? Let me give a few brief suggestions:

1)   Sinner-friendly churches talk freely about sin in both prayers and teaching. It is not offensive to name things for what they are. Sins are not mere mistakes or indiscretions, but thoughts, words, and deeds that go

against God's will for our lives. If we all have a problem with sin, it helps no one to avoid talking about it. Instead, we help each other name what ails us.

2) Sinner-friendly churches talk about sin in the context of grace. Our goal is not to send people on a one-way guilt trip from which they never return. Nor is it our goal to smash self-esteem or humiliate any soul. Instead we talk of sin so that we might experience the Lord's forgiving grace and press on in being changed into the likeness of Jesus.

3) Sinner-friendly churches will continue to love people when they fall, even when they fall so far they don't (yet) feel like getting back up. We don't approve of sinful behavior, but ours is a steadfast love that persists even when others give us reasons to not love them. After all, that's how God loves us.

4) Sinner-friendly churches will try to avoid ranking sins. Although there is an indication in Scripture that some sins are worse than others,[2] most of the time creating a list that ranks sins is unhelpful. That's because we usually stack the deck so that our own sins are on the better end of the scale, while the sins of others get shoved to the worst end. Sinner-friendly churches, however, will treat all sins—gossip and greed, legalism and lesbianism—with the same amount of grace and truth.

5) Sinner-friendly churches will learn to confess their sins to one another and share their struggles with temptation. In most churches it's a safe thing to pray about bodies that are unhealthy, but if it's our spirit that's unhealthy we are afraid to let each other know. However, if we really want to be sinner-friendly, the church should be a place where it's safe to admit your struggles.

May all our churches be given the same label Jesus had: the friend of sinners.

---

[2] For more on this, see the essay "It's no worse than..." on page 137.

Specks and logs

There she sat on the couch, an elderly woman talking about all her pains and aches, with her husband dutifully sitting nearby in silence. She had had a lot of practice giving this recital of agony, although to look at her you wouldn't think that she had a lot of problems. She was known by other church members as a chronic complainer, which is why many people did not like to drop by for a visit.

As we talked, the conversation somehow turned to funerals, and she looked me in the eye and said, "Well, when my time comes, I want you to mention at my funeral that even though I suffered a lot, I never complained." I didn't respond, but inside I was thinking, "What?! You honestly think that you never complain?" And once again I was amazed by our sinful tendency to overlook our own flaws.

Jesus spoke of this tendency in the very vivid imagery of Matthew 7:3-4, "Why do you see the speck that is in your brother's eye, but do not notice the log that is in your own eye? Or how can you say to your brother, 'Let me take the speck out of your eye,' when there is the log in your own eye?" (ESV).

Some of us can remember celebrity preachers who made a name for themselves by their tough talk about sin, only to have it come out that they themselves were involved in plenty of sexual shenanigans. Rank hypocrisy.

Long ago, when I was entering the ministry, a wise person told me that if someone in the church is very vehement in their opposition to a sin, perhaps insisting that you need to preach on it more or wanting someone to be disciplined for it, the odds are pretty good that they themselves have something to hide. That parishioner who wants to hear more sermons about hell just might be beating his wife. That elder who is eager to discipline a church member living with his girlfriend just might be cheating in his workplace.

So what might it mean when conservatives sound the alarm about same-sex behavior? What might at least some of us be hiding?

In some cases it could be that a conservative is frightened by his own same-sex attractions. He is appalled by it and drawn to it at the same time. He hasn't acted on this attraction, but to help ward off this temptation, he rails against the same-sex behavior of others. He is trying to convince himself and others that this just isn't him. After all, look at how he takes up the banner against this sin.

In other cases, it could be that a conservative is tempted by other sexual sins. Again, she hasn't succumbed to them, but she realizes that if the church gives the green light to same-sex sins, it will only crumble her own weak defenses against other sexual sins. She thinks she needs the church to stand strong so that she can stand strong.

Other conservatives may have actually given in to other sexual sins—same-sex and otherwise—and so to appease their own sense of guilt, they have taken up the banner against same-sex behaviors. In their own mind, they are somehow atoning for their own moral failures.

Others who have succumbed may have a different motive for opposing same-sex sins. They think that if they shine the spotlight on the sexual sins of others, their own sexual sins will remain hidden. By deflecting attention elsewhere, they figure they are even less likely to come under suspicion for wrongdoing.

Then there are those conservatives who do not wrestle with sexual sins at all, but they love to go after others who do. By spending so much effort opposing the sexual sins of others, they blind themselves to their own non-sexual sins. This may be one reason why many conservatives get all upset about sexual permissiveness in society and yet fail to notice their own involvement with greed, racism, and social injustice.

And perhaps most common log in the eye of conservatives is a big plank called pride. We are all looking for some way to prove to ourselves (and maybe others) that we are better than they are. We want to be higher in the heavenly pecking order than other people. But focusing on the sexual sins of others quickly turns us into Pharisees who pray, "God, I thank you that I am not like other men—extortionists, addicts, adulterers, or even like that gay man over there" (see Luke 18:11).

So what should our response be when we notice that others are involved in something we regard as sinful?

Well, the gist of Jesus' teaching is not that we come to an implicit agreement with others which would say, "I won't point out the speck in your eyes, if you don't point out the log in mine. Let's just agree to let sleeping logs lie." No, Jesus' goal is not that we let sin do its own thing in our hearts, without any intervention from others.

Instead Jesus would contend that the first step is for us to examine ourselves in the light of Scripture and ask the Holy Spirit to point out the logs and specks in our own eyes. And when we face the awful truth of our sins, then we can seek God's forgiveness offered to us through the blood of Jesus on the cross and call upon God to send his Spirit to transform us.

But we will always have blind spots, so it's important that we invite others to help us bring them to light. Conservatives might learn a lot about themselves if they were to ask the LGBT community what logs they see in our own eyes. How do others perceive us? I would not be surprised if a progressive were to point out some of my flaws after reading this book. Not that we have to agree with every outside assessment, but we need to keep an open heart so we can have open eyes.

Then—after some careful discernment with the help of brothers and sisters in the Lord—then we might have a role to play in helping others find the specks in their eyes. After all, Jesus did conclude this teaching by saying, "First take the log out of your own eye, and then you will see clearly to take the speck out of your brother's eye" (Matthew 7:5, ESV).

We probably should not interpret this too much in a sequential sense because that gives the impression that you can help others remove specks from their eyes only if you have successfully removed all specks and boards from your own eyes. In other words, you would have to be sinless before you can help others with their flaws. But that doesn't appear to be what Jesus is teaching. Rather, there is to be more of a mutual helping in this respect. It's not "you scratch my back and I'll scratch yours," but, "you help me spot my flaws and I'll help you do the same."

But even here, caution is absolutely essential. No one is being given general permission to let others know what their sins are, not even if you have rooted out your own. Besides approaching this with a lot of humility, it's probably best to confront people with their sins only if you have some kind of authority in the church to do this (as elders do) or if you have the kind of relationship in which you know the other person would want your help. Otherwise, your best bet is to keep your mouth shut and pray for them.

In any case, the most important part of Jesus' words is that we be very much aware that the temptation to point out the sins of others is rooted in the sinful lumberyard of our own hearts.

Teachings of the Spirit

We might like to think that Jesus told us everything we need in order to understand and live out the gospel, but he did not. On the last night of his earthly life, he explicitly told his disciples that he had not yet told them all they needed to know. It's found in John 16.

After telling his disciples that he would be going away, they were understandably sad (verse 6). That's when he told them that his departure would actually work to their advantage, for then he would be able to send the Holy Spirit to them (verse 7). He called the Spirit the Paraclete, a notoriously difficult word to translate—as evidenced by the variety found in common English translations: Counselor (original NIV), Advocate (NRSV and NIV 2011), Helper (ESV), and Comforter (KJV). This Spirit will convict the world concerning sin, righteousness, and judgment (verse 8-11).

It's then that Jesus says, "I still have many things to say to you, but you cannot bear them now. When the Spirit of truth comes, he will guide you into all the truth, for he will not speak on his own authority, but whatever he hears he will speak, and he will declare to you the things that are to come. He will glorify me, for he will take what is mine and declare it to you. All that the Father has is mine; therefore I said that he will take what is mine and declare it to you" (John 16:12-15, ESV).

This Spirit of truth will not be an independent operator in this. Rather, the Spirit will only declare what Jesus and the Father want to have declared. It will not be new truth at all, but an expansion upon what Jesus had been saying all along. By saying "all the truth," Jesus is presumably not referring to every true fact about the entirety of the universe, but the fullness of truth about sin, righteousness, and judgment that he had just mentioned. During his earthly life, Jesus himself had not shared all this because the disciples were not ready for it.

This intriguing statement explains why the disciples soon would be teaching things that were not explicitly taught by Jesus. In the Gospel of John, for instance, Jesus himself does not talk about being the Word of God in human flesh, but the Spirit led John to connect the dots and teach about the incarnation of Jesus. Also, the book of Revelation was inspired by the

Spirit to reveal to John more about the Last Days than Jesus had said during his earthly life.

And other things found in the New Testament must also have been taught to the early church by the Spirit of Jesus. We have no record of Jesus explicitly teaching about speaking in tongues, spiritual gifts, eating meat offered to idols, being crucified with him, circumcision, slavery, justification, the church as his body, salvation by grace through faith, and more. And he only gave minimal teaching (bare hints in some cases) on predestination, atonement, resurrection, the future of Israel, church discipline, family life, the new covenant, the role of the law, evil powers, leadership in the church, the Second Coming, how to view the Old Testament and its institutions, the atoning power of blood, the Scriptures, etc. So the Spirit of truth was very busy teaching the early church.

And even after the apostles had died and the canon of Scripture was closed, the church continued to be led by the Spirit to understand more fully the Trinitarian reality of God, as well as more on the person and work of Jesus. So we can be thankful that the Spirit did just what Jesus said—led his church into all truth.

Unfortunately, this wonderful promise also turned into a very large door through which a lot of heresies and odd teachings entered the church. Every false teacher out there, whether they explicitly cited John 16 or not, believed that the Spirit of truth was leading them to teach new ideas not found in the Bible. So the Spirit not only had to reveal truth to the church, but also had to expose lies. This is why, with the exception of the short note to Philemon, every New Testament book deals with the issue of false teaching. In fact, the Christians were commended for not departing from what they had learned from the apostles (see Colossians 2:5-6).

Currently we are in a time of discernment, trying to sort out whether some new ideas about same-sex behavior is new teaching from the Spirit or old lies from the father of lies. Some are saying that just as the Spirit led the church into mission to non-Jews by removing the laws about circumcision, so the Spirit is leading the church into mission to the LGBT community by setting aside biblical texts about same-sex behavior (or at least interpreting them through a new lens)—or so the argument goes.

A number of church members believe that this is now what the Spirit is teaching the church, but the majority of the worldwide church does not. It is true that the Spirit has been teaching things to help the church reach out to the world with the gospel—and in some cases removing unnecessary barriers, like circumcision and food laws. But the Spirit has not removed all barriers. Although the church was called to reach all the idolaters of the Roman Empire, the Spirit did not teach that idolatry was now acceptable. Although the church is called to bring the gospel to all the greedy people of the world, the Spirit does not teach that greed is now good. Although the church is called to proclaim Good News to all the sexually immoral people of the world, the Spirit does not preach that such sins are now acceptable behavior. The same applies to same-sex behavior.

Although some think the Spirit is leading us into new teaching on same-sex behavior, I think, instead, that a good case can be made that the Spirit has already done this. As many have pointed out, Jesus himself never said anything about same-sex behavior. It was one of those many things that he wanted to say to them, because they would soon be preaching in a non-Jewish world that was much more accepting of same-sex behavior. But that didn't make Jesus anxious, for he knew he would be sending the Spirit of truth to lead the disciples in this matter. And the Spirit did just that when he inspired Romans 1:24-27, 1 Corinthians 6:9-20, 1 Timothy 1:8-11, and Jude 7.[1] The Spirit has led us to know things about same-sex behavior that Jesus did not reveal during his earthly ministry. And now it's incumbent upon us to follow where the Spirit has led.

---

[1] For more on these verses, see the essay "Seven texts" on page 211.

Theology

From time to time, a progressive person in the LGBT debate will say, "Why are we spending so much energy on such a minor issue? It's not found much in the Scriptures, and it's more of a minor moral matter than a major theological issue." I suppose someone could have said similar things about that little ritual issue of circumcision in the early church. But I would like to set forth here how this "minor" issue of same-sex behavior actually impacts or is impacted by what we might call "major" theological themes.

I will simply be presenting questions that LGBT issues raise for other areas of theology.

CREATION & HUMANITY:
• **General Revelation**: In what way does God reveal himself in creation in this matter? Through scientific studies of the nature of same-sex behaviors? Through the "creation order" of man and woman? How do we respond if science and Scripture seem to contradict?
• **Humanity in the image of God.** What does being made male and female contribute to our understanding of the image of God? Are there more genders than male and female, and if so what impact do they have on our understanding of the image of God? How do questions of complementarianism and egalitarianism impact the issues of same-sex behaviors?
• **The body and sexuality**. To what extent should anatomical reality determine morality? To what extent is same-sex attraction genetic? Do people have a God-given right to sexual love and intimacy, even those who are same-sex attracted?
• **Creation/nature.** What do the biblical writers mean when they describe a behavior as "against nature"? Is doing "what comes naturally" always a part of God's plan for human life?
• **Creation and fall.** Is same-sex attraction a natural part of creation or a sinful distortion of created reality?
• **Marriage.** What is marriage and what are the goods of marriage? How does marriage reflect God's love for humanity, and can same-sex marriages fit into that understanding?

FALL & SIN

- **Sin.** What is sin and does same-sex behavior qualify as sinful?
- **Comparisons.** Are some sins worse than others? Is injustice worse than same-sex behavior? Are sexual sins worse than other sins?
- **Freedom and responsibility.** To what extent can it be said that we choose to sin? Can we choose to sin and then lose our freedom because of those choices? And what does it mean that we are in bondage to sin and cannot choose otherwise? When we try to explain what caused us to do something morally questionable, are we actually just looking for excuses? To what extent are we responsible for our actions when they were influenced by genetic factors, cultural factors, family factors, negative and positive experiences, moral training and our will?
- **Misery.** Are the miseries experienced by the LGBT community (promiscuity, substance abuse, sexually-transmitted diseases, depression, suicide) due to the fact that sin always brings its own misery, or due to the fact that they have been mistreated as outcasts, or a bit of both? Are these miseries any different than found among the rest of the population? Will these miseries lessen as same-sex behavior becomes regarded as more acceptable in society?

SCRIPTURE

- **Revelation.** Does the Bible include not only the primary gospel message, but also other culturally-conditioned statements that do not bind us? Is the Bible *the* primary resource for Christian ethics, or only *a* resource? To what extent should the Old Testament have a role to play in the LGBT debate?
- **New situations.** Is it really true that same-sex behaviors today are so different from those in the first century that the biblical texts have little bearing on the contemporary situation?
- **Tradition and experience.** To what extent should we be following traditional understandings of Scripture, and to what extent should we look for new truths? What role does experience play in how we interpret the Bible?
- **Interpretation.** Can we say that our differences need not bother us because it's just a matter of biblical interpretation? Are there some interpretative moves that would clearly be out of line?
- **The Holy Spirit.** Since Jesus did say that the Spirit would guide us into all truth, are we at the point that the Spirit is now leading us in a new direction concerning same-sex behaviors? If the Spirit reversed some Old Testament laws, will the Spirit also ever reverse moral teachings found in the

New Testament)? Will the Spirit lead us to call other things clean that were once regarded as unclean?

CHRIST
• **Jesus as prophet.** Is it significant that Jesus said nothing explicit about same-sex behavior? To what extent is the way Jesus dealt with the Old Testament a model for us?
• **Jesus as the friend of sinners.** If Jesus reached out to all kinds of marginalized people (the sick, the lepers, women, children, Samaritans, extortionists, adulterers), how would he have reached out to the LGBT community?

SALVATION
• **Grace.** Does showing grace mean overlooking sin? What is the relationship between God's grace welcoming us as we are and transforming us into someone new? What is more loving and gracious: to affirm people as they are or to call them to repentance and change? Are we tools of God's wrath if we give people over to follow their sinful inclinations? How do we know when we have perverted grace into a license for sin (Jude 4)?
• **Repentance**: What role does repentance play in coming to faith? If a person claims to be trusting in Jesus, but has not repented of anything, what does that faith mean? When we call people to repent and come to Jesus, are we imposing a new kind of legalism on them?
• **Law**: What is the role of biblical law with respect to same-sex behavior?
• **Union with Christ.** If we are primarily defined by who we are in Christ, then how do our other forms of identity (race, family, marital status, gender, profession, interests, etc.) coordinate with or rebel against our identity in Christ?
• **Sanctification**. Since we are righteous in God's sight through justification, how much does Jesus expect his church to actually live in a holy way? What should purity and holiness mean for the believer? Is real transformation toward opposite-sex attraction possible for a person with a long (life-long?) history of same-sex attraction?

CHURCH
• **Always reforming.** How do we know whether the church is reforming according to the spirit of the age or the Spirit of God? When is a change not a good one? Does the Spirit tend to loosen moral standards or tighten them?
• **Past controversies.** How do we distinguish between important controversies and spats that in the future we will realize were frivolous?
• **Unity.** When Jesus prays for the church to be one, does that mean that organizational and bureaucratic unity needs to be maintained? What would

ever warrant leaving a church or denomination (or moving to evict a false faction within the church or denomination)?

• **Trajectories**. Since we do see a trajectory in the New Testament which would eventually undermine slavery and the oppression of women, is there a similar trajectory that will open doors to the full affirmation of the LGBT community?

• **Discipline.** What does church discipline (about any moral issue) look like in today's context? How should it function with regards to same-sex behaviors (assuming that all Christians can agree that some forms of same-sex behaviors are out of bounds)? Were the Reformers wrong to make discipline, but not love, a mark of the true church?

• **Sacraments.** Baptism and communion are open to sinners who come to Jesus, but are they open to people who have sworn to continue in their actions which the majority of the church would regard as sinful, but which they themselves regard as right and good?

• **Leadership.** The church has always ordained sinners (who trust in Jesus) as leaders, but should we ordain those who have sworn to continue in their actions which the majority of the church would regard as sinful, but which they themselves regard as right and good?

MISSION

• **Contextualization.** If we live in a society that increasingly accepts same-sex behavior, do we need to adjust our moral positions in order to gain a hearing for the gospel?

• **Distractions from mission.** Are same-sex issues distracting the church from its true mission or sending us into mission?

And these are just some of the theological issues posed by the same-sex debate. I hope you can see that it's not wrong for the church to spend time and energy on these issues. Please pray that the church finds clarity in the midst of polarity.

Unconditional love [1]

Many products on grocery store shelves have a date stamped on them, often with some warning like, "Do not use this product after *x*." I usually don't bother to check the date on products like mixed nuts or potato chips, because the worst that can happen is that they'll be a little stale. But I do check products like milk and yogurt for the expiration date, because it might not only taste bad if it's too old; it might make me ill. The time period from when the product was made until its expiration date is called the shelf life of a product.

Words and phrases also have a shelf life. Some have a long shelf life. You can use words like hope, joy, and peace year after year and they never sound dated. Other words and phrases, however, have a short shelf-life. They are used by many people for a short period of time, and then they quickly disappear—relics of a bygone era. If you say "far out" or "right on" in a conversation, you quickly date yourself as an old hippie.

What's not so good is when many people continue to use a word as if it has a long shelf-life, but in actuality the word has gone sour long ago. One of the phrases that I think should've gone out of style long ago is the term "unconditional love." It's an extremely popular term, especially among Christians. We often use it as a way to define what God's love is like and how we ought to love one another.

The original impulse behind using this term is a good one. "Unconditional love" was our way of saying that no matter what the conditions of a relationship may be, love will prevail. True love will not set up "if...then" conditions for it to operate, such as, "If you behave, then I'll love you." Unconditional love keeps on loving even if the other person misbehaves.

I want to preserve that meaning for true love, but I think the term "unconditional" is not the best word to describe this kind of love and actually ends up distorting love. What started off as a nice fresh loaf of a word has gotten a little moldy, and it threatens to do more harm than good.

---

[1] Based on an editorial entitled "Unconditional Love," which I wrote for *The Sunday School Guide,* Vol. 85, September 10, 2006, 17, 30-31. Used by permission.

It's risky business putting the concept of "unconditional love" under the microscope. Some may feel like I'm attacking Mom and apple pie, and assume that the only result of such a probe would be a return to a Pharisee's kind of love that must be earned. Yet I think it's important to consider what might be going bad in the concept of unconditional love.

First, there's the problem that "unconditional" is not a biblical term. By itself that does not disqualify it for usage—after all, the term "Trinity" is not found in the Bible either. But the fact that it's not a biblical term should raise some warning flags for us. It may be introducing some philosophical conceptions that truncate the full counsel of God.

For instance, using the word "unconditional" implies for many people that setting conditions in a relationship is automatically not allowed. Supposedly when we love unconditionally then we're not allowed to say, "If you do this, then that will be the consequence." Yet we find in Scripture that terms and conditions are frequently a part of God's relationship with us. His words of promise and warning are loaded with conditions.

When Moses preached in Deuteronomy, he declared, "If you pay attention to these laws and are careful to follow them, then the LORD your God will keep his covenant of love with you..." (Deuteronomy 7:12, NIV11), but "If you ever forget the LORD your God and follow other gods and worship and bow down to them, I testify against you today that you will surely be destroyed" (Deuteronomy 8:19, NIV11). In the prophets we read that if a "nation I warned repents of its evil, then I will relent and not inflict on it the disaster I had planned," but if a nation "does evil in my sight and does not obey me, then I will reconsider the good I had intended to do for it" (Jeremiah 18:8, 10, NIV11).

These conditional statements do not disappear in the New Testament. In the Gospels, for instance, Jesus said that if we do not forgive others, God will not forgive us (Matthew 6:15). If we cause little ones to stumble it would be better if a millstone were hung around our neck and we were cast into the sea (Matthew 18:6). If we are ashamed of Jesus, he will be ashamed of us (Mark 8:38). If we do not believe, we will die in our sins (John 8:24). And if we do not abide in Christ, we will be thrown into the fire (John 15:6).

The epistles continue along this same vein. According to 1 Corinthians 3:17a, "If anyone destroys God's temple, God will destroy him" (ESV). Later Paul adds in 1 Corinthians 16:22, "If anyone does not love the Lord—a curse be on him" (NIV). One of the most dire conditional warnings is found in Hebrews 10:26-27, "If we deliberately keep on sinning after we have received the knowledge of the truth, no sacrifice for sins is left, but only a fearful expectation of judgment and of raging fire that will consume the enemies of God" (NIV11).

These verses don't exactly fit with today's ideas about God's unconditional love. And unfortunately, people are often more committed to their idea of what unconditional love means than they are to the kind of love described in the Bible. Therefore, most people conveniently figure out ways to ignore or re-interpret these verses in ways that ensure "unconditional love" wins out over the biblical love of God.

Another problem with the concept of love being "unconditional" is that it actually makes God's love lose its intensity. Instead of divine love being a passionate commitment that cares very deeply about the condition of our relationship with God, it turns into a bland all-encompassing blanket of approval that is indifferent to what's happening in the relationship. Some, for instance, might think it's unconditional love to say, "Hey, I don't care that you're abusing drugs, I love you anyway." Or "it doesn't matter to me that you're cheating on your spouse, I will love you always." But notice how the phrases, "I don't care" and "it doesn't matter to me" are hiding in those previous examples. Those phrases actually imply indifference, not love.

But if you look in Scripture, you'll find that God cares very deeply about the condition of our relationship with him. Our faith, morality, and theology is not a matter of indifference to God. God would never say, "I don't care if you sin, I love you anyway." Rather, God would say, "I do care if you sin—it hurts me deeply, it angers me terribly—but I love you anyway." Just look at Hosea 11:1-9 for an example of how intensely God cares about the condition of our relationship with him. God moves from deep love to sorrow to frustration and bitter anger, and then in the end, back to love.

Clearly, God cares very much about what is happening in His relationship with his people, and with each of us. God's love is not an "unconditional love" that overlooks the condition of our relationship. But neither is it a "conditional love," with God waiting to decide if he'll love us based on our performance. I think a better word to describe God's love is found frequently in the King James Version, which often refers to the "steadfast love" of the Lord (Psalm 117:2). Maybe at one time, the shelf life of the word "steadfast" had expired, but it could be time for its renewal. Steadfast love is a love that stands through thick and thin. It's a love that presses on in spite of all our sin. Steadfast love is not indifferent to sin, but contends with sin. Steadfast love holds fast like glue when human sin threatens to pull everything apart. Steadfast love is everything good about "unconditional" love without the negative baggage that implies our relationship with God is a matter of indifference to him.

Some will think I'm just quibbling about words (which Paul said not to do in 2 Timothy 2:4), but I think the wholesale adoption of "unconditional" as the preferred way to describe God's love has actually pulled us away from the gospel. If the concept of unconditional love prevails, there's no sense in talking about the need for faith or obedience—why bother with either, if God loves you anyway? If the concept of unconditional love prevails, there's no need to talk about final judgment or hell, because if God loves you no matter what, there's no need for punishment. If God loves you no matter what, there is not even a need for a cross. To say that sins can only be forgiven by the shedding of blood would mean that we have set a condition, which according to the popular understanding is not permitted with unconditional love. Worse yet, the concept of unconditional love removes the drama of salvation. Instead of being amazed at the grace of God shown to sinners, we start to think of God's love as something we're entitled to and that it would be offensive to us if he dared to give us anything else. This wrong approach is evident in the lyrics of "Unconditional Love," a pop song by Donna Summer from the Christian phase of her career: "Give me your unconditional love, the kind of love I deserve." But God's grace is not a deserved love.

In an essay entitled, "Conditional and Unconditional: A Misleading Distinction," Walter Brueggemann writes against those who dismiss the OT emphasis on obedience because it strikes them as a wrongful condition of salvation. He responds thus: "If this relationship [between God and Israel] is indeed one of passionate commitment, as it surely is, it is undoubtedly the case (by way of analogy) that every serious, intense, primary relationship has within it dimensions of conditionality and unconditionality that play in different ways in different circumstances...Of course Israel was to respond in love to the self-giving love of Yahweh. As in any serious relationship of love, the appropriate response to love is to resonate with the will, purpose, desire, hope, and intention of the one who loves...Israel's proper response to Yahweh's inexplicable love is obedience."[2]

This issue is important because some progressives give the impression that God's unconditional love means that God is not that fussy about how people behave, especially how they behave sexually. God might regret some of the things we do, and might even try to change our ways, but ultimately it doesn't matter because God loves us no matter what. At least that's the thinking. But I'm not finding that kind of mood or message in the Bible. It certainly takes the "amazing" out of amazing grace and replaces it with a "what else would you expect" grace. I'd rather talk about the steadfast love of the Lord any day than this negatively-defined term "unconditional love," which smacks more of indifference than passion.

---

[2] Walter Brueggemann, *Theology of the Old Testament: Testimony, Dispute, Advocacy* (Minneapolis: Fortress Press, 1997), 419-21.

Unity

My denomination is on the verge of splitting over the issue of same-sex behavior. The smaller progressive side often appeals to the conservatives to stay together because Jesus prayed for the church to be one as he and the Father were one, so that the world would know that Jesus was sent of the Father (John 17:11, 20-23). Our witness to the world, they insist, will be hurt if we become another group of Christians that cannot learn to live together. Division will undercut our message. It's often thrown in at this point that there are already 33,000 denominations out there, and we should not add to that tragic total.

It's a very emotional appeal and very effective.

While I do not intend to be an apologist for church divisions, we need to look more closely at the unity of the church.

First, the statistical numbers often cited don't mean what we might think they do. That number comes from *The World Christian Encyclopedia*, (edited by David B. Barrett, 2001, Oxford University Press) which has its own way of totaling up numbers. According to this book, world Christianity has six major blocs: Roman Catholics (242 denominations), Orthodox (781 denominations), Anglicans (168 denominations), Protestants (9,000 denominations), Independents (22,000 denominations) and Marginals (1,600 denominations).

Some have wondered, though, how the books counts denominations, especially since they divide the one Roman Catholic Church into 242 denominations. It appears that even when a church is organizationally and doctrinally one, if the churches within that larger church body are part of different nations or use different rites, then they are counted as separate denominations. This inflates the count tremendously. Also, you can't help but notice that over 71% of the "denominations" come from Independents and Marginals. This means that all the independent churches out there (at least the ones they found) get counted as separate denominations. It's also questionable whether the Marginals should count toward the total because this includes groups that most of us would not regard as Christian, including Mormons, Jehovah's Witnesses, Unitarians, Masons, Christian Scientists, some spiritists, and more. So the total of actual organizational denominations is much smaller than 33,000—and many of these groups do talk to one another, work together on many levels, and regard each other as Christians. So there's a lot of unity within the plurality of denominations.[1]

At this point, we should delineate between (1) the types of unity and (2) the bounds of unity.

(1) The **types of unity** could include:

worship unity: a willingness to worship God together
theological unity: a recognition of the basic validity of the theology of other churches, even though there may be different emphases
fellowship unity: a warmth of fellowship and friendship between churches/denominations
confessional unity: a recognition of the validity of the confessions of other churches/denominations
sacramental unity: a recognition of the validity of each other's forms of celebrating the sacrament and a willingness to share in those sacraments together
missional unity: participation in a common mission of service and/or evangelism
organizational unity: a sharing of resources, staff and programming within one organization that follows a set of guidelines
educational unity: joint ventures in curriculum development and seminary training
leadership unity: a recognition of the leaders of other churches/denominations with minimal difficulty involved for leaders moving from one denomination to another
respectful unity: a recognition of others as Christians even though there is a strong disagreement on theological matters

(2) The **bounds of unity** on the other hand indicate the participants in the envisioned unity. These would include:

unity between individual Christians
unity within a local congregation
unity within an area between churches in the same denomination
unity within a denomination

---

[1] This analysis is based on an essay "We Need To Stop Saying That There Are 33,000 Protestant Denominations" written by Scott Eric Alt in his blog for The National Catholic Register. Although the essay is written from the perspective of a Roman Catholic and does chide Protestants for their divisiveness, the writer thinks we need to be more truthful about the statistics.

unity between churches in the same community or area that stand in
the same theological tradition

unity between denominations in the same theological tradition on a national level

unity between denominations in the same theological tradition on a
global level

unity between different denominations in the same community or area

unity between different denominations on a national level

unity between denominations on a global scale

All this unity takes place within amazing levels of diversity with regards to age, race, ethnic group, language, geographic area, social status, and wealth.

Unity across the board in all these respects has never been achieved, although we might look on it as a vision for God's desired future for his church. Of course, when we look far enough into the future—when all God's diverse children are gathered around his throne—about the only types of unity that will still be needed are the unity of worship, theology, and fellowship. Other types of unity will not be needed anymore. There will be no need for missional unity or educational unity for everyone around the throne already knows the Lord (Jeremiah 31:34). When we experience the full reality of God, and not just signs of it, then sacramental unity will not be necessary either. Nor will a unity of leadership or confessions. And while God will always be a God of order, I doubt that there will be anything like a bureaucratic or organizational unity in the new heavens and new earth (at least not in the way we experience it today). But at present, all these one-day-will-be-unneeded forms of unity can serve as pointers to the ultimate unity of God with his people.

My small denomination has a reputation for joining nearly every ecumenical group that comes along. We are eager to acknowledge that other denominations, which have theological perspectives and practices that differ from ours, are nonetheless our brothers and sisters in Christ. So we do fairly well in nearly every denominational category listed above concerning the bounds of unity, with one glaring exception—we do not have unity within our denomination. Our internal denominational disunity has had a long history. Every so often some issue comes up that not only divides us theologically, but threatens to split us organizationally into two denominations. Other than the fact that some churches have left us, we have mostly managed to stay together.

In recent years, however, we have not been managing to stay together very well. With regards to our latest—and long—controversy over same-sex behaviors, it's not so much a case of each side feeling *pretty strongly* about the issue. It's more a case of each side feeling *certain* about the issue.

Conservatives feel that if the denomination officially gives at least some forms of same-sex behavior a stamp of approval, then it would be an act of defiance against God with serious, eternal consequences for many involved in the defiance. Progressives, on the other hand, feel that if the denomination officially takes a stand against all forms of same-sex behavior than it would be like committing a gendered version of racism, a rejection of a whole people group called the LGBT community, which could result in many of them turning away from the gospel of Jesus Christ. The stakes are high for both sides.

But why is my denomination able to tolerate other denominations who have practices with which they do not agree—even on the issue of same-sex relations—but finds it very difficult to tolerate other perspectives on this issue within the denomination?

I think it has something to do with my denomination's emphasis on covenant. Although we know we are part of the worldwide church (and in a vague sense in covenant with them all), we are especially in covenant with each other in our denomination. We have covenanted to be a people in mission together, offering our own unique witness to the gospel of Jesus. Because we are in covenant together within our denomination, we are responsible to and accountable to one another in a way that is not true with other denominations. If those other denominations teach something in error or are involved in a practice that we regard as sinful, we might comment about it, but we mostly let those other groups answer to Jesus. We are not running the whole body of Christ. But we do feel more responsible for what happens in our part of the body. If we are the elbow in the body of Christ, we want to make sure the elbow is working well. We would love to have the whole body be fit and whole, but we really can't deal with the infection in the big-toe denomination, nor can we provide much relief to the sore left-shoulder denomination. We just have to be the best elbow we can be. And right now, we are not being the best elbow we can be because we don't agree on what that should look like—at least with regards to the LGBT community in our midst.

Because of this, many on the conservative end have talked about going our separate ways, while progressives have likened that move to a wrongful divorce. We should not split apart, say the progressives, just because we can't get along. It's understandable why the divorce analogy is used because it conveys well how traumatic a split would be. We're not just efficiently dividing up a business, but painfully rending apart long-established relationships. But there is a sense in which the divorce analogy doesn't work. When the churches in a denomination covenant together, we are not marrying each other. The entire worldwide church is already married to Christ, who functions as the groom. When churches separate from each other, they are not separating from Christ (unless they have renounced their faith altogether). If we wanted to insist on sticking with the marital imagery, then a denominational split would involve the bride splitting into two, which is too odd a thought to be helpful.

We may be on better footing if we stick with the "body of Christ" imagery mentioned above. If we have covenanted together to function as, say, the skin cells on the elbow, then, when we are no longer functioning well together in that capacity, Christ (the Head of the Body) has the prerogative to move us around. We can be separated and grafted on to a different, more fitting, part of the body of Christ. We're still both a part of the body of Christ, but in a new place in that body—unless we have so rejected the Lord that he must amputate us (or, as he says to the churches in Revelation 2:5, remove our lampstand from its place).

Of course, that imagery can be taken in weird directions too (imagine a stomach moved to replace the ear). So how about another image? What if we were to think of each denomination as a group of people who are on an extended mission trip together? When we look at each denomination, we are seeing that the Lord has all kinds of mission trips happening all over the world. In a sense, they are organizationally separate, but in another sense, they are one, for they are all following the one Lord in mission. If we were to view the early church from this perspective, we could think of the Apostle Paul, his co-workers, and the churches associated with him as being on one mission trip, while the Apostle Peter and those associated with him were on another trip. The twelve apostles had twelve mission trips going from the very beginning. There was some coordinating of all this in the beginning when they were small, but it was fairly free-flowing. It wasn't a perfect system; but what is? There was some rivalry, some conflict, and some groups promoting false teaching. Yet part of the one church of Christ, with each group on a different mission trip.

In the early church, some of those mission trip groups would subdivide further, sometimes with some conflict mixed in. Acts 15:36-41, for instance, tells of such an incident involving Paul and Barnabas, who had been together for a number of years and had recently completed what is now called Paul's first missionary journey. But when Paul suggested they return to visit the new churches they had helped start, they got into a squabble over who else to take along on their mission trip. Barnabas wanted to take along John Mark, who had gone on part of the first trip, but then abandoned the mission. Paul did not want to give him another chance. They had a sharp disagreement, selected new mission partners, and went on separate mission trips (Acts 15:39-41). Years later Paul had a change of heart about John Mark and wrote appreciatively of him (2 Timothy 4:11). Although we have no record of Paul explicitly acknowledging it, Barnabas ended up being right about John Mark's potential.

But the thing to notice is that Paul and Barnabas did not sit on the dock and argue for the next twenty to thirty years about who was best qualified to be a mission partner. Nor did they anathematize each other as they went their separate ways, disparaging each other's faith. Nor did they insist on staying together for the sake of the unity of the church, with either Paul or Barnabas having to give in concerning Mark. No, the church remained one even though they had disagreements and went on separate mission trips.

I look at my own denomination's conflict in light of that story. The conservatives and progressives are in conflict over who makes a suitable partner for the mission trip. The progressives want to take along members of the LGBT community, and the conservatives do not think they are qualified for it without further transformation. We have already been arguing on the dock long enough about this. It's time to select new mission partners and get going. Yes, this will disrupt an organizational unity, but I don't look on that as being all that crucial to the overall unity of the church. Both mission trip denominations would still be part of the one church of Jesus Christ.

Some may wonder whether a denomination that goes on a mission trip with a message of full affirmation of same-sex behaviors is still part of the Christian church. In spite of my firm convictions that denominations who do so are wrong, I am not prepared to say that they are not even Christian churches. As long as they still are calling on Jesus to be their Savior, confessing that he died on the cross for their sins and rose from the dead to bring them eternal life (and perhaps some other gospel basics that I don't want to pursue at this point), then I have to acknowledge them as brothers and sisters in Christ. They may be wrong in their convictions, but they are still Christians. Could their message slowly (or quickly) pull them away from the basic gospel of Jesus? I think that's a real possibility—and they may think the same of me. Nonetheless, at this point, I must entrust them to the Lord of the church to keep them in his care—and I hope they will do the same for me.

For the past few centuries my denomination has covenanted together to be accountable to one another within our own denomination's mission trip, but we have reached the point at which the progressives no longer think it's a good thing to be accountable to the conservatives, nor the conservatives to the progressives. We both believe we're hearing God's call to take a certain path with regards to same-sex issues, and it's more important for us both to obey our perception of God's call rather than to obey the men and women with whom we have been in covenant. So I believe it's time for each group to find new mission partners and carry on with our perception of God's call. Conservatives may think the progressives' mission trip will fail, and progressives may think the conservatives' trip will fail. But we don't know. Perhaps both of us will succeed, and someday the conservatives will have a change of heart concerning the progressives' LGBT mission partners (as Paul had a change of heart about John Mark). Because of my certainty about this issue, I doubt it; but I must always remain open to what God has in store. But in the meantime, for the sake of the unity of the church, we need to go on separate mission trips. We'll be connected because we're still both part of the one body of Christ, but we won't be organizationally connected.

I have noticed, however, that while the conservative side of my denomination is more willing to contemplate going in separate directions, the progressives have a greater desire to stay together. I can only guess a number of reasons for this:

(1) Perhaps it's because progressives tend to operate under more of a big tent view of truth. For them, there are many grey areas with regards to truth, and a smaller block of black and white issues. Conservatives, on the other hand, lean toward larger blocks of black and white truths. Progressives, then, are more willing to stay together because they are more tolerant of divergent views. This one confuses me a little, because if the refusal to affirm at least some forms of same-sex behavior is really a kind of gendered racism, as progressives seem to think, then why should they put up with conservatives in this matter? They wouldn't tolerate other overt forms of racism, so why would they want to be with us if we truly are the heterosexual supremacists they think we are?

(2) Perhaps progressives are less willing to separate because they place a higher value on the *accepting* side of love than the conservatives who also value love, but greatly appreciate its *correcting* side (such as found in Proverbs 27:6, "Faithful are the wounds of a friend; profuse are the kisses of an enemy," ESV). Progressives like the warm love of continued fellowship, while conservatives not only value that, but also tough love.

(3) I know that at least some progressives—in my denomination anyway—are more eager to stay together because they actually do value some of what conservatives bring to the table, such as evangelistic zeal. They suspect that if the denomination was just comprised of progressives, some of the Jesus-focus of conservatives would be missed. Conservatives, on the other hand, don't think they'd be missing much if the progressives were to leave—although my guess is that it would be a lot easier for us to become Pharisaical.

(4) Although I'm not sure they would say this aloud (or even to themselves), but it's possible that progressives are more eager to stay together because they think the tides of history are moving in their favor, and if we just manage to hold together long enough, the conservatives will come

around to accepting their approach to same-sex behavior (or at least enough people will come around that the votes will start going their way). They might be right about what the future holds, but conservatives would not see that as a sign of progression, but regression to a pagan past.

(5) The wealthier and more populous part of our denomination (with notable exceptions) is on the more conservative end of the spectrum. So progressives might also want to remain together because, if we separate, financial sustainability is at risk—maybe for us both.

(6) My denomination prides itself on being the oldest evangelical church with a continuous ministry in North America (since 1628). The progressive part of our denomination tends to be located on the eastern end of the United States where it all began, so they have a greater sense of heritage and history than the conservative areas. They see no reason to throw this away over one theological squabble.

Like I said, this is just how I'm perceiving things. And even among the progressives, some reasons may be more cogent for some than others. I have the most sympathy for reason three, but do not see it as sufficient to stay together.

At present, we are still organizationally united, but our current theological division is also fracturing the other kinds of unity we could be living out. We are confessionally united on paper, but our understandings of those confessions are drifting apart. We still have worship and sacramental unity, but since our theological division is somewhat tied to geography, the opportunities for both sides to worship together seldom happen. Our missional unity suffers because we are so focused on our conflict. Leadership unity has also been harmed, as churches on both sides are reluctant to call pastors from the other side. The level of respect and warmth of fellowship is also at a pretty low level. When staying together on an organizational level only seems to be driving us further apart, you have to wonder if organizational unity is really the best way to live into Jesus' prayer for his church to be one.

Who's to blame for all this division? Both sides tend to blame each other. From my perspective, it's a case of the progressives disrupting theological unity, and the conservatives responding by disrupting organizational unity. For me, the bigger problem is that of disrupting theological unity, for organizational unity is not enough of a reason to be on the same mission trip. It's not that theological unity means theological uniformity, for there is plenty of room for different understandings, perspectives, emphases, and nuances. But the theological division over same-sex behavior is not just a changed perspective, but a shockingly stark division. We are no longer weeping with those who weep and rejoicing with those who rejoice. Instead, what one group is celebrating causes the other group to mourn in horror over such defiance of God.

So rather than continuing to beat each other up over the issue of same-sex behavior in order to preserve some kind of organizational unity, I believe it's time to for the two sides in my denomination to drop their direct accountability to each other, find new mission trip partners, carry on with their sense of calling, and submit to Jesus' rule over his church.

Upcoming generations [1]

Some people wonder what will happen to the church in the future if it refuses to flow with the current tidal wave of acceptance of same-sex behaviors. Polls suggest that upcoming generations are no longer disturbed by same-sex relationships, and so, if the church clings to the past on this issue, the upcoming generations will abandon the church at an even more rapid pace than we have seen.

I don't think the church should cave in to this fear. For one thing, I doubt the upcoming generations are as monolithic on this matter as some suggest. My generation at one time was called the Woodstock Generation. Indeed, you can still find a few old hippies around, but most of the Baby Boomers never got into the hippie scene, and even if they did, a lot of them ended up becoming conservatives who take in a steady diet of conservative talk shows.

I can't remember when I first learned that I was a baby-boomer. But I do know that it didn't mean much to me. It just explained why I had 30 other students in my elementary class—a lot of babies were born about the same time.

But then somebody out there suggested that because I'm a baby-boomer, therefore my values and aspirations would be this, that, and the other thing. But this idea (that you can tell what a person will be like by the year they were born) sounded to me as flawed and fatalistic as astrology (which says that you can tell what a person will be like by the month or even day they were born). I was born at the end of March, which astrologers say puts me under the sign of Aries and means that I will be impulsive and hasty. The only trouble is, their assessment is a bunch of baloney. And now the generation-ologists try to do the same by telling me that because I was born under the sign of the Baby-Boom, I will be a big spender and want to buy luxury sports cars—which is just more baloney.

Now I'd be the first to admit that I—along with others born in the same time period,—was shaped by the events of the day when I was growing up. I

---

[1] Partially based on an editorial entitled "Beyond Generation X, Y & Z," which I wrote for *The Sunday School Guide*, Vol. 85, June 10, 2007, 13, 22-24. Used by permission.

was affected by rock and roll, the threat of communism, the assassination of JFK, the race to the moon, and the Vietnam War. But that doesn't at all mean I was affected in the same way as everyone else in my generation. The differences within my baby-boomer generation were already obvious when I was in high school. While some were passing out from drug abuse, others were passing out evangelistic tracts after school. While some were TARS (Teen-Age Republicans), others were fiercely anti-war. While some lost their virginity in middle school, others waited until they were married. We were not all alike (except for the fact that nearly all the boys had long-ish hair).

And yet the generation-ologists keep doing research to put us all in the same basket. It's become big business to study the baby-boomers, the busters, Generation X, the Millennials, Generation Z and who knows what's next. Much of this research is done for the sake of marketing. Businesses want to know what products they need to attract the next generation's dollars. If businesses don't pay attention to the next Big Thing desired by the next generation, then they'll get left behind with all the other obsolete businesses stuck with inventories of horse shoes, 8-track tapes, and Beanie Babies. But I wonder if it's really the case that new generations are asking for new stuff, or if, instead, it's a case of businesses training us to think of ourselves as a new generation, so that it's easier for them to sell us new stuff.

And, of course, the generation-ologists pitch their latest data to the church, too. Wanting to fulfill the promise of Psalm 78:4 ("we will tell the next generation the praiseworthy deeds of the Lord," NIV11), many churches are anxious to avoid being left behind. The baby-boomers supposedly wanted seeker-sensitive worship (which bordered on entertainment). But today's Millennials want something different; after all, being seeker-sensitive is so 80's. And so the church keeps scrambling to keep up with what the newest generation is looking for.

But it's my inclination to step back from this whole mad scramble and ask, "Is it really that helpful to make all these generational categories?" It's true that Paul said he wanted to become all things to all people so he might by all means save some (1 Corinthians 9:22), which implies that he was attuned to cultural differences in presenting the gospel. But isn't there also some wisdom in emphasizing how alike the generations are instead of how different they are?

My heart has always resonated with the proverb, "People are people wherever you go," and I think it's also true that "people are people whenever they were born." For example, no matter what generation someone might belong to, every person wants to be loved. It's been amazing for me to see how when an elderly person gets dumped by a boyfriend or girlfriend, their heartbreak is very similar to what happens when a teenager gets similarly dumped.

Every person, no matter what their generation, struggles with the same temptations. Pride, greed, vengefulness—the external circumstances of the temptations change with technology, but the dynamics of the temptation are the same. Whether they are retirees talking at the coffee shop or young people text-messaging each other, the temptation to gossip is one and the same. Whether it's old men sharing a dirty joke or young lads viewing pornography on YouTube, lust can trip them both up.

I could go on and on. Both old and young need hope, purpose, and truth. They all confront decisions about when to be assertive and when to be passive, how to share in someone else's joy or sorrow, when to speak and when to be silent in witnessing. No matter how "new" each new generation might be portrayed by the media, we all have the same old human heart. But when we forget this, it's not helpful to the Lord's church.

For one thing, by following the emphasis on generational distinctions, the church ends up caving in to the whole consumer mentality of society. As I mentioned earlier, the generational research is fueled by marketing. When we give each new generation a name and a description, we end up telling that generation, "You have a right to demand that churches cater to your unique needs. You shouldn't have to settle for boomer styles or Gen-X services. You need your own style of church." Consumerism wins the day again.

Second, by emphasizing generational distinctions, we end up creating churches that are dominated by a certain age group. Today we see more and more churches that are either mostly old or mostly young, and not as many that have a broad cross-section of ages. The elderly churches miss out on the new ideas, new music, and new energy of the young. The young churches miss out on the ancient wisdom, valuable traditions, and solid hymns of the old. The church has a harder time being the family of God when it's mostly filled with one's peers.

Third, when we emphasize generational distinctions, evangelism quickly becomes indistinguishable from marketing. The lost are no longer treated as individuals with their own unique situations and personalities. Instead, each person becomes just a part of a vast generational herd branded by an X or a Y, and the church only needs to figure out how to best herd them toward the cattle chute of salvation.

Fourth, by stressing generational distinctions, we give people excuses for their bad behavior. Instead of learning to express her emotions in worship, an elderly woman can just say, "Well, in my generation, we just didn't do things like that. You can't teach an old dog new tricks." That elderly person is just using her year of birth to give herself permission to be passionless in praise. On the other end of the age spectrum, a millennial might say,

"Well, our generation just isn't into that absolute truth stuff," and then without even having to think it through, he easily tosses out important theology. If we define ourselves by our generational label, we'll likely miss out on the full counsel of God.

Fifth, all this business (and it is a money-making business) of trying to keep up with the latest generational changes has made the church exceedingly anxious. So many church leaders run from one seminar to another, only to be told that what was working two years ago is now obsolete. Since the Lord is King and Head of the church, we would do better to follow the words of that famous church planter named Paul, "Do not worry about anything," but instead pray (Philippians 4:6, NRSV).

But lastly, and most importantly for the concerns of this book, when the church pays too much attention to generational changes, it's very tempting to change the message so that we sound more appealing. Every generation has ears itching for what they *want* to hear (2 Timothy 4:3). But it's not our job to scratch whatever itches. Rather, we must focus on what every generation's ears *need* to hear, which is the gospel. And when we do that, we will not fear for the future of the church.

Some might say that the church is on the wrong side of history with the LGBT issue. But I can easily people in Paul's day thinking that the church was on the wrong side of history with regards to the Roman Empire. Yet that empire came and went. Meanwhile the church of Jesus continues. With the Lord on the throne, the gates of hell cannot prevail against the church. So there's no need to change the gospel message in order to reach this generation. Since "Jesus Christ is the same yesterday and today and forever" (Hebrews 13:8, NRSV), then we should also heed the very next words in that letter, "Do not be carried away by all kinds of strange teachings" (Hebrews 13:9, NRSV).

Violence

Furious debates over same-sex behaviors were happening during our denomination's 2016 annual meeting. On the floor of meeting, a lot of zingers were being thrown in all directions. When there's a microphone in your face, and you are only given two minutes to say something in a large room full of people you don't know, it's pretty tempting to express yourself harshly on a controversial issue. It's akin to the way people get nasty on social media. To alleviate this somewhat, the denomination arranged for a number of small group meetings in which we'd discuss these matters face-to-face.

It was during one of these meetings that someone knocked on our door and broke the news that someone had killed forty-nine people in a gay nightclub in Orlando, Florida. Just like that, the issue of same-sex behavior was no longer just a theological issue or a debate topic. We could see that the words spoken and the stances taken have real impact on the way people treat each other, and sometimes with deadly impact.

We were all stunned, but what stood out for me was that a pastor whom I really respect began to openly sob. I get teary-eyed just thinking about his response as I'm writing this. It was a cry like Paul talked about in Romans 8:22-23: "We know that the whole creation has been groaning in labor pains until now; and not only the creation, but we ourselves, who have the first fruits of the Spirit, groan inwardly while we wait for adoption, the redemption of our bodies" (ESV). When we see the devastation caused by bigotry and hatred toward the LGBT community, you just have to join creation in groaning over this senseless violence.

We still had another round of debate on the floor ahead of us the next day, and I have to admit I was expecting to hear someone say, "See what happens when conservative views on this prevail? Conservative views are born out of hatred and spawn violence." But no one said anything about the previous day's horrendous event. We all just kept bashing each other about the issue.

That next night, with synod ending the next morning, I felt God telling me that something needed to be said against the violence directed toward the LGBT community. So the next day I brought this resolution to the floor.

No matter what position we as Christians have taken on the moral status of same-sex behavior, we reject all forms of mockery, degrading words and thoughts, economic oppression, abuse, threats, and violence made against members of the LGBTQ+ community, and we call on anyone involved in such behavior to repent and immediately begin walking in obedience to Jesus' command to love.

At first it was ruled out of the order, which was not surprising because the war-weary delegates were ready to go home. But the parliamentarian later told me that he had only glanced at my resolution and thought I was trying to have synod once again declare that same-sex behaviors are sinful. But a progressive delegate must have felt some agreement with my resolution and challenged the chair on the ruling. It was then open for debate.

The first person to speak was a progressive woman who said that the resolution felt like the conservatives had been kicking her down for the past week and now at the last minute (out of guilt?), they were offering her a helping hand to get up. So even though she liked the substance of the resolution, she was going to vote against it. I could understand her feelings. Many conservatives had not been very nice to the progressives or the LGBT community at that meeting. Maybe we did need to sit a little longer and contemplate how the LGBT community experiences our words. And maybe words like ours did contribute to the violence that had shocked the nation that week. But I didn't take her words personally and wrote her a note when I returned home to express that I could understand why she felt the way she did.

The debate did not go on long—it was, after all, nearly the last thing we did before we adjourned—and it did win the support of most of the delegates.

I still believe the words of the resolution. No matter where I stand on the question of God's assessment of same-sex behavior, no one deserves the kind of treatment that many in the LGBT community have experienced. I'm well aware that my positions (many of which are in this book) could be perceived as violent to some people, for it does "push back" (to use a violent term) against many of the ways that the LGBT community views same-sex behavior. I feel badly if anyone feels hurt by my words, but I don't know any other way to express how I see Scripture on this matter. I want the best for the LGBT community, but I'm pretty sure most of them are not liking what I see as the best. Nonetheless, let me repeat myself here.

No matter what position we as Christians have taken on the moral status of same-sex behavior, we reject all forms of mockery, degrading words and thoughts, economic oppression, abuse, threats, and violence made against members of the LGBTQ+ community, and we call on anyone involved in such behavior to repent and immediately begin walking in obedience to Jesus' command to love.

What's the big deal?

C urrently my denomination is involved in ecumenical partnerships with denominations that allow for same-sex marriage and ordination. While chairing a denominational task force that was re-evaluating that partnership, I could tell that some who were more affirming of LGBT behavior were puzzled by those of us who were not. So I said something like this, "Those of us who regard LGBT behavior as sin need to answer the question of why this sin in particular causes us to speak out at our national meetings, initiate disciplinary actions in our regions, and even consider withdrawing from the denomination and some of its ecumenical partnerships."

I would like to attempt to answer that question. I will not, however, be dealing with other important questions such as "Why do I think my interpretation of relevant biblical texts is correct and those of others are wrong?", nor "Why do I think the currently popular explanations for same-sex attraction and behavior are wrong?", nor "Is our denomination's polity adequate for situations like this?" Those issues are for another time. Rather, I want to focus on helping progressives at least understand why this is a "big deal" to me and many others.

First, I want to be clear about what is *not* causing me to consider LGBT issues a "big deal."

1. Some may think I am taking a stand on this because it's a sexual matter and that people like me are uncomfortable with physicality, sexuality, and the body. To support this contention, they might point out the fact that the church often seems to be more eager to discipline sexual sins than any other sins. Why, for instance, is no one disciplined for greed?

While this charge may be accurate for some today, it does not reflect my thinking. The reason that sexual sins seem to be more frequently disciplined is not because they involve sexual organs, but because they are easier to detect than most other sins. It's very difficult to tell with a high degree of certainty whether someone else is greedy, but it's relatively easy to tell (though not fool-proof) if they have committed a sexual sin, especially if there is a record of motel bills, phone texts, videos, or a pregnancy.

I am completely comfortable with physicality, sexuality, and the body—as long as these realities are lived out within the parameters of God's will for human life.

2.   Some may think I am taking a stand on this because I consider LGBT sexual sins as worse than heterosexual sins. To support this contention, they would point out the fact that the church today forgives others sins like adultery and divorce—we allow pastors who have committed adultery to receive calls to other churches, and we baptize, offer communion to, and ordain people who have been divorced. So why can't we offer the same grace to the LGBT community?

While this charge may accurately describe some who might think of themselves as my "allies" in this debate, it does not reflect my thinking. I do not consider same-sex sins to be worse than heterosexual sins.

But the objection that conservatives treat same-sex sins differently from other sins is actually an odd one, because most progressives would still not be satisfied if we actually did treat all sins alike. That's because what they really want to say is that same-sex behaviors are not necessarily sinful at all. And that's a whole different question. If an adulterer thought that I was treating him unfairly and said, "My sin is not worse than yours," we could probably have a helpful conversation about that. But if the adulterer's next line was, "Actually, I don't think adultery is even a sin," we'd have other things to talk about first. There's little reason to talk about whether or not we are dealing equitably with same-sex sins if we don't even have consensus on whether it's a sin at all.

3.   Some may think I am taking my stand because I fear the Other, the one who is different and outside the norm.

I would be fooling myself if I thought I was immune from this fear. Nobody is immune from this fear. This fear may have come into play when the issue first started garnering more attention in the media, but I am well beyond that point. For decades now the media has been introducing me to people who are Other, who are outside the norm. In the last forty years, I have been inundated with information about the LGBT community and introduced to people from it, with the pace of such information picking up rapidly. So none of this is different or outside the norm anymore, because in the greater society (with plenty of small-scale exceptions) I fail to see any sense of normality portrayed anywhere. Ab-normality is the new normality.

Although the labels of "homophobe" and "homophobic" have been thrown my way, I refuse to accept such labels. I am not afraid of the members of the LGBT community, but love them as part of the world so loved by God.

If I have any fear, it's a rightful fear of the Lord, a fear of rebelling against the Lord's will, and a fear for the temporal and eternal consequences of those who have rejected that will. There may be some of my "allies" who also are afraid of losing "Christian-based America." But I know that all was not well in the so-called "Christian America" of an earlier time. The Lord's goal for us is not to make the United States a Christian nation, but to be the church of Christ, standing for God's truth and justice and mercy.

4. Some may think I take my stand because I have a simplistic understanding of sexual identity issues. To support this contention, they would quote Christians who have said something like, "People in the LGBT community are there by choice," to which those favorable toward the LGBT cause respond, "What do you think? That LGBT people just got up one morning and decided to be gay? Who in their right mind would choose something that brought such misery into their lives?"

I must confess that some of my "allies" do have a simplistic understanding of sexual identity issues. And I am trying to understand these issues more and more, as is everyone else.

But I also believe that many of those who disagree with me also have a simplistic view of these matters. Their common mantra seems to be "they were born this way," which strikes me as simplistic and often serves as an excuse for moral irresponsibility. The interaction of freedom, biological determination, inherent tendencies, family of origin experiences, and moral responsibility should not be reduced to such simplistic slogans on either side of this issue. We all have much to learn about these matters, but I do not think any theory about why we are the way we are exempts anyone from submitting to the Word of God.

5. Some may think I take my stand because I am an unloving person who doesn't really understand grace. To support this contention, they would point out how Christians and churches have shunned, shamed, verbally abused, economically oppressed, and even acted violently against the LGBT community. If we were gracious, they say, we would instead recognize how the LGBT community has been sinned against, and that we need to extend our open arms and welcome them into every aspect of the church, bringing peace, reconciliation, and healing.

I recognize with sadness and anger that some of my "allies" on this issue have acted in these ungracious—horribly sinful—ways. I repudiate them thoroughly. I want to be a person who lives out the grace of the Lord Jesus, and I want the same for the church.

But if so many Christians want to live out the grace of Jesus, why is there still division on this matter? It may be because we put different emphases on how Jesus' grace operates. Some emphasize the *accepting* aspect of grace as an unconditional love extended to people in need. They see how LGBT people have been mistreated, and so reach out with this accepting grace. Others emphasize that God's welcoming grace is extended *to sinners*, with the implication that those who will experience it most fully are people who acknowledge they are sinners. To them, the LGBT community will not experience the fullness of God's grace until they face the truth that they are not just sinners in general, but also sinners with respect to same-sex behavior. Still others will emphasize the *transformative* power of grace. People can come to Christ just as they are, but they should fully expect to be transformed by Christ. It is transforming to be accepted as you are, but this transformation is incomplete if not accompanied by a calling to be so transformed that one's desires and behaviors fit with God's will. I believe all three aspects of grace should be present in how the church ministers. Some may accuse me of lacking sympathy or being legalistic when I encourage the LGBT community to find this fuller transformation in Christ, but I think that's an important element of grace. It may be a tired cliché that has become an exasperating slogan to some, but I think Jesus speaks richly to this issue when he said to the woman caught in adultery: "Neither do I condemn you; go, and from now on sin no more" (John 8:11, ESV).

So what is it that causes me to take the stand I do on LGBT issues? The main reason is my sense of biblical clarity on this matter. I am fully aware that many matters of Scripture are less than clear, subject to a wide variety of interpretations and perspectives. Christians read Scripture differently with regards to warfare, baptism, predestination, eternal security, the Lord's Supper, God's wrath, capital punishment, and much more. Even the formulation of the doctrine of the Trinity was less than clear during the first few centuries of the church (and my hunch is that the typical Christian today is unable to articulate the orthodox formulation on this).

Most of these different perspectives are based on the fact that Scripture itself includes different perspectives on God's truth to us. It could be likened to an art class in which the students form a circle around a still life object in their midst, and each student draws the object from his or her own angle. What they draw will vary, partly because of their level of skill, but mostly because of their different perspectives on the one object. This multi-faceted aspect of God's truth, however, does not mean that all ideas are true. In the art class, some students might not be drawing the correct object at all, but instead are drawing something across the room, or their own hand, or an object from their own imagination. Likewise, some who attempt to sketch out their ideas of God might not be offering merely another perspective, but instead be offering false images of who God is. God's truth is not an amorphous blob that has no shape or contour and incorporates every idea or behavior into itself. Some ideas are clearly false and deserve to be called so. Some actions are clearly wrong and deserve to be called sin.

Because of this, I believe that our responsibility as people who believe and follow the Word of God is to learn to become as black-or-white as Scripture *and* as grey as Scripture. An important part of discipleship is learning when to take a firm stand against sin and deception, and when to appreciate the perspective of other believers in their reading of Scripture. If I were to insist that every issue must be black-or-white, I would be unnecessarily divisive and proudly asserting that I alone know the dividing line of truth. And on the other hand, if I were to dissolve everything into a blob of greyness, I would proudly insist that no one really knows the truth and I would no longer have ears to hear the specifics of God's Word.

Given this perspective, someone might think that I'd be open to the interpretations of those who affirm at least some forms of same-sex behavior. I have been open in the sense of listening and trying to understand, but I have been completely unconvinced that there's biblical allowance for same-sex behaviors. With respect to many other issues in the Bible, countervailing truths help me see the multi-facetedness of Scripture. For instance, Paul speaks harsh words about not allowing women to speak in church, but he also speaks about women praying with heads covered and says there is no male or female in Christ. Jesus calls us to non-resistance, but the warfare imagery of the book of Revelation shows that God's violence is still operative. Jesus says that nothing can snatch his followers out of his hand, but then Hebrews reminds us that there's no hope if we turn our back on Christ. But when it comes to same-sex behaviors, the only thing I read in the Bible—Old Testament and New—is an unrelenting negative assessment. I see no crack in the wall that stands against this. Is it talked about a lot? No, but when it is mentioned, it is always regarded as sin.

Of course, the Bible does speak to other aspects of the issue besides whether LGBT behavior is sinful or not. I am called to love sinners (including myself among them). I am called to confess my own sexual sin. I am called to be merciful, helpful, kind, welcoming—and also truthful. I am also called to not be proud, arrogant, Pharisaical, self-righteous, mean-spirited, mocking, or abusive. But these biblical callings are in the context of an unrelenting negative assessment of same-sex behavior.

I understand that those who interpret the Bible differently on this matter claim that it's just a matter of hermeneutics—that in the mash-up of personal experiences, cultural differences between biblical times and ours, historical criticism, big picture issues in looking at the Bible, and more, that it's not surprising we see things differently. But simply to claim that we are using different hermeneutics resolves nothing. Arius had a different hermeneutic from Athanasius. Pelagius had a different hermeneutic from Augustine. Martin Luther had a different hermeneutic from the pope. Even the devil likes to be involved in biblical hermeneutics. Different hermeneutics lie behind every heresy ever devised. It's the next question that we must ask: are we using the right hermeneutic and are we using it in the right way?

Those who want the church to be more affirming of same-sex behaviors might say I have the wrong hermeneutic—that I'm stuck in some kind of legalistic approach. Or I'm content with simple proof-texts and neglect the big picture. That I subscribe to some kind of bibliolatry. Or I don't understand how Christ has transformed the meaning of purity laws. Or I have failed to see how the Holy Spirit still has things to teach me and the church. I am well aware of how these factors can distort one's hermeneutic, but I don't think I have succumbed to these problems.

Some might say I am only seeing in the text what I want to see. That's always a temptation. But if truth be told, I would actually prefer it if those favorable toward same-sex behaviors were right. I am a tender-hearted person. If I could avoid situations in which I had to confront someone with their sin (like gossip, greed, adultery, living together unmarried), I would welcome the opportunity. The conversation on such matters, even though I try so hard to be gracious and understanding, seldom goes well (although occasionally it does). It would be a blessing to not have to have those conversations. So I can understand why it's tempting to either look the other way or redefine actions as non-sinful. But I must be faithful to God's Word and to my calling in helping people see where they are straying from the Lord, and I want others to do the same for me.

I am firmly convinced that the Bible clearly opposes all same-sex behavior. Given that certainty, I cannot help but think that those who teach and live differently on this matter are not merely wrong, but they are wrong in a way that represents a defiant rejection of God's Word. As noted above, I can bear with many different interpretations of Scripture, even when I think they are wrong. But because of the biblical clarity on the same-sex issue, I see no reason for the church to create any space for such defiance.

There's all kinds of room for people to come before the Lord with sins they have not yet conquered and with theological errors they have not yet corrected—my own included. The person who has same-sex attraction is welcomed into the Lord's presence when they acknowledge their sin and seek transformation, even when they often lose the struggle. But it's a different situation when people insist that their sin is not sin, when they specifically justify their own sin. Then it becomes hard-hearted defiance–at least in this matter.

And what "ups the ante" is when those who insist it is not sin are also insisting that this defiant perspective should be celebrated in churches, taught in our seminaries, preached from our pulpits, and even be lived out by our pastors. For me to go along with this would mean that the church as a whole would be hardening our own hearts in a defiant rejection of God's Word.

Some might say, "No one is stopping you from interpreting the Bible and practicing your Christian life as you see fit in this matter, so why should you stand in the way of those who approach this matter differently?" And in my denomination, our polity gets wrapped up in this question. Some argue that each regional grouping of churches is free to live out its own interpretation of Scripture. The thought is that each regional grouping is allowed to decide on its own if they want to ordain those who are actively involved in same-sex relationships. But this is a "silo" approach because pastors are not merely ordained by that regional group; they belong to the whole denomination. Once they are ordained in one place, they are able to minister in other locations. When this defiance of the Lord is introduced into the body of Christ, it grieves the Holy Spirit of God, and it poses a threat to us all. It's hard to be united when we don't have a united confession or a common witness.

Others have suggested the acceptance of same-sex behaviors and the rejection of same-sex behaviors are simply two arms in the body of Christ, each doing ministry in different ways. I am all for using different models of ministry, for there is room within Scripture for that. But there is no room for models of ministry that refuse to call sin for what it is. While we recognize that there may be differences over what constitutes sin in other areas of moral discernment, I do not believe this to be the case with same-sex behavior.

It has been tempting to soften my words throughout this essay with the hope of making a more persuasive case, and to signal my own recognition that I may be wrong. For instance, something in me would like to say, "*From my perspective*, it *seems to me* that the Word of God is *pretty* clear that same-sex behavior is *not quite in line with* God's will." But in my heart and mind, to phrase it this way actually misrepresents my position. My stance here is more accurately stated thus, "The Word of God clearly teaches that same-sex behavior is sinful and stands in opposition to God's will."

It's because of this biblical clarity that I feel compelled to oppose all efforts to move the church in a direction of affirming and celebrating same-sex behavior. I am not trying to win a political battle or just "get my way." I am attempting to be faithful to the Lord Jesus Christ. I love my denomination. We have covenanted with each other as brothers and sisters. But if the denomination ends up being unfaithful to the Lord in this matter, I will be in the difficult situation of having to choose between a loyalty to the Lord or a loyalty to the denomination. I must obey God.

And this same perspective applies to our other ecumenical partnerships. I love being theologically hospitable, enriching and being enriched by the theological perspectives of other followers of Christ. Living together with our diversities in Christ testifies to the power of the gospel. My denomination, for example, is in covenant with some brothers and sisters of the Reformation. We have learned from their diverse perspectives on the *solas* of the Reformation, the structure of their churches for ministry, their confessions, and their theologians. But when another denomination strays from such a clear biblical command, I feel once again that it is incumbent upon me to try to help them reverse course. And if they refuse this counsel, we dare not walk with them into blatant disobedience.

Given my stance, you might wonder if I would be an eager heresy hunter, pressing charges whenever and wherever I could against those who believe differently on this matter. And in some cases, my "allies" have done that. But I find myself in a dilemma. I like and respect many of the people that I oppose. I believe they are Christians who follow Jesus in many other areas of their lives. I believe they have a genuine love for the LGBT community. I believe them when they say that they too believe the Bible, though their interpretations completely befuddle me. And I regard myself as being in covenant with them.

So now what? I see only five main roads to take: (1) Capitulate and abandon Scripture. This is a bad idea. (2) Co-exist by allowing this evil to persist and yet telling myself that at least in my heart of hearts I still have the right beliefs. For me, this is about the same as capitulating. (3) Continue on in the present morass of attack and counter-attack, which is definitely sapping our energy from our greater mission to the world. (4) Aggressively seek to correct or possibly discipline those in our denomination who think differently on this matter—but this would be very difficult to do in a way that would be perceived as loving. Or (5) quietly depart so that I (and my "allies") can begin a new mission trip with a different circle of believers. I frequently wonder if the last option would be the best.

Why do you ask?[1]

M ost of us have had the experience of asking a question, only to be greeted by the counter-question, "Why do you want to know?" The person suspects an agenda hiding behind our question, and their answer will depend on what our agenda is.

Jesus had the same attitude when he came under questioning. He seldom gave straight-forward answers because he detected an agenda hidden in the questions. A simple study of how Jesus responded to questions would reveal three basic strategies he used to get at that agenda.

Sometimes Jesus gave a command instead of an answer. After being asked if only a few would be saved, Jesus responded, "Make every effort to enter through the narrow door" (Luke 13:24, NIV11). When the Pharisees wanted to know if the woman caught in adultery should be stoned, Jesus replied, "If any one of you is without sin, let him be the first to throw a stone at her" (John 8:7, NIV). In response to the question of why he ate with sinners, Jesus said, "Go and learn what this means, 'I desire mercy, not sacrifice'" (Matthew 9: 13, NIV11).

Occasionally Jesus would hint at an answer, but wrap it inside a stinging rebuke. To the religious leaders who wondered about the marriage arrangements in the after-life, Jesus said, "You are in error because you do not know the Scriptures or the power of God" (Matthew 22:29, NIV11). When asked why his disciples did not wash their hands according to the tradition, Jesus replied, "Isaiah was right when he prophesied about you hypocrites; as it is written: 'These people honor me with their lips, but their hearts are far from me'" (Mark 7: 6, NIV11).

Jesus was especially adept at answering questions with questions. A short list of Jesus' counter-questions would include:

"How can the guests of the bridegroom fast while he is with them?" (Mark 2:19, NIV11).

---

[1] Based on an article I wrote entitled "Our Motives and the Message," that I wrote for the now-defunct *The Church Herald*, 58 (September 2001), 22-23.

"Have you not read that the one who made them at the beginning 'made them male and female'?" (Matthew 19:4, NRSV).

"Why are you trying to trap me?...Whose portrait is this [on the coin]? And whose inscription?" (Matthew 22:18-20, NIV).

"Why does this generation ask for a miraculous sign?" (Mark 8:12, NIV11).

"Which is easier: to say, 'Your sins are forgiven,' or to say, 'Get up and walk'?" (Luke 5:23, NIV11).

"What is written in the Law? What do you read there?" (Luke 10:26, NRSV).

Perhaps the most telling incident which illustrates Jesus' avoidance of straight-forward answers is found in Matthew 21:23-27. The chief priests and elders of the people wanted to know by whose authority Jesus had just cast the money-changers out of the temple. Jesus would not answer their question until they first answered his question about the source of John's authority to baptize. Since the religious leaders did not want to commit themselves to an answer out of fear of the people's response, Jesus would not give them an answer either. Jesus was not about to give the truth to people who did not really want to know the truth, commit themselves to it, or allow themselves to be changed by it.

Because we are wary of sound-bite politicians skilled in giving non-answers, we might suspect that Jesus is just another artful dodger. But we would err in that assessment. Jesus does not avoid straightforward answers in order to steer clear of the truth. Rather, he avoids straightforward answers to probe the truth even more fully. For the truth is, there is an agenda lurking in the shadows of these questions, and Jesus would rather speak to the agenda than to the question.

The people of Jesus' day were asking agenda-oriented questions. When they asked about divorce, resurrection, or taxes, they did not do so in order to draw near to Jesus. They did not want answers from him that would affect the way they lived. They did not want answers that would apply to the specific condition of their own soul. They did not want to hear narratives or metaphors that would cause a revolutionary paradigm shift in their relationship with God. They just wanted to follow their own agenda.

But Jesus does not give people what they ask for. He draws near to his questioners. He looks into their eyes and sees their needs and agendas. He knows this questioner wants to kill him and that one wants to justify himself. He knows this interrogator is seeking God and that one is seeking power. Jesus doesn't want to give anyone mere information, but transformation. Jesus avoids straight answers because he is not speaking to the question, but to the agenda behind the question. He gives no answers to out-of-context questions, but instead tells parables of ordinary life so that his questioners will never again see anything as ordinary.

Jesus still operates that same way when we lay our theological questions before him. He asks us, "Why do you want to know?" Do you want to know about the perseverance of the saints so that you can complacently rest in the slogan of "once saved, always saved" or so that you can find security in the grace of Jesus? Do you want to know about the Return of Jesus so that you be one of the inner circle who knows the secret schedule of the universe, or so you can face the unknowns of the future with confidence? Do you want to know about forgiveness so that you feel justified in holding a grudge or because you are looking for how to let go of a painful incident in your past?

Jesus knows the agendas lurking in our questions. Sometimes our agendas are excellent. We want to know how we can be saved, how we can serve, love, or live in a God-pleasing way. Sometimes our agendas stink to high heaven. In order for us to best hear Jesus' response to our questions, we as individual Christians, churches, and denominations need to let him expose the agendas behind our questions.

For instance, we might be surprised how many different agendas might lie behind the question, "Is it a sin to smoke?" An adolescent whose parents smoke has a different reason for asking than a young person who is tempted to be Joe Cool. Some ask because they are compiling a list of rules to tell true Christians apart from hypocrites, while others ask because they wonder if they should include tobacco companies in their stock portfolio.

We will also find many different agendas lying behind the question of whether or not same-sex behaviors are sinful. A college girl is tempted to engage in her first lesbian encounter and wants to know what God would think of that. A male heterosexual porn addict wants to know so he can shine the light on someone else's sin instead of his own. A political junkie wants to know so that he can justify the position of his favored political party. A mother of a gay man wants to know so that she can best know how to talk with her son. A scholar wants to know so that he can accurately teach college students what the Bible actually says. A denomination executive wants to know so that she can find a way forward between warring factions in the church. And on and on it goes.

Jesus' answer to our questions will vary depending on what our agenda is. Sometimes he will give a command, sometimes a rebuke, sometimes a counter-question, and every so often a straight-forward answer.

This does not mean that the truth is like Silly Putty, capable of being bent and shaped in any direction, depending on the situation. Situational theology would be just as misguided as situational ethics. God's truth is solid, firm, and sure. But God's truth is not solid and firm like an abstract object. It is solid and firm in a living, active way. God's truth moves toward us to speak to the real condition of our soul. Only in that way can information bring transformation.

Of course, our temptation will always be to think we know the agendas of other people and what they need to hear from Jesus. We are ready and willing mouthpieces to speak for the Lord—too willing. While it's true that some of us (like pastors and counselors) are in a position to do a little probing—helping people uncover their agendas and speaking the Word of the Lord to them—our main job is to figure out how Jesus is speaking to us with our own agendas.

Dave Landegent is on a lifelong adventure of conveying God's Word in everyday language—as a pastor of an evangelical church, a weekly columnist in The Sunday School Guide, *and a lyricist rewriting over 4,000 pop songs to reflect biblical truth. He has written two other books:* Colossians: A Commentary *and* A Year in Colossians: a 365-Day Devotional Commentary *(both available through Amazon).*

Made in the USA
Monee, IL
26 November 2019